D0824604

*'Thus there is a certain bloom of newness in each building
and an appearance of being untouched by the wear of time.
It is as if some ever-flowering life and unageing spirit had
been infused into the creation of these works.'*

Plutarch, *Life of Perikles, c.* AD 100

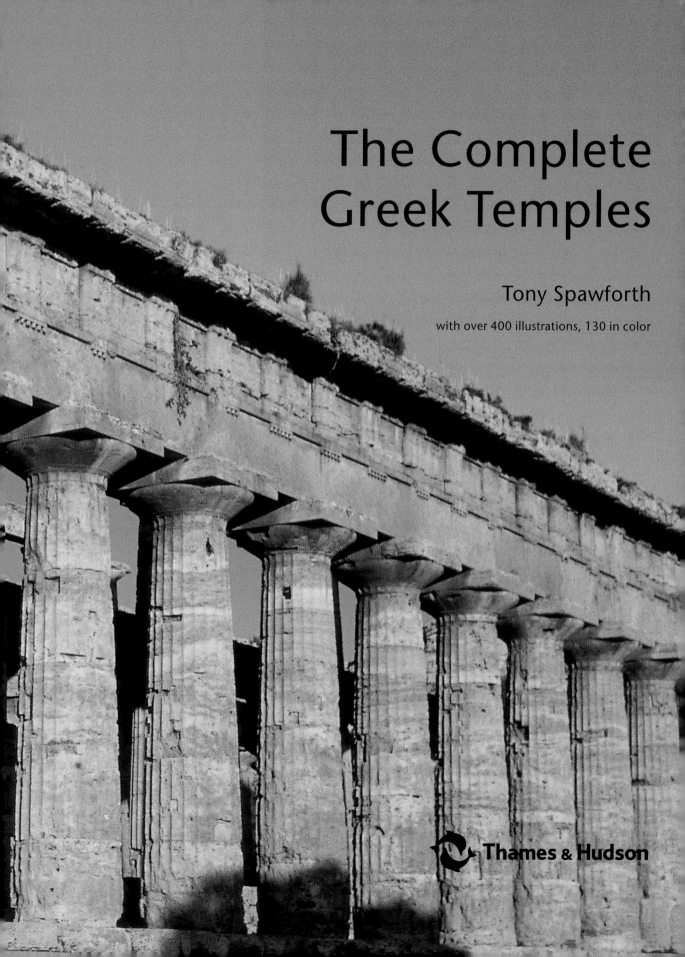

# The Complete
# Greek Temples

Tony Spawforth

with over 400 illustrations, 130 in color

Thames & Hudson

For my parents

Half-title: *Ionic column, Erechtheion, Athens.*

Title-page: *Temple of Poseidon, Sounion, near Athens.*

This page: *Temple 'of Concord', Agrigento, Sicily.*

First published in 2006 in hardcover in the United States of America by Thames & Hudson Inc., 500 Fifth Avenue, New York, New York 10110

thamesandhudsonusa.com

Library of Congress Catalog Card Number 2005906236

ISBN-13:  978-0-500-05142-9
ISBN-10:  0-500-05142-9

Printed and bound in Singapore by Craft Print International Ltd

# Contents

# Introduction:
# Temples, Lands and Gods

*The Parthenon, Athens. A massive manmade platform permitted the building of the Parthenon on a natural slope in the southern part of the Akropolis. Such terracing, to create sufficient level ground on a conspicuous site, is common in ancient Greek temple construction.*

To worship their gods the ancient Greeks created a sacred architecture regarded nowadays as one of the supreme glories of their civilization. For over eight centuries they reserved for their major temples a unique all-stone design comprising a free-standing rectangle of columns raised on a stepped platform and framing an inner building closed by a door, the whole topped by a pitched roof and triangular gables. Over the centuries Greek architects honed and adapted this monumental form, but the essentials never changed. The colonnaded Greek temple constitutes a cultural phenomenon in itself.

The Greeks called such a building a *naos*, the dwelling of a deity, whose sacred images normally stood (or sat) inside. They applied this same term to a range of structures on a sliding scale of size and prestige, from the one-room shrine tucked inside a larger public building to the lavish colonnaded temple. This book is concerned with the *naos* in the fully blown sense just defined, of which nowadays the Parthenon in Athens is the most famous survivor.

This emphasis is justified by the attitudes of the ancient Greeks themselves. As we shall see later, the conspicuous sites assigned to colonnaded temples, their architectural intricacy and their cost, their place on the cutting edge of Greek building technology, the importance of the state cults which they served, and the decades or even centuries doggedly devoted to their completion, are all pointers to their exceptionality in their day.

So, too, is the very fact of their monumentality and the sense of permanence exuded by tier upon tier of finely dressed masonry. In their heyday no other public building in Greece could compare with them in impact and majesty. When simpler shrines were upgraded, the natural route to follow was the addition of a prestigious colonnade (for examples see pp. 138–39, 207–8, 209, 225).

The fad for neo-Greek architecture in more recent times (see Epilogue, p. 228) has seen the distinctive forms of the ancient Greek temple adapted for purposes far removed from the original: churches, museums, memorials, even private houses.

Partly as a result of this more recent appropriation of ancient Greek sacred architecture, we are in danger of forgetting that colonnaded temples first and foremost were monuments to the god-fearing piety of the communities which built them. Even the stones which constituted them were sacred and inviolate. According to an ancient anecdote, when a

R. Eridanos (Po)

ADRIATIC SEA

Rome

Pompeii
Epidamnos
Foce del Sele    Metapontion    Taras
Poseidonia                              Apollonia
Eleia                                    E

KERKYRA

TYRRHENIAN SEA                Krimis(s)a    Kerkyra
Lakinion                                Ambrakia

Hipponion                              Kassop

Kaulonia
Lokroi Epizephyrioi

Segesta    Himera
Selinous        SICILY
Akragas    Akrai
Gela    Syracuse

IONIAN SEA

Thessaly

eiros        Pherai
Demetrias

Metropolis

Aitolia

Stratos                Lokris
Elateia
Thermon        Phokis    Hyampolis    EUBOIA
Kalydon    Velvina    Delphi    Orchomenos    Eretria
Lebadeia        Ptoion
Ano Mazaraki        Boiotia    Thebes
Lousoi    Aigeiria        Plataiai
Elis    Achaia    Sikyon        Rhamnous
Corinth    Megara    Attike
Olympia    Orchomenos    Nemea    Pallene
Makiston        Isthmia    Athens    Loutsa
Alipheira    Gortys    Tegea    Argos    Cape Zoster    Thorikos
Lepreon    Vigla    Peraitheis(?)    Epidauros    AIGINA
Bassai    Arkadia    Troizen    Sounion    KEOS
Kalaureia
Messene    Hermione
Messenia

Lakonia

N

0        50 miles
0        100 kilometres

0        250 miles
0        400 kilometres

Olbia

Pantikapaion

**BLACK SEA**

R. Istros (Danube)

**Macedonia**

Neapolis

Amphipolis

Thessalonike

Thasos

Stageira

**Bithynia**

Bithynion-Claudioupoulis

**Galatia**

Kyzikos

Ankyra

**Thessaly**

Passaron

Torone

Aphytis

Chrysa

Ilion

Neandria

Assos

Klopedi

Messon

**LESBOS**

Pergamon

Aizanoi

Pessinous

**Phrygia**

Aigai

**Lydia**

Antioch-near-Pisidia

Smyrna

Sardis

**CHIOS**

Teos

Kato Phana

Klaros

Ephesos

Nysa

Sagalassos

**Kilikia**

**SAMOS**

**Karia**

Aphrodisias

Selge

**Pisidia**

Samos

Alabanda

Termessos

Diokaisareia

Elaioussa-Sebaste

**DELOS**

Lagina

Side

**NAXOS**

Seleukeia-on-
the-Kalykadnos

Seleukeia in Pieria

**KOS**

**Lykia**

Priene

Letoon

Myous

Labraynda

Didyma

Kastabos

Miletos

Mylasa

Knidos

Euromos

Diktynnaion

**RHODES**

**CRETE**

Triopion

Magnesia-on-the Maeander

R. Orontes

**MEDITERRANEAN SEA**

Apollonia

Cyrene

Alexandria

R. Nile

Hermopolis Magna

**RED
SEA**

corrupt overseer of works in Sicilian Syracuse pur-
loined for private use stone hewn for a local temple
of the goddess Athena, 'the deity revealed herself to
mortals: for Agathokles was struck by lightning,
and he, along with his house, went up in flames'
(Diodorus Siculus, *c.* 40 BC).

By the same token, we must beware of thinking
that the ancient Greek way of experiencing a
temple was – like ours today – mainly aesthetic.
This register of response was open to the ancient
Greeks when viewing their temples, especially in
later antiquity, and Greek architects certainly
sought to incorporate Greek ideals of beauty into
temple-design: it is modern admiration for the
results which accounts for the neo-Greek strand in
Western architecture today. But, as we shall see, the
Greeks thought of a temple first and foremost as
the god's personal house.

The divine images inside were not just symbols
of deity: they were, or could become, alive – idols in
the true sense. In antiquity Greek temples were
mysterious spaces, where things could go bump in
the night. One aim of this book is to rescue the
ancient Greek temple from its use and abuse by
more recent classicizing movements and, as far as
possible, to reconstruct its original religious context.

*The deities of Mount
Olympos. Sculptured frieze
from the Parthenon, East
Pediment. Shown here (left to
right) are Poseidon, Apollo,
and his sister Artemis.*

As we shall see in Chapter IV, the now-vanished deities who resided in these temples were mainly the extended family whose seat the Greeks placed on Mount Olympos in northern Greece. Given human form and foibles in the stories which the Greeks told about them, the quarrelsome Olympians can all too easily seem to us to cut ludicrous figures, their obsolescence inevitable. But the traditional religion of which they constituted the vivid centre retained the allegiance of the Greeks for centuries, needing all the resources of the Christian Roman Empire before being finally swept away in the 5th and 6th centuries AD.

Polytheism, the worship of many gods, is at the heart of a number of living faiths in the modern world. It attracts less Western condescension in a multi-cultural age than in the 19th century, when historians of religion were unable to shake off their Christianizing prejudices against 'inferior' idol-worshippers.

For the ancient Greeks, conceiving divine power as a multitude of deities, each with a specific field of influence over human affairs, offered a means of comprehending, systematizing and communicating with the unseen forces governing the human condition. Made sacred by the presence of the god, Greek

*Mount Olympos in northern Greece, home of the gods.*

# Chronology of the Temple Builders

BC

| | |
|---|---|
| c. 1575–1200 | Mycenaean civilization in Greece |
| c. 1100–776 | 'Dark Age' of Greece |
| c. 1050–950 | migration of Ionian Greeks to the Eastern Aegean and Asia Minor |
| c. 825–750 | Greek colonization of Italy and Sicily begins |
| c. 800–700 | the first Greek poleis or citizen-states develop |
| 776 | the first athletic games at Olympia |
| 753 | traditional date for the foundation of Rome |
| c. 700 | Greek colonization of the Black Sea area begins |
| c. 700–600 | strong eastern influence on Greek culture |
| c. 610 | Greek colony of Cyrene in North Africa founded |
| c. 560–510 | tyranny of Peisistratos and his sons at Athens |
| c. 557–530 | Cyrus the Great founds the Persian empire |
| c. 546/545 | Persians conquer Ionian Greeks |
| 499 | Ionian Revolt against Persian rule |
| 490 | first Persian invasion of Greece; battle of Marathon |
| 480 | Carthaginian invasion of Sicily; colonial Greek victory at Himera |
| 480–447 | second Persian invasion of Greece; battles of Thermopylai, Salamis, Plataia |
| 478/7 | Athens founds Delian League against Persia |
| c. 460–430 | Herodotus writes his history |
| c. 460–429 | Perikles dominates Athenian politics |
| c. 431–400 | Thucydides writes his history |
| 431 | Second Peloponnesian War begun between Athens and Sparta |
| 406 | Carthaginians sack Akragas (Agrigento) |
| 404 | Athens surrenders to Sparta |
| 386 | King's Peace restores Persian rule over the Greeks of Asia Minor |
| 377–353 | Maussolos rules Karia in Southwest Asia Minor |
| 359–336 | Philip II rules as king of Macedon |
| 338 | Philip defeats Athens and other poleis at Chaironeia |
| 336–323 | Alexander ('the Great') rules as Macedonian king |
| 332/331 | Alexander founds Alexandria in Egypt |
| 323– c. 281 | Alexander's 'Successors' divide his empire |
| 323–31 | Egypt ruled by the Ptolemies |
| 321 | beginning of Seleukid empire in Near East and Central Asia |
| 281/280 | Achaian Confederacy revived in mainland Greece |
| 272 | Rome completes conquest of Italy |

temples were places apart, offering a focal point for the encounter between humans and the divine.

After religion, Greek temples were about the political. It is no coincidence that the zenith of Greek temple-building overlaps with the period from the 6th to the 4th centuries BC. This is often seen as an age when more Greek states were more successful on the political and military front than at any other time in antiquity. The rate of colonnaded temple-building in this period seems to reflect this Greek corporate dynamism in a range of ways.

On the other hand, a third of the colonnaded Greek temples which can be dated belong to later antiquity, the period from roughly 300 BC to AD 200. Historians of religion used to believe that from the 4th century BC on the ancient Greeks gradually lost much of their faith in the traditional deities who inhabited their temples. The statistics for later temples hardly bear out this – admittedly, now old-fashioned – view. Nor do the repairs to older temples, which could extend their working life as

naoi for up to eight centuries – as long as the great cathedrals of medieval Europe.

Greek temples offered a vehicle for the assertion of Greek religious identity. No other Greek building had the unique feature of a surrounding colonnade, which at once identified a temple for what it was.

By the same token, it is often pointed out that from a distance all Greek temples must have looked much the same. The way in which the colonnaded temple was instantly recognizable architecturally made a powerful visual sign of cultural identity as well – of a community's claim to Greekness.

After the eastern conquests of Alexander the Great, the number of non-Greek communities which wished to represent themselves as culturally Greek expanded. Previously the Greek-speaking world had comprised the Greek mainland and the Aegean islands and coasts, and colonies sent out from these areas to northern Africa, Italy and Sicily, and the Black Sea. Now it was spread, if thinly, as far east as Afghanistan.

| 241 | Sicily becomes the first Roman province |
| 241–197 | Attalos I rules Pergamon in Western Asia Minor |
| 212 or 211 | Rome allies with Aitolian Confederacy |
| 167 | Rome destroys kingdom of Macedon at battle of Pydna |
| 149–146 | Third Punic War; Rome destroys Carthage |
| 146 | Roman destruction of Corinth; Greece loses its independence |
| c. 118 | death of Greek historian Polybios |
| 64 | Rome expels the last Seleukids; Syria a Roman province |
| 44 | Caesar made perpetual dictator at Rome; murdered (15 March) |
| 31 | Octavian defeats Antony and Cleopatra at Actium |
| 30 | Egypt a Roman province |
| 28–23 | Vitruvius writes his work on architecture |
| 27 | Octavian is given the name Augustus |

**AD**

| after 21 | death of Strabo, the Greek geographical writer |
| 41–54 | Claudius emperor |
| 54–68 | Nero emperor |
| c. 65 | death of St Paul in Rome |

| 79 | death of the elder Pliny, Roman encyclopaedist |
| c. 100 | Greek writer Plutarch active |
| 117–138 | Hadrian emperor |
| 150 | Pausanias the travel writer active |
| 235–284 | period of anarchy in the Roman empire |
| 267 | Athens sacked by Herulian Goths |
| 306–337 | Constantine I emperor |
| 313 | Edict of Milan: Christianity tolerated |
| 324 | Constantinople (Istanbul) founded |
| 391 | Theodosius I closes pagan temples |
| 393 | athletic games at Olympia abolished |
| 395 | division of the empire between East (Byzantium) and West |
| Early 1400s | Cyriaco of Ancona travels in Greek lands |
| 1453 | Ottoman Turks capture Constantinople; fall of Byzantine empire |
| 1460–1830 | Ottoman occupation of Greece |
| 1762 | first volume of Stuart and Revett's *Athenian Antiquities* published |
| 1787 | Goethe visits Poseidonia (Paestum) |
| 1801–1805 | Lord Elgin removes sculpture from Athenian Akropolis |
| 1833 | Kingdom of Greece founded |

## Temple Highlights

| c. 1000 BC | apsidal building at Lefkandi, Euboia |
| 700s BC | earliest colonnaded temples |
| c. 600–409 BC | Temples of Selinous, Sicily |
| c. 580 BC | first all-stone colonnaded temple, Kerkyra (Corfu) |
| c. 550–450 BC | temples of Poseidonia (Paestum) |
| c. 500–405 BC | temples of Akragas |
| c. 470–c. 457 BC | Temple of Zeus, Olympia |
| c. 450–c. 405 BC | Temple of Hephaistos, Parthenon, Erechtheion at Athens |
| c. 429–c. 400 BC | Temple of Apollo, Bassai |
| 356 BC | 6th-century temple of Artemis, Ephesos burns down; new temple (an ancient Wonder of the World) begun soon after |
| 323 BC | Alexander's temple-building plans set aside |
| c. 300 BC | Temple of Apollo, Didyma, begun |
| 30 BC–AD 15 | restoration of Greek temples under Roman emperor Augustus |
| AD 117–138 | Hadrian builds last generation of Greek mega-temples |
| c. AD 150 | Temple of Zeus, Aizanoi |
| AD 263 | Goths plunder temple of Artemis, Ephesos |
| c. AD 500–600 | conversion of Parthenon into a church |

*The massive temple of Apollo at Didyma on the west coast of Asia Minor, begun around 300 BC by the nearby Greek city of Miletos. The oracle here made Didyma one of the centres of Greek religious life in Asia Minor.*

*Oil painting by Archibald Archer (1819) showing the temporary Elgin room on London's Park Lane where Lord Elgin's marbles were displayed before their purchase for the nation and installation in the British Museum.*

Especially in the hinterland of ancient Asia Minor (modern Turkey), building a colonnaded temple was one way of feeding the desire among indigenous peoples to 'go Greek' – even if the result did not always look quite as a homeland Greek would expect (as at the Letoon in Lykia: pp. 214–15).

Among non-Greek neighbours who succumbed to the lure of Greek culture, the Romans are in a class apart. Their admiration for Greek temples would take paradoxical forms, as befitted a military superpower which saw itself as both the political master and the cultural protégé of Greece.

In the worst cases, Greek temples became booty. But the last wave of Greek temple-building was prompted by the patronage of the Greek-loving emperor Hadrian (AD 117–38). When in 1807 a British connoisseur mistook Lord Elgin's newly displayed sculptures from the Athenian Parthenon as Hadrianic work, in a wrong-headed way he had a point.

Much later, after Christianity became the official religion of the Empire, it was Roman law which decreed the closing of Greek temples. Their long history since has been mainly one of degradation, sudden or gradual. But fifteen or so temples (see pp. 16–17 overleaf) are still well enough preserved to inspire wonder at their beauty and execution, and prompt reflection on who built them all those centuries ago, and why.

# The Best Preserved Colonnaded Greek Temples

## Greece

Aigina, temple of Aphaia, *c.* 510–?480 BC
Athens:
   temple of Athena Parthenos (Parthenon),
      447–432 BC
   temple of Athena Polias (Erechtheion),
      end of the 5th century BC
   temple of Hephaistos, *c.* 450–415 BC
Bassai, temple of Apollo, *c.* 429–400 BC
Sounion, temple of Poseidon, 440s BC

## Asia Minor

Aizanoi, temple of Zeus, *c.* AD 150
Didyma, temple of Apollo, *c.* 300 BC–early 3rd
   century AD
Diokaisareia, temple of Zeus Olbios, *c.* 150 BC
Euromos, temple of Zeus Lepsynos, 2nd century AD

## Southern Italy and Sicily

Akragas (Agrigento), temple of 'Concord',
   *c.* 450–440 BC
Poseidonia (Paestum):
   temple of Hera, *c.* 550–530/20 BC
   temple of Athena, *c.* 500 BC
   temple of 'Poseidon', *c.* 474–450 BC
Segesta, Doric temple, *c.* 460–450 BC
Syracuse, temple of Apollo, *c.* 565 BC

*(Below) Aizanoi (mod. Çavdarhisar) in Turkey, the
best-preserved Ionic temple from antiquity.
(Opposite, top) Bassai, Temple of Apollo. Lying on a ledge
of Mount Kotilion, Bassai is visible for many kilometres.
(Opposite, bottom) Segesta, Doric temple (unknown cult),
southwest of Palermo, Sicily, c. 460–450 BC.*

## Development, Glory and Decline

The colonnaded Greek temple was invented around 600 BC. Driving its creation was a dynamic new society formed in Greek lands from the 8th century BC, a young world pioneering its identity in a range of media, from poetry to architecture.

The colonnaded temple quickly established itself as the architectural flag of the Greek polis or 'citizen-state'. Its numbers multiplied rapidly, and the 5th-century Athenians brought its design and execution to a sophistication and artistry which would never be surpassed.

As foci for the religious traditions of the ancient Greeks, colonnaded temples survived the fall of successive Greek empires and were protected by the Romans. After Christianity's triumph, they mostly fell into neglect and ended up, prosaically, as quarries. For a minority, conversion into churches preserved the fabric and the aura of holiness.

From the 15th century on Western scholars began to rediscover ancient Greek temples. Their precise recording began, and countless artists made their ruins more widely known. Knowledge of them inspired a revival of Greek principles in Western architecture, echoes of which are still heard today.

*Aerial view of the temples of Hera (left) and 'Poseidon', Poseidonia (Roman Paestum), southern Italy.*

I   Homes of the Gods

# The First Temples

(Below left) Reconstructed wall
section by Robin Rhodes of
the first, pre-Doric, temple of
Apollo at Corinth, built
around 660–650 BC. The
mudbrick walls rested on a
base of squared masonry,
and the roof, covered with
clay tiles, was hipped – that
is, it sloped on all four sides.
There was no colonnade.
On the outer walls a timber
framework enclosed panels
of fine white plaster.

(Below right) At nearby
Isthmia, where the first temple
of Poseidon was of strikingly
similar plan and date, these
panels were decorated with
brightly coloured geometric
designs and – perhaps –
animals.

## Beginnings

Architecturally the direct ancestors of the colonnaded stone temples were the simpler *naoi* which appear in Greek sanctuaries only from the later 9th and 8th centuries BC. These developed from the building traditions of the early Greek iron age, and mostly their materials were perishable wood and bricks of sun-dried mud, with thatch for the roofs.

An imposing appearance by the modest standards of the time was mainly achieved by elongating them well beyond the norm. Hera's earliest temple on the island of Samos, for instance, and the temple at Ano Mazaraki in the northwest Peloponnese, had respective dimensions of nearly 33 x 6.75 and 29.5 x 7.5 m (108 x 22 and 97 x 25 ft). Units of measurement varied locally, but both temples may have aimed to impress as 'hundred footers' (*hekatompedon*, a term used by Homer).

More modest in scale than these, the 8th-century temple of Artemis at Ephesos also featured an external colonnade – the earliest certain example of this defining feature of classic Greek temple-design, but one already found in Greece in the 10th century BC, albeit in a different context (p. 22).

The early 7th century saw increasing experiments in the use of blocks of cut stone, still a rarity in Greece at this time, and the replacement of thatch by the invention – at Corinth, it seems – of mould-made clay rooftiles, which at first seem to have been reserved for temple use only. Exterior decoration could be painted onto plaster or fired-clay attachments.

Finds hint at the functions of these first temples. The display and protection of sacred objects was clearly one, as shown by finds from Ephesos, including likely traces of a sacred image. Ritual cooking and feasting was another, to judge from finds of hearths. But these messy and perhaps unseemly activities were soon relegated to the

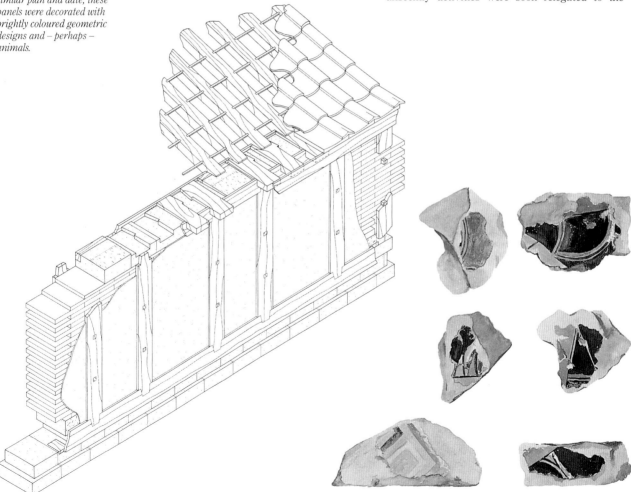

outside altar and – in some sanctuaries – to purpose-built dining rooms. In the standard temple of later times, altars for burnt sacrifice, as at Olympia or Delphi, seem to have been very much the exception.

Why did these first temples emerge precisely when they did? The previous 400 years or more had seen the mainland revert to relative poverty following the mysterious collapse of the palace-based civilization of the Mycenaean Greeks. But by the 8th century BC Greece was becoming more prosperous, more populated and more in touch with neighbours.

Yet a straightforward picking up where the Mycenaeans left off cannot be the explanation. Although their Linear B records show that the Mycenaeans worshipped many of the same Greek gods, the architectural emblem of the Mycenaean way of life was not a communal temple but a mighty palace.

*This dining room from the sanctuary of Artemis at Brauron, in the rural hinterland of Athens, dates from the late 5th century BC. Diners reclined on wooden couches set against the walls, with food and drink placed before them on the marble-topped tables visible in the picture. By this time, such separate facilities for sacred banquets were the norm in Greek sanctuaries.*

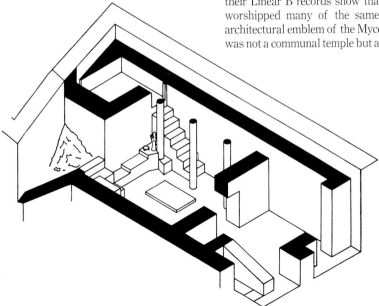

*Restored view of a cult-centre on the southwest slope of the citadel of Mycenae (13th century BC). Both in its position and its modest architecture, this little complex was clearly subordinate to the grand palace of the ruler on the higher ground above.*

Mycenaean rituals may have differed too. The normal combination from the 8th century on of a temple housing divine statuary and an outside altar for blood-sacrifice (pp. 84–85) cannot be identified in Mycenaean cult. It may only have been introduced into Greek lands after the Mycenaean collapse, under the influence of the Near East, where this so-called triad of temple, statue and altar was an ancient one.

The particular significance of the 8th century BC for the emergence of the *naos* seems to lie with an intensified sense of religious community among Greeks of the time, in turn linked to a new political dispensation. By the 700s BC, and under a variety of stimuli, Greeks had begun once more to form themselves into more complex polities. Of these, the polis or 'citizen-state', based on a given territory and the political dominance of a male warrior group, started to become the most widespread.

Each new polis turned to the Greek gods for protection of its interests, performing rituals to achieve this at local sanctuaries in which the community came together to celebrate common festivals and strengthen its social bonds.

A need was now felt for a new type of collective religious building. It has been suggested, although there is no real proof, that these first *naoi* housed functions taken over from the halls of 10th- and 9th-century priestly leaders and chieftains. Such halls may also have provided architectural inspiration for some of the earliest *naoi*.

*Restored view of a huge early-iron age building (c. 1000 BC), excavated at modern Lefkandi, Euboia, in 1981. Measuring almost 50 x 14 m (164 x 46 ft), it had an outside colonnade of wooden posts, a pitched roof, a gable at one end and an apsidal plan at the other, as well as internal columns. All these features recur in the earliest* naoi *on the mainland (e.g., pp. 150, 166). The building may have been a chieftain's home, although it has also been claimed as a shrine.*

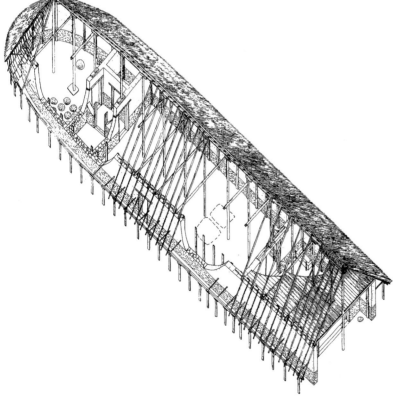

The *naos* was always a sacred space first and foremost, in ways to be explored in Chapter III. Providing communal access to the cult objects, it also symbolized the collective identity of the new polis: the equivalent, it has been suggested, of its 'birth certificate'. This essentially political frame for the building of public temples in ancient Greece is crucial for understanding the dynamic of their diffusion.

## Revolutions in design

'Kleomenes, son of Knidieidas, made the temple for Apollo. And he executed columns – [?] fine works'

Inscription on the steps of the temple of Apollo, Syracuse, about 565 BC

The energizing adoption of the communal *naos* as a key material embodiment of Greek state-identity drove the rapid technological and stylistic

advances in temple-building which mark the 600s and earlier 500s BC.

Although Greek builders became more proficient at working in stone during the 7th century BC, around 600 BC the earliest colonnaded temple in the prime religious site of Olympia could still be built largely of mudbrick and wood. But, only a generation later, temple-builders were able to quarry, transport and manoeuvre 35-ton megaliths. The boastful inscription of the early temple-builder Kleomenes, cited above, shows how the Greeks themselves marvelled at this achievement.

The all-stone *naoi* which started to appear in the earlier 500s BC provide the earliest certain examples of what became the standard colonnaded plan. Another apparent innovation was their decorative finish in the uniquely Greek styles of ornamentation later known as Doric and Ionic.

All these developments reflect the fact that the early Greeks were becoming richer, producing a sufficient surplus to shoulder the costs of building on a more monumental scale. They must also have felt sufficiently stable and confident of the future to embark on building projects which could take years or decades to complete.

The intellectual and artistic climate capable of responding creatively to the challenge of devising a new monumental architecture must also have been in place. As crucially, so was the exposure to more sophisticated neighbours. In the later 8th and especially the 7th centuries BC, increased contact with the older civilizations to the east had a profound impact on Greek cultural life, including architecture. For the development of the colonnaded Greek temple the crucial influence may have been the Egypt of the 26th Dynasty

*Cut-stone colonnade in the temple of Hatshepsut at Deir-el-Bahri near Luxor in Egypt (c. 1460 BC). The square capitals, and the line of horizontal blocks resting on them, both have echoes in the Doric style of Greek temple-building.*

23

Here Greek visitors in the later 7th century BC confronted an age-old tradition of vast temples made of cut stone which far outdid in magnificence anything which the Greeks would see elsewhere on their Mediterranean travels, let alone at home (see illustration, p. 23).

Archaeologists continue to debate how far early Greece's temple-builders were indebted to Egypt. On the technical side, underlying the appearance of the first known stone colonnaded temples in Sicily and Corfu early in the 6th century BC may well have been Greek absorption of Egyptian techniques for cutting, lifting and fitting large stone blocks. The Greek use of iron clamps to tie neighbouring blocks together is also a technique first found in Egypt.

In terms of design, Greek temple-designers may have been inspired by other features of Egypt's temples such as their rows of columns, their use of painted decoration, and the idea itself of translating perishable building materials into stone. The Egyptian temple was a symbolic form, and this aspect may also have influenced the Greeks, as we shall see in Chapter II. In a process of transmission impossible to recover in any detail,

the innovative Greeks could have grafted these foreign ideas onto local traditions.

The distinctive Doric and Ionic systems of ornamenting Greek temples were once seen as the result of a lengthy evolution. In fact, working out the essentials of these new styles in stone probably occurred fairly rapidly in a phase of intense architectural innovation: the late 7th and earlier 6th centuries for Doric, extending beyond 550 BC for Ionic.

No names of individuals can be linked to these momentous changes, or even specific localities, although creative matrices could well have been the northeast Peloponnese for Doric, and for Ionic the Cyclades and the southeastern islands and coast of the Aegean. In the former lay Corinth, an early centre of Greek craftsmanship with extensive overseas contacts, in the latter Samos and Ephesos, two nearby sites where archaeological finds disclose interaction with Egypt and the Near East as early as the 8th century BC.

### Dates and numbers

The table on the right is a first, and inevitably provisional, attempt to quantify numbers of Greek

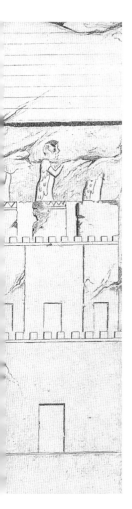

*This lost Assyrian relief of 714 BC shows a temple with a triangular gable at Musasir in the ancient kingdom of Urartu (eastern Turkey). According to the Greek poet Pindar (around 490 BC), the Corinthians were the first Greeks to build a temple with gables.*

able, but on attested temple remains. It charts all known sites of colonnaded temples and dates them – where the indicators are available, and these are often only approximate – by the latest temple on the site.

The proportion of all colonnaded temples represented by these known sites is a more intractable issue. In regions where archaeologists have been active over a long period, such as southern Italy and Sicily, the Greek mainland and islands, and western Turkey, it may be relatively high. But in these regions as everywhere, there is less chance of finding temple-remains located under areas of modern habitation. There again, a temple-site brought low by stone-robbers can still disappear from view even in open ground, as with the remains of the Triopion in southwest Turkey, unearthed in 1998–99 (p. 213).

In other regions where archaeologists have been less active in their search for Greek remains, such as the Black Sea coasts or much of the Near and Middle East, the data have a decidedly provisional air.

Even so, the table presents rough orders of magnitude over time which seem inherently credible on historical grounds. The building of colonnaded temples rapidly swells to a crescendo in the 6th and 5th centuries. A general diminuendo sets in from the 4th century, modest at first but becoming more marked, before a last surge of activity in the 2nd century AD.

Within this big picture are significant regional variations. In Italy and Sicily, new colonnaded temples virtually ceased to be built after 400 BC. On the Greek mainland, the heyday of temple-building fell in the 6th, 5th and 4th centuries BC. In Asia Minor, there was a renewed surge in temple-building from the later 4th century BC, sustained into the 2nd century AD – far longer than in any other part of the Greek world.

colonnaded temples and to distribute them by date and geography, based on the sites collected in Chapter V. It requires a brief explanation.

Its picture is not, of course, based on the absolute totality of ancient Greek temples, which is unknow-

# Approximate chronology and numbers of dated Greek colonnaded temples

| century BC/AD | 7th | 6th | 5th | 4th | 3rd | 2nd | 1st BC | 1st AD | 2nd | Total by area |
|---|---|---|---|---|---|---|---|---|---|---|
| Italy & Sicily | 0 | 20 | 22 | 0 | 1 | 0 | 0 | 0 | 1 | 44 |
| Mainland | 3 | 24 | 22 | 17 | 8 | 1 | 2 | 0 | 2 | 79 |
| Aegean & Black Sea | 1 | 7 | 2 | 1 | 2 | 3 | 0 | 0 | 2 | 18 |
| Asia Minor | 1 | 4 | 0 | 6 | 8 | 7 | 8 | 6 | 11 | 51 |
| Syria & Africa | 0 | 0 | 0 | 1 | 3 | 0 | 0 | 0 | 0 | 4 |
| *Total by century* | 5 | 55 | 46 | 25 | 22 | 11 | 10 | 6 | 16 | 196 |

# Temples and Community

## Temple and polis

'A temple shall be constructed as Kallikrates shall prescribe, and an altar of marble.'

Inscribed decree of the Athenians, 5th century BC

*Segesta, near Palermo, Sicily. Doric temple, c. 420 BC. The temple was unfinished, as shown by unfluted columns and the lifting bosses left on the steps.*

The Greek colonnaded temple was always an assertion of community. A minority were commissioned by the type of polity which the Greeks called a 'people' (*ethnos*) or 'commonality' (*koinon*). But the table on p. 25 points to a broad chronological and geographical correlation between the surge in temple-building in the 6th and 5th centuries BC and the rise of self-determining polis-communities and their colonies, including necklaces of rich Greek settlements around the Black Sea and the coasts of southern Italy and Sicily.

This mutual evolution reflects the fact that, in a very straightforward and fundamental way, temple-building was by and large a polis affair. As we shall see in the next chapter, on the rare occasion where we catch sight of the decision-making process behind temple-building, it was the citizens of the polis who normally took the decision to build a temple, and who then supervised the project. This remained true right through antiquity, even if Greek cities under Roman rule were ruled by rich oligarchs and no longer the citizens as a whole.

We must allow, therefore, for the probability that public works in Greek states, as in other historical periods and places, were vehicles for political statements, over and above their explicitly religious functions. The idea that the temple served as a highly visible symbol of communal identity has already been broached (p. 12). Archaeologists nowadays consider choice of location, discussed at greater length in Chapter II, as highly revealing. Striking here is the fact that, time and again, temples were placed on highly visible sites.

This penchant for erecting a temple in what the ancient Greeks called *ho epiphanestatos topos*, 'the most manifest place', makes sense if the temple was thought of as a communal beacon, visible from the farmland or home-waters, or dominating the built-up nucleus.

## Markers of territory?

But a conspicuous setting visually confronted outsiders as well as insiders. Given the prevalence of disputes over land in ancient Greece, neighbours posed a particular problem for Greek states. About half the known sites of colonnaded temples were rural, and in turn many of these were erected in sanctuaries marking one state's frontiers with another.

It is often assumed that a major temple on a boundary was meant – among other things – as a territorial marker. This interpretation can be applied to Greek colonies too. Here the incomers often acquired their land at the expense of, or even under threat from, the indigenous peoples, and a monumental temple could serve as a strong statement of possession in the face of threatening neighbours.

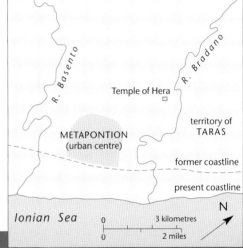

*(Below) Temple of Hera, Metapontion, Italy. The colonists at Metapontion placed this rural temple at Tavole Palatine on an eminence by the Bradano river, the frontier with the neighbouring Greek colony of Taras (Tarentum) to the east (see map, right).*

### 'Peer-polity interaction'

Greek disputes over land were just one aspect (albeit major) of the intense rivalries which were a hallmark of Greek interstate relations at all times – even when the polis had dwindled to being no more than the local authority of a Roman province. It is widely believed nowadays that temple-building intersected with these rivalries in a crucial way.

The extraordinary sameness of Greek temples, already commented on, suggests how keen early Greek states were to copy each other. This behaviour – 'peer-polity interaction', as some call it – was crucial to the rapid diffusion of the monumental temple in the 6th and 5th centuries BC. In this period, the early Greeks came to see the colonnaded temple as a symbol of state sovereignty in itself. Investing in one advertised the claim of a community to be an independent polis and offered a medium for political self-legitimation.

### Size matters

'I have dwelt longer on the affairs of the Samians, because three of the greatest works in all Greece were made by them… The third is a temple, the largest of all the temples known to us.'

Herodotus, Greek historian, 5th century BC

In the 6th century, after the initial novelty of all-stone temples, giant proportions seem to have become a new way of 'upping the ante', at least for rich Greek states with the requisite resources. In the mid-century the Samians, followed by the Ephesians across the water on the Turkish mainland, had built huge new Ionic temples for Hera and Artemis, their respective patron goddesses. When Hera's temple burnt down not long after, the Samians replaced it with a new temple which was fractionally wider than that of Artemis – the one which so impressed Herodotus. This looks like a deliberate attempt to outstrip a neighbour.

In Sicily, a similar race was on. The rich polis of Selinous (Selinunte) began a huge Doric temple ('G') in the later 500s BC. The men of Akragas (Agrigento) along the coast responded with a behemoth for Olympian Zeus, a mite wider.

*Plans of the mid-6th century temple of Artemis at Ephesos (above) and the later 6th century temple of Hera on Samos (below). Both temples were enormous by Greek standards, but at 55.16 m, the Samian temple is just that bit wider than that of Artemis (55.10 m).*

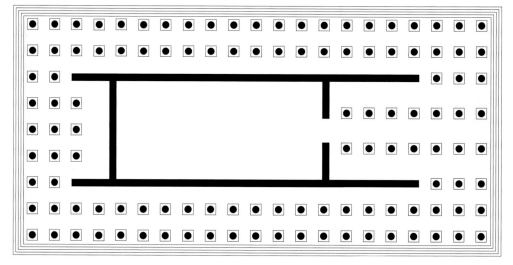

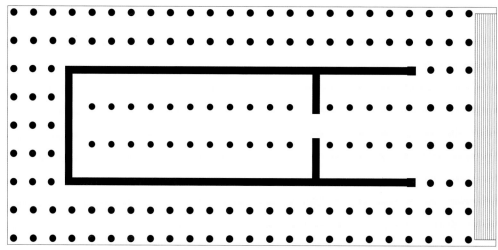

According to Diodorus, four centuries later, it was the huge size of this Olympieion which allowed its comparison 'with the temples outside Sicily'. The fact that neither of these Sicilian temples, nor the Samian one, was ever finished suggests the strain of huge ambitions on the host cities.

The sheer number of colonnaded temples stacked up by a minority of Greek states also looks suspiciously like a form of display. In the 6th century pretensions expressed in this way were marked among the rich colonies of southern Italy and Sicily (pp. 110–33), with major colonnaded temples lined up in a pair at Poseidonia (Paestum) and a trio in Metapontion. Akragas and Selinous finished with six and seven colonnaded temples respectively, in both cases in close and visible proximity to each other.

*Reconstructed elevations of temple 'G' (right) at Selinous and the temple of Olympian Zeus at neighbouring Akragas (below), as they would have looked if they had been finished. There is a significant difference in width: 55 m (164 ft) at Selinous compared with 52.74 m (173 ft) at Akragas.*

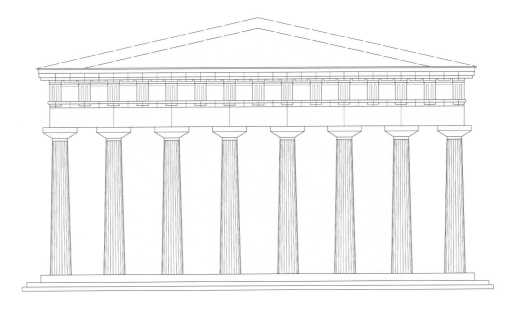

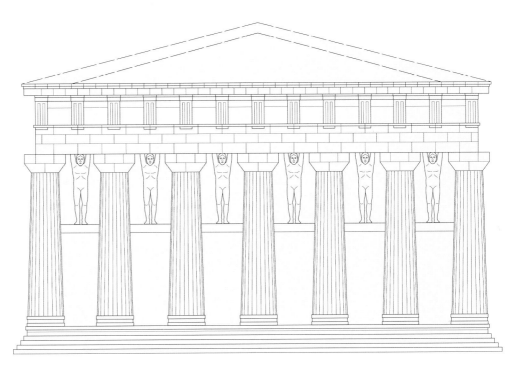

# Tyrants, Rivalry and War

## Tyrants and temples

'As examples of works instituted in order to keep subjects perpetually at work and in poverty we may mention the pyramids of Egypt, the numerous offerings made by the Kypselids, the building of the temple of Olympian Zeus by the Peisistratids, and public works under Polykrates of Samos.'

Aristotle, Politics

In the 7th and 6th centuries BC a number of Greek states saw the usurpation of local power by rulers whom the Greeks called 'tyrants' (*tyrannoi*). The jaded quotation from the tyrant-hating 4th-century BC philosopher Aristotle, likening tyranny in Corinth, Athens and Samos to pharaonic autocracy, makes the important point that tyrants were major patrons of public works, not least temples.

The temple of Zeus begun by the Athenian tyrant-family of the Peisistratids (ruled about 560–510 BC) shows their concern for the glorification of themselves and their state: this was by far the largest temple ever attempted on the Greek mainland. In modern times the Samian tyrant Polykrates has been linked to the last Heraion, just mentioned (p. 28), as has his contemporary, Lygdamis of Naxos, to a Naxian temple, the largest in the Cyclades (pp. 181–82).

Because rule by tyrants was unstable, there was a danger that their grandiose projects could be repudiated by hostile successor-regimes. This is precisely what happened at Athens, where the fledgling democracy which replaced the last Peisistratid left the temple of Zeus a building-site.

## Temples and 'Greekness'

'Again, there is the Greek nation – the community of blood and language, cult-buildings and sacrifices, and similar customs.'

Herodotus, 5th century BC

In this passage the 5th-century historian offers a famous definition of what it meant to be 'Greek'. It is striking that he emphasizes cult-buildings (*hidrumata*) as well as the rite of sacrifice in articulating the religious dimension to Greek identity.

The idea that shared religion was central to Greek ethnicity had already found expression in the

*These unfinished column-drums from the Peisistratid temple of Olympian Zeus at Athens were reused by the Athenians in their new city-wall, built in 479 BC.*

emergence on the mainland of a few sanctuaries – above all Olympia, Delphi, Isthmia and Nemea – which were (a modern coinage) 'panhellenic', or common to all Greeks. These were locales where Greek communities vied in splendid offerings, and in athletic and musical contests at the sacred festivals. In doing so they could assert their claims to prestige and identity before the widest possible audience of fellow-Greeks.

It is hard to prove, but likely enough, that the appearance of the first colonnaded temples in Olympia, Delphi, Isthmia and Nemea consolidated the authority of this particular type of sacred structure as a marker, not just of polis identity, but also of what Herodotus called *to Hellenikon*, 'Greekness'. This process was somewhat slow: an all-stone Doric temple with colonnades first appeared at Delphi in the later 6th century, in Olympia only in the early 5th century.

The sense of religious unity which crystallized around these temples found expression in their mode of funding. For Apollo's 6th-century temple 'the Delphians wandered around the poleis seeking donations' – according to Herodotus, from as far afield as the Greek community in Egypt, which contributed the sizeable sum of 2000 drachmai.

When the temple was rebuilt in the 4th century BC another 'panhellenic' collection was organized.

In the nostalgic atmosphere of later antiquity, these temples became objects of pilgrimage for Greeks (and Romans) in search of the most sacred aspects of the Greek tradition. The Greek travel writer Pausanias (2nd century AD) gave relatively short shrift to the Parthenon, passing over its architectural sculpture apart from a cursory mention of the gable groups. By contrast he wrote a reverential description of Zeus' temple at Olympia which included a figure-by-figure account of its sculpture, and detailed even the sculptured metopes (for this term see the diagram of a temple's parts, p. 62).

## War

'Thanks to these gods the men of Selinous are victorious in war. We are victorious thanks to Zeus and Phobos and Apollo…'

This Greek inscription was carved by the men of Selinous in Sicily on the doorway into the back room of their temple of Apollo around 480–470 BC. The text chillingly includes Phobos, terror in battle personified, among the gods who conferred success in a local war.

*The stadium in the sanctuary of Zeus at Olympia. The 'panhellenic' contests staged here every five years brought together athletes from all over the Greek world.*

*Impression left by an oval shield attached to a metope from Apollo's 4th-century BC temple at Delphi. The shield, part of a larger display, was captured by the Greeks from Celtic bands who attacked Delphi in 279/8 BC.*

Greek temples and Greek warfare were intimately related. After his victory over the Carthaginians at Himera (480 BC) the Syracusan tyrant Gelon 'put to one side the fairest part of the booty, since he wished to embellish the temples of Syracuse with the spoils' (Diodorus). Some temples ended up looking like war trophies, ostentatiously parading rows of captured shields over their colonnades.

In a more specific way Greek temples commemorated Greek victories. In Sicily once more, construction of two new temples formed part of the war indemnity imposed by the victorious Greeks on a humiliated Carthage. Unsurprisingly, when Carthage next gained the upper hand, Greek sanctuaries were a particular target. At Akragas in 409 BC the enemy not only set them on fire but made a point of 'mutilating the sculptures and everything of rather exceptional workmanship' (Diodorus).

On the other hand, the destruction of Greek temples by fellow-Greeks seems to have been extremely rare, thanks to the universal horror of sacrilege (in this respect the Macedonian king Philip V did not behave as a Greek: see Sounion and Thermon, pp. 146, 174). Robbery of temple-treasures (*hierosulia*) was a heinous crime too, although as the Greek writer Strabo (1st century BC) wryly observed, 'since riches inspire envy these are hard to protect, even when they belong to the gods'. There is no shortage of stories of Greeks plundering sacred property, especially in war.

Where Greek temples were damaged by Greeks, it was more likely because they were in the line of fire. In 364 BC, Arkadians and Eleians slugged it out inside the sanctuary at Olympia from the roofs of the temples. Rooftiles – even ones of fired clay weighed up to 30 kg (66 lb) – could then become lethal missiles.

Back in the early 5th century, just as the Sicilian Greeks were beating off the Carthaginians at Himera, the mainland Greeks – allies for once – were themselves fighting a foreign invasion by the world's greatest empire at the time, Persia. In this epic struggle Greek temples came to figure as symbols of Persian barbarism and Greek renewal.

The Persians burnt Greek temples as legitimate targets of war both in western Turkey and on the mainland. After they captured the Akropolis in Athens (480 BC), 'they stripped the temple of its treasures and burnt everything' (Herodotus).

Ejected from the Greek mainland in 479 BC, the Persians remained objects of fear and loathing. Sight of the violated temples played an important part in keeping alive Greek hatred. Shrines supposedly left in deliberate ruin from the Persian wars were still visible at Phaleron near Athens and Haliartos in Boiotia in the 2nd century AD.

Soon afterwards work began on Zeus' great temple at Olympia, mentioned earlier. This too was conceived as a thanks offering for a victory by the builders, the men of Elis, over some neighbours, the men of Pisa. But by 457 BC the apex of the main gable advertised what would turn out to be a far more destructive inter-Greek enmity, displaying a gold shield with this inscription below it:

'The temple keeps the golden circle: Lakonians and allies dedicated the gift from Tanagra: the tenth of Argos, of Athens, of Ionia, for victory in war.'

The 'Lakonians' were the Spartans, and this victory over Athens in 457 BC marked the beginning of the open hostility between the two which dragged on until the decisive Spartan defeat of Athens in 404 BC. In the intervening half-century an efflorescent Athens assembled a magnificent array of new buildings, including the Parthenon. Thanks

to them, commented the contemporary Athenian historian Thucydides, if his countrymen's city ever fell into ruins, 'we should infer their power to have been twice as great as it really is'.

## 'The works of Perikles'

'Thus there is a certain bloom of newness in each building and an appearance of being untouched by the wear of time. It is as if some ever-flowering life and unaging spirit had been infused into the creation of these works.'

Plutarch, *Life of Perikles, c.* AD 100

Thus the Greek writer Plutarch rhapsodized over the monuments raised in Athens under the leader-ship of the 5th-century BC statesman Perikles. He had in mind above all the Propylaia, the grand entrance to the sanctuary on the Akropolis, built in 436–432 BC, the Parthenon and (probably) the Erechtheion (pp. 140–44).

These were the architectural keystones of a larger effort by Athens under Perikles to assert its superiority over other Greeks by reinventing itself as what today would be called a 'capital of culture'. This aspiration helps to explain the technical perfection at which the Parthenon and Erechtheion so clearly aimed.

The Parthenon was, on a grand scale, an expression of the inter-state rivalries and triumphalism which, as we have seen, were such a powerful dynamic behind temple-building in the 6th and 5th centuries. Built when the Athenians were at loggerheads with the Spartans and their Peloponnesian allies, it may have been a deliberate attempt to outdo Zeus' temple at Olympia. It was bigger, it was better built, in marble instead of coarse limestone, and it had masses more sculpture – including 92 carved metopes against Olympia's more normal 12.

For contemporaries, the Parthenon may also have symbolized Athenian dominance of other Greeks since it was paid for – according to ancient tradition – from the defence budget of the Athenian alliance (the so-called Delian League), which in this and other ways came more and more to resemble an Athenian empire. In the 4th century, if not before, Athenians also understood it as a memorial to ancestral successes in the Persian wars. No other Greek temple was built in circumstances more conducive to the acquisition of layers of historical meanings.

*The Athenian Akropolis viewed from the gateway or Propylaia. This was one of the famous 'works of Perikles', as was the Parthenon (right) and the colossal open-air statue of Athena (left of centre) by Pheidias.*

# The Spread of
# Greek Culture

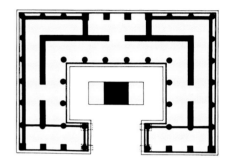

*Reconstruction of the architecturally unique Spartan sanctuary at Amyklai. Soaring above a surrounding colonnade, the colossal statue of Apollo stood in the open air on an elaborate carved 'throne'.*

## Diffusion and its limits

In this classical heyday the colonnaded temple makes its first appearance in a non-Greek context. In Sicily the indigenous people of Segesta, neighbours (and enemies) of the Selinountines, had been acquiring a taste for the material trappings of Greek culture since the 7th century BC. In the 5th century BC they started to build colonnaded Greek temples – one in the mid-century, another a generation later.

In contrast, it is salutary to reflect that, for the 6th and 5th centuries BC, well over twice as many Greek states are attested as colonnaded temples. Over 200 Greek states alone were members of the 5th-century Athenian alliance (p. 33). But the total number of known colonnaded temple sites in the 6th and 5th centuries is just over 100.

Even allowing for the gaps in our archaeological knowledge, the statistic is a reminder of the continuing exceptionality of these structures, which on grounds of cost must always have been a limited option. Their relative rarity only underlines the likely kudos available to possessors of such outstanding buildings.

In Macedonia there is evidence for stone temples, probably but not certainly colonnaded, in the Greek cities fringing the coast. But the Macedonians themselves never seem to have favoured this building type, which was conspicuously absent from their ethnic sanctuary at Dion near Mount Olympos. Until the late 4th century BC the same held true for the Greek-speaking tribes of northwest Greece.

North of the Corinthian gulf, there were early temple-building efforts by the Aitolian tribes in their communal sanctuary at Thermon, but a temple with a colonnade appears for certain only in the later 3rd century BC (pp. 173–74). In the southern two-fifths of the Peloponnese, no colonnaded temple has been found at Sparta, and none in Messenia before the 3rd century BC. They are a rarity in the Cycladic islands (one on Naxos, one on Delos), and all but unknown on Crete (one possibly, from the 2nd or 1st century BC).

Geologically Greece and the islands are largely limestone or marble, and anyway Greek states were willing to import stone for temple-building in spite of the huge transport costs (p. 58). Rather than being a matter of practicalities, these absences suggest cultural variation.

Regional preferences in architecture reflecting ingrained local traditions were certainly a factor, as in Crete and the Cyclades, where temples without surrounding colonnades were favoured, and possibly Sparta, where local shrines, although imposing in their way, could look quite different from any other Greek cult-building.

The north and northwest contained populations considered politically and culturally backward by southern Greeks because they were not organized into poleis but formed polities based on 'peoples' or hereditary monarchies (or both). These types of Greek state may not have felt the need for this particular form of political symbol, or not as urgently.

## Fourth-century crises

The 4th century BC witnessed profound changes in the Greek world. Over in the west, protracted conflict with indigenous peoples in Italy and the Carthaginian empire in Sicily put the Greek colonies there on the defensive and for most marked the end of their days of greatest confidence and prosperity.

In these conflicts with western 'barbarians' Greek temples were once more casualties, as with the Heraion at Foce del Sele, burnt in the 4th century, or the sanctuaries of Akragas, targeted in the Carthaginian sack of 409 BC. The last major temple in a western colony, at Kaulonia on Italy's instep, dates around 430–420 BC.

On the mainland, the period after the wars between Athens and Sparta, leading to the overthrow of Athens in 404 BC, is often seen as one of relative decline. 'Relative' needs stressing where temple-building is concerned. Somewhat fewer colonnaded temples were indeed erected than in the previous two centuries (see Table on p. 25). But they included major projects in the panhellenic sanctuaries of Delphi, Epidauros and Nemea, as well as Tegea's new temple of Athena, considered by Pausanias the finest in the Peloponnese, and a group in the northwest, including the regions of Akarnania and Epeiros, where the colonnaded temple now appears for the first time.

The Macedonian kingdom's unexpected rise to dominance on the mainland culminated in Philip II's decisive victory over the allied Greeks at Chaironeia (338 BC). Macedonian power would overshadow Greece until the early 2nd century BC. Along with economic problems, political instability on the mainland was a factor in the decline in major temple-projects here in the 3rd century.

But it needs stressing that in the parts of Greece which prospered in this period, such as those dominated by the powerful Aitolian and Achaian confederacies, based in northwest and central Greece respectively, or well connected at the royal courts, as with Athens, new colonnaded temples continued to be commissioned. Most, as before, were in the Doric style.

## Persian Asia Minor

'As a true testimony to the magnificence of Greece there is still extant the temple of Ephesian Diana…'

Pliny the Elder, Roman writer, c. AD 60

In the rich Greek cities of the east Aegean and Asia Minor (western Turkey), temple-building had got off to a dazzling start in the 6th century BC with the creation of the Ionic style and the building of huge temples at Ephesos and Didyma and on Samos.

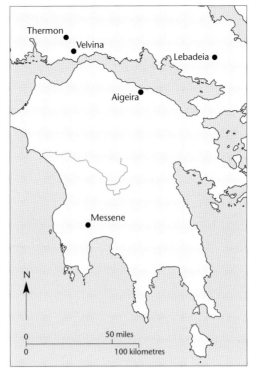

*Distribution of new Doric temples on the Greek mainland begun in the 3rd or 2nd century BC.*

*(Below) Artist's impression of the huge temple of Artemis (Roman Diana) at Ephesos (pp. 199–200), rebuilt in the 4th century BC and hailed by the Greeks as one of the Seven Wonders of the World.*

The Persian conquest, and subsequent Greek dissatisfaction with Persian rule, leading to a great revolt in 499–494 BC, threw this early trajectory off course. More unexpectedly, the region's 'liberation' by Athens and entry into her alliance in the years after 479 BC do not seem to have recreated local conditions, economic or political, which favoured the resumption of temple-building. In stark contrast to the mainland and the western colonies, not a single colonnaded temple in the region can be assigned to the 5th century.

After the defeat of their Athenian protectors in 404 BC the Greeks of Asia Minor became Persian subjects once more until their next 'liberation', this time by Alexander the Great (334 BC). Persia ruled with a light touch, offering no hindrance to the first really big major temple-building project in the region for nearly two centuries: rebuilding the huge Artemision of Ephesos, which burnt down in 356 BC. It was to this building, a marble forest of 117 Ionic columns, that later Greeks gave the accolade of inclusion – as the only temple – on their list of the world's Seven Wonders (see p. 35).

Temple-building had already reappeared in Asia Minor during the 4th century BC as a result of non-Greek patronage. The Karia region in southwest Turkey was in the hands of a family of indigenous viceroys based on Halikarnassos (Bodrum). One of them, Idrieus (351–344 BC), upgraded the temple of the local Zeus in the Karian sanctuary of Labraynda (p. 209) by adding an Ionic colonnade. Highly unusually, on the front above the columns was an inscribed dedication in Idrieus' name – a piece of self-advertisement which no true Greek polis at this date would readily permit, as Alexander the Great was to learn.

## Alexander and the kings

In eleven short years Philip II's son Alexander utterly transformed the Greek world. On his death he left behind a joint Macedonian and Greek colonial empire stretching as far as what is now Pakistan. In deliberate contrast to Persia, Greek temples were very much a part of Alexander's imperial vision.

At little Priene he persuaded the citizens to let him dedicate a new Ionic temple of Athena (pp. 202–3). A much grander piece of public relations beckoned him in the Ephesian Artemision. He offered to pay the costs 'both past and future, on

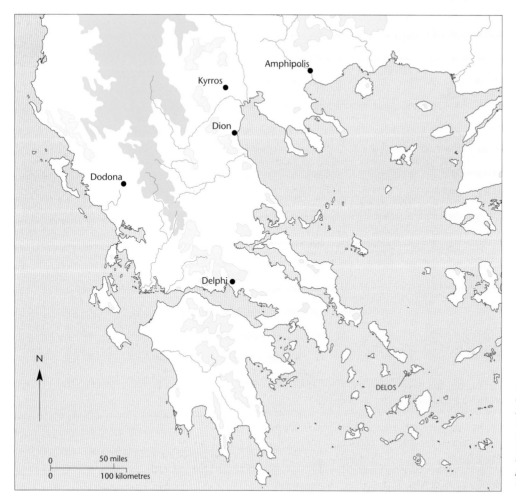

*The new Greek temples allegedly being planned by Alexander in 323 BC. Three (Delos, Delphi and Dodona) were panhellenic sanctuaries. The other three sites were all in Macedonia – at last to be put on the map in terms of major Greek-style temples.*

ΒΑΣΙΛΕΥΣΑΛΕΞΑΝΔΡΟΣ
ΑΝΕΘΗΚΕΤΟΝΝΑΟΝ
ΑΘΗΝΑΙΗΓΟΛΙΑΔΙ

condition that he should have the credit thereof on the inscription' (Strabo). The condition prompted the Ephesians to rebuff the king – an indicator of extreme Greek sensitivity to the placing of individual donors' names on temples conceived as expressions of communal prestige (see illustration above).

At his death Alexander was said to be planning 'six most costly temples, each at an expense of 1500 talents' (Diodorus Siculus). Although the authenticity of this ancient tradition is debated, it is certainly in keeping with Alexander's earlier interest in dedicating temples. Temple-building in the Aegean area was now to become an instrument of royal public relations, emphasizing the kings' Greek credentials and giving their rule the imprimatur of the Greek gods.

Among the Macedonian successor kings, the dynasties of the Ptolemies, based in Egypt (323–30 BC), and the Seleukids in Asia (305–64 BC), both supported temple-building in the Aegean heartland.

The Seleukids provided crucial start-up funds for what, after the new Artemision at Ephesos, would be the greatest monument to the revival of temple-building in Asia Minor: Didyma's new mega-temple (pp. 204–7) of Apollo, who was claimed by the dynasty as its progenitor. Here gigantism, as with the earlier tyrants and, centuries later, the Roman emperor Hadrian, served to advertise royal power.

A later Seleukid, Antiochos IV (ruled 175–164 BC), gave another huge temple, the Olympieion, to the Athenians (pp. 134–35). This was a public relations exercise if ever there was one, since Athens at the time had long been rendered politically powerless, but remained a powerful symbol of Greek culture. The more ornate Corinthian style in which the Olympieion was built may have been thought of by Greeks of the time as the royal style par excellence.

## The new colonies

'[Alexander] himself marked out where the city's agora was to be built, how many sanctuaries there were to be and of which deities… and the wall which was to be built all around.'

Arrian, Greek historian, c. AD 140

As this passage shows, describing the founding of Alexandria in Egypt (332/331 BC), communal temples were an integral part of the foundation of new cities for Graeco-Macedonian colonists by the kings in Asia and Egypt. But the traditional colonnaded temple has so far made a sparse showing in the archaeology of these regions.

Although care is required here, since new finds may change this picture, it may also reflect some historical reality. The founders and the colonial elites of these new cities were usually ethnic

'King Alexander dedicated the temple to Athena Polias.' The citizens of Priene may have let the king dedicate the temple of their patron-goddess, but they placed his Greek inscription in a strikingly inconspicuous position – some 6 metres (20 feet) off the ground, at the top of a dimly lit pilaster or wall-terminal as you entered the front porch.

(Right) The temple of Sarapis
in Alexandria, hugely famous
in its day, has left only scrappy
remains. This possible plan of
the earliest structure was
suggested by Michael Sabottka
in his unpublished Berlin
dissertation (1985). It is a
Greek-style naos, but of the
simplest kind. (Far right) A
Graeco-Egyptian image of
the god Sarapis himself.

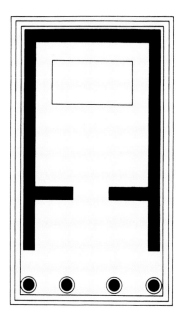

Macedonians, in whose religious traditions, as we saw (p. 34), the Greek colonnaded temple had hitherto played little or no part.

It is striking that in the royal capital of Alexandria (admittedly in Rhakotis, the Egyptian quarter), the temple built by Ptolemy III (246–221 BC) for his dynasty's divine patron, the Graeco-Egyptian Sarapis, may have been a modest affair – no more than 22 x 12 m (72 x 39 ft) according to the latest study, without a colonnade.

The one attested temple with a colonnade, at Seleukeia in Pieria (p. 224) in Syria, has a crypt – a feature recalling the colonnaded mausoleum found at Ai Khanoum, a Graeco-Macedonian colony founded around 300 BC on the banks of the Oxus River (Amu Darya) in northeast Afghanistan. Here the traditional three-stepped platform and colonnade was adapted for a grandiose funerary monument, its crypt yielding finds of sarcophagi and skeletons.

It is just possible that the temple at Seleukeia was likewise a tomb – that of Seleukos I. It should not perhaps surprise us if the most prestigious type of Greek religious monument was now appropriated for the burial of Macedonian kings, who were widely hailed by the Greeks themselves as gods.

### The 'Ionian renascence'

In contrast to mainland Greece, the Table (p. 25) tells a different story for the eastern Aegean after Alexander. In western Turkey alone, well over twenty major colonnaded temples date to the last three centuries BC, not just in the old areas of Greek settlement but also among indigenous neighbours in the regions of Mysia, Lydia, Karia, Lykia and even Pisidia.

Broadly speaking this mushrooming reflects the revitalization and multiplication of the Greek poleis in this region, in turn based on the region's natural wealth and the more encouraging political and cultural climate ushered in with Alexander's 'liberation'. As we saw, kings can be closely linked to the funding of one of these projects (Didyma), and their hand can be suspected in numerous others.

The deities which these temples served were overwhelmingly the old-established Greek deities, even if in non-Greek communities their names mask Anatolian origins. Time and again the new temples turn out to be serving the chief cults of the cities in question (Artemis at Sardis and Magnesia-on-the-Maeander, Apollo at Alabanda, Asklepios on Kos, and so on). This same point is made by the overlap with the distribution of rights of inviolability (p. 91), usually granted only to major sanctuaries in these and later centuries.

Among these new temples were two major oracles of Apollo. Didyma with its huge temple, never completed, has already been mentioned. The other was Klaros (pp. 197–98). These are the first two colonnaded temples where the special architectural arrangements for consulting the oracle can be studied – if not always understood.

The renewed prestige of the colonnaded temple in Asia Minor triggered more developments in temple-design. Roman writers mention a number of famous Greek architects working in the region in Alexander's time and later, including Hermogenes (p. 64). Their preference for the Ionic style reflects a self-conscious regional identity and perhaps too a certain 'Ionian' chauvinism. This may also be echoed in the technical criticisms of Doric for its 'faulty and ill-fitting proportions' attributed by the Roman architectural writer Vitruvius (late 1st century BC) to Hermogenes and his colleagues. For all that, Doric was in no sense outlawed for temples in the region. The most notable example is Ionian Klaros, where the choice of Doric may have paid homage to Apollo's oracle at Delphi.

*One of the two dimly lit passages inside the temple-walls at Didyma, leading down into a huge inner court where the oracle was located. Exactly how they were used is a mystery.*

# The Coming of Rome

*Repairs to the temple of Zeus at Cyrene (pp. 225–26) by the Roman proconsul are indicated by this Latin inscription above the columns of the facade. 'Zeus' has become 'Jupiter Augustus': the Greek supreme god and the Roman emperor were now worshipped together.*

## The Romans arrive

Conquering what was left of the Greek west in the 3rd century BC, the Romans went on to become masters of mainland Greece and western Turkey in the 2nd century BC, the interior of Asia Minor, Syria and Egypt in the 1st century BC. The impact on the Greeks was profound.

Early on the Romans found it expedient to be 'Greek-friendly' (philhellene). Roman warfare, unlike Persian or Carthaginian, was not harsh in its treatment of the fabric of Greek temples. The Roman general Sulla behaved unusually when he made off with marble columns from the (unfinished) Olympieion at Athens (86 BC).

A greater threat was the Roman craze for old Greek objets d'art, fed by war, unscrupulous Roman officials (see p. 59), and, increasingly, art-dealers. Roman activities anticipated Lord Elgin's onslaught

*This marble figure is Greek work of around 450–425 BC. But it was found in Rome, along with other figures from the same set of gable-figures. They were reused to decorate the temple of Apollo Medicus (30s BC), perhaps after being removed 'to order' from Apollo's temple at Eretria (pp. 166–67).*

on the Parthenon, and some Greek temples were now forcibly parted from their sculpture.

But it was not all doom and gloom for Greek temples at this time. In Asia Minor, even in the more turbulent days of Roman rule in the late 2nd and 1st centuries BC, Greek cities felt confident enough to embark on major temple projects, like Stratonikeia's for Hekate at Lagina (pp. 211–12). Good relations with Rome as well as local prosperity lay behind such initiatives, as with the temple at Aigai (p. 193) which celebrated the city's 'salvation' by the Roman governor (46 BC), or the temple at Aphrodisias, sponsored by Zoilus, a rich freedman of the future emperor Augustus (pp. 207–8).

## Preserving the old

'After my victory I replaced in all the temples of the cities of Asia the treasures of which they had been robbed…'

This action of Augustus, the first Roman emperor (30 BC–AD 15), recorded in his *Deeds*, was meant to advertise his piety for the gods, Greek as well as Roman. From Augustus on, Roman rule was allied to an increased show of respect for Greece's sacred heritage, including temples.

Roman governors sponsored repairs to venerable colonnaded temples, as did emperors themselves. A favoured form of sprucing up was the veneering in coloured marbles, Roman-style, of floors and walls. The conserving trend reached a climax with the emperor Hadrian AD 117–38), whose careful restoration of Hermogenes' dilapidated temple at Teos

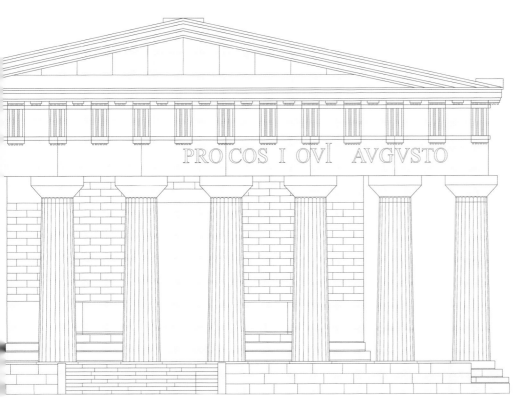

PRO COS I OVI AVGVSTO

(pp. 196–97) amounted almost to a new building.

A more extreme form of conservation was the careful and costly dismantling of a temple and its reerection on a new site. A well-documented case under Augustus is the temple of Ares at Athens (pp. 136–37). An operation of this kind can be interpreted as an act of homage by later Athenians to the prestigious 'works of Perikles'. But it also points to the disruption and abandonment of the older cult places – some of them in the countryside – where these temples had originally stood.

### The Hadrianic 'renascence'

Hadrian, a great builder as well as ardent Hellenist, built from scratch the first and only explicitly Greek temple in Rome itself (p. 121). Like the Olympieion at Athens, which he finally finished, this was a mega-temple, as were others which he funded at Kyzikos (p. 188–89) and Smyrna (p. 196) in Asia Minor. In matters of size, Hadrian sought to emulate the kings.

It was perhaps inconceivable for such huge new sacred architecture to ignore the Roman emperor, now the most manifest form of god-like power in the Greek world. In Athens, and probably Kyzikos too, Hadrian seems to have been worshipped alongside Zeus as his earthly counterpart.

Hadrian's patronage helped to stimulate a final wave of Greek temple-building in the Roman empire's 'high noon' during the 2nd century AD, mostly in Asia Minor. The cult of the Roman emperors was an important factor in this activity, as we

shall see in Chapter IV. Among the latest Greek colonnaded temples to be built, however, were those of Athena and Apollo at Side (p. 216) on Turkey's south coast. They show how, right to the end, this building type retained its primary association with the traditional deities of Greek civic religion.

*Bronze portrait of Hadrian combined with the body of an older statue, found in Israel. His un-Roman beard announced his Greek interests.*

# Decline and Rediscovery

### The coming of Christianity

Constantine I died in AD 337 as the first Christian emperor. The pagan emperor Julian (361–63) tried unsuccessfully to turn the clock back. In 391, Theodosius I closed all temples and banned all forms of pagan ritual.

The fate of surviving Greek temples in this twilight of the old religion seems to have varied considerably. In Ilion, it was the local bishop who acted as protector and guardian of Athena's temple and cult objects (p. 189). Elsewhere in the east, Christian fanatics destroyed temples before 391 – although the clearest evidence archaeologically for the impact of ancient religious fanaticism on a colonnaded Greek temple relates to Jews, not Christians, during a revolt in Cyrene in AD 115 (pp. 225–27).

### Conversion

In the two centuries after 391, many colonnaded temples were converted into churches – in the case of the temple of 'Concord' at Akragas, we are told, after the bishop had first 'chased away the demons who were there, hiding in the idol of Ebert and Raps'. Here the retention of the outer colonnade disguised the transformation. In more radical conversions like the former Athena-temple at Syracuse (pp. 123–24), the outer colonnade was immured in the outer fabric of the new building.

In Greek lands, many early churches failed to survive the upheavals marking the transition from late antiquity to the Middle Ages (7th and 8th centuries). Among those that did are the best-preserved temples today. Under Ottoman Turkish rule, these ancient buildings might undergo further adaptation, into a mosque (the Parthenon) or medrese (Ankyra), or a private residence, complete with harem (the Erechtheion).

### Quarrying

The majority of temples experienced sadder fates. Few today preserve much of their upper structure in place; most are mainly foundations, or not even these: just the trenches for them. Once abandoned by the communities which they had served, temple-sites were usually pressed into service as quarries.

Even before Christianity, this had already been the fate of disowned temples like those of Apollo Daphnephoros in Eretria (p. 167), or Tavole Palatine in Metapontion (p. 120). Only rarely did extreme remoteness protect a temple, as at Bassai.

Abandoned temples were irresistibly handy suppliers of ready-made building materials. Their masonry could be reused, in late antiquity often finding its way into new churches nearby. Marble was burnt to make lime for mortar. In late antiquity kilns for this purpose were set up by the ruins of Sardis' temple of Artemis (p. 194). Finally temples could be 'mined' for the iron clamps which held their blocks together.

*The Parthenon was first converted from a church into a mosque in 1460. After the Venetians accidentally blew it up (1687), the small mosque shown here was built inside the shell.*

## Rediscovery

In the Middle Ages the lands once inhabited by the ancient Greeks were controlled by a patchwork of Christian and Islamic states. Apart from some erudite Greeks in Constantinople, few people at this time took much interest in the physical debris of classical antiquity all around them. But, during the 15th century, indifference changed to enthusiasm as Italian scholars and artists rediscovered the Roman roots of western, Christian culture.

In this new atmosphere of inquisitiveness about the antique, occasional travellers began to penetrate the lands east of the Adriatic with drawing boards and a vague inkling of 'the glory that was Greece'. The earliest drawings of Greek temples to survive, including the Parthenon and Hadrian's now-vanished temple at Kyzikos in northwest Turkey, were made by a certain Ciriaco Pizzicolli, from Ancona, on the Adriatic coast of Italy. Ciriaco paid repeated visits to Greek lands in the first half of the 15th century, and was sufficiently smitten with classical Greece to learn the ancient tongue.

Until the mid-18th century, however, educated westerners knew much more about ancient Rome than ancient Greece. People making the Grand Tour at this time rarely visited Greece proper. If they had seen a Greek ruin, it was likely to be in southern Italy or Sicily, where the temples of Paestum were a fixture for visitors to the kingdom of Naples. At a time when 'Roman' and 'Greek' were commonly confused, the site of these sturdy Greek temples came as a shock to travellers fresh from a visit to the elegant wall-paintings of ancient Pompeii. 'I found myself in an utterly unfamiliar world,' recalled Goethe after his visit in 1787.

By this date a thaw in diplomatic relations between the Ottoman empire and the western powers was putting Greece firmly back on the cultural map of the west. In 1762 the first volume appeared of an English publication, *The Antiquities of Athens*, in which James Stuart and Nicholas Revett published

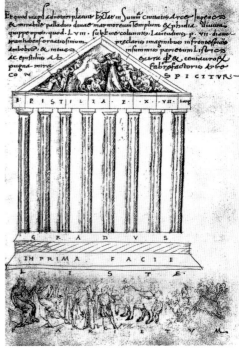

*(Right) Cyriaco's sketch of the west front of the Parthenon, preserving important details of the gable-sculpture before it was damaged in the explosion of 1687.*

*(Below) Here James Stuart (foreground, right) has painted himself sketching the Erechtheion, while its pipe-smoking proprietor, the Ottoman commandant of the Akropolis, looks on (1751).*

measured drawings, as well as sketches, based on a visit to Athens in 1755. This major work offered Western readers accurate images for the first time of the Parthenon and the Erechtheion. In Britain it triggered a new appreciation of things Greek. This included a growing fad for neo-Greek architecture, at its height from 1770 to 1820.

In the Napoleonic era, as Ottoman power continued to wane, Western treasure-hunters began the first excavations at temple sites in Greece. Digs at Bassai (1811) and Aigina (1810), not to mention the controversial activities of Lord Elgin on the Akropolis (1801–5), all resulted in the export of important collections of Greek temple sculpture from Greece to European capitals.

The new kingdom of Greece, founded in 1833 following a successful Greek uprising against the Ottoman sultan, identified itself closely with Classical Greece. Its first king, Otho, was a prince of Bavaria, where Munich, the capital, was a centre of the new Western idealization of ancient Greece. Unsurprisingly, archaeology in Greece from the outset was a matter of state interest. As early as 1834 the restoration of the temples of Athens was officially taken in hand, under the aegis of a German archaeologist, Ludwig Ross.

In the 19th century, temples were the most admired and the most imitated models of ancient Greek architecture. Their study now enjoyed a heyday. Fuelled by new discoveries, scholarly debates raged about whether they were unroofed, and about the extent and the effect of their paintwork. Pioneering work was done on the so-called refinements of temple architecture and on their orientation – Francis Penrose, the first Director of the British School at Athens, was particularly active in these two areas.

Founded in 1886, the British School was one of a number of foreign archaeological missions based in 19th-century Greece. In prestige it was overshadowed somewhat by the French School, founded in 1846, and the German Archaeological Institute, dating from 1873. These two well-funded institutions secured the right to excavate respectively at Delphi (from 1892) and Olympia (from 1875). Here, remains of some of the ancient Greek mainland's most famous temples outside Athens were now brought to light.

In the same century, the eastern Mediterranean became increasingly opened up to the west. Foreign archaeologists conducted expeditions to Greek lands further afield; the British expeditions to Cyrene (1860–61), Epheso (1863–74) and Priene (1868–69) deposited parts of the Ephesian Artemi-

*Drawing by the young British architect Charles Cockerell of finds from the first investigations at Bassai in 1811, including the enigmatic Corinthian capital (p. 156). The rifle suggests the dangerous conditions in Greece at this time.*

sion and the Prienian temple of Athena Polias in the British Museum, where they are still on display.

In the rediscovery of Greek temples, the 19th century has some claim to be considered the age of pioneers. Although the pace of new discoveries has since slowed down, the potential for exciting revelations is far from exhausted. Turkey (Asia Minor) continues to be one of the richest seams in Greek archaeology, as shown by the excavations of Aphrodisias in Karia, begun in 1961 on a site where a few columns of the temple of Aphrodite have managed to stay upright for nearly 2,000 years. At the dawn of the 21st century, the continuing liveliness of temple research is shown by the revelation of new colonnaded temples in Epidamnos (Albania), Metropolis (Thessaly, central Greece) and Triopion (southwest Turkey).

In the later 20th century, more methodical techniques of excavation have allowed archaeologists to reconstruct the complex history of even badly preserved temple-sites, such as Kalapodi (Hyampolis) in central Greece (pp. 169–70). In addition, archaeologists continue to return to more famous sites. In the last half-century, for instance, American archaeologists active in the Peloponnese have conducted major new investigations at Bassai, the Argive Heraion, Nemea and Isthmia.

At Nemea, the Americans have reerected two of the fallen columns of the temple of Zeus, based on a careful survey of the ruins. Ever since the work of Stuart and Revett, the accurate recording of the remains of Greek temples has been a concern of those who study Greek temples closely. Nowadays, archaeologists normally carry out block-by-block studies of temple-remains, including measuring, drawing and photographing of individual elements which have fallen from their original positions. As at Nemea, this kind of exact work creates the potential for partial reconstruction.

The modern restoration – including rebuilding – of Greek temples began with the work of Ross in the Athens of the 1830s. In most of the modern states which find themselves heirs to Greek archaeological sites conservation is now encouraged. In the past Greek temples have sometimes been conserved with more concern for the picturesque than for accuracy or with construction techniques which have failed to stand the test of time. The high standards of modern work are exemplified by the conservation programme carried out by Greek archaeologists on the Athenian Akropolis since 1979. The careful examination of every identifiable block in a programme of this kind also helps to provide new information about Greek temple-design and construction, to which we turn next.

*Painting by Hugh William Williams of the temple of Aphaia on Aigina (1820). With its artful rearrangement of the surrounding landscape, it captures the Romantic spirit in which Westerners approached Greece's Classical ruins from the later 18th century on.*

# Siting, Construction, Decoration and Finance

For the ancient Greeks, building a colonnaded temple was a complex challenge. Communities had to assemble unfamiliar expertise and exotic materials in order to raise temples on sites which were often lofty and inaccessible, chosen by religious diktat and a competitive compulsion to show off.

In origin the form of the colonnaded temple may have been a built symbol of the cosmic order. Once established, the design varied little in essentials, although as late as the 2nd century BC it was the site for a continuing experiment with Greek ideas about harmony and proportion in architecture. From early on, the most talented artists were brought in to create the religious sculpture forming an integral part of the temple's fabric and to apply the bright washes of colour without which no Greek temple was complete. A temple might remain in religious use for centuries and be subject to repeated repairs, nowadays hard to reconstruct.

Fund-raising for temple building was an art in itself. The pious paid what they could. More often it was the profits of war which tipped the financial balance, or the helping hand of the rich and powerful. The local officials who handled these huge sums of money were held to account by their fellow citizens. Today building records, meticulously inscribed on stone for all to see, are sometimes the best record of long-vanished Greek temples.

*The temple of Apollo at Delphi in its ancient setting.*
*In this archaeologically precise reconstruction, note the shields on display*
*above the temple columns, and the painted mural on the inner building.*

S D'APOLLON

II    Building for the Gods

# Selecting the Location

## Choosing the site

The invariable setting of a colonnaded temple was a sacred space, a sanctuary (*temenos* or *hieron*). Since Greek sanctuaries were usually older than their monumental temples, the choice of temple site could be broadly predetermined. In the case of Olympia, for instance, the cult of Zeus there can be traced back to the end of the 10th century BC – some three centuries before the construction of the first monumental temple, later dedicated to Hera. That said, certain common factors, social and religious, can be observed in the placing of temples on their specific sites.

## 'The most conspicuous place'

General statements in ancient Greek writers about the ideal site for temples and sanctuaries stress the desirability of conspicuousness and loftiness. Archaeology amply bears out the texts. Among the ancient Greeks a preference for placing temples on or next to the civic centre (agora), on natural eminences, or overlooking plains and sea (or all these things, as at Priene), was widespread.

This preference, often noted for Greece proper, is in fact found everywhere. In southern Italy a majority of Greek colonnaded temples were built on the sea's edge, such as Kaulonia, Kroton and Krimis(s)a, or commanded superb views from high ground (Eleia, Hipponion, Lokroi's Marafioti temple), or both.

The same tendency can be observed in Sicily, especially at Syracuse, Selinous and Akragas – where seven colonnaded temples are strung out like a chain on an eye-catching ridge, easy to see both from inside the ancient city and from the sea. It is

*Part of the 'temple ridge' at Agrigento (ancient Akragas).*

found, too, in many colonnaded temples in the Aegean islands and Asia Minor: Naxos, Kos, Assos, Pergamon, to name but a few.

The assertion of group solidarity and identity, as discussed in Chapter II, was by no means the sole explanation for this emphasis on conspicuousness. Ancient writers state, or imply, as reasons the inspiration to prayer of seeing a temple from afar, the security provided by a high place, and also religious cleanliness – Pausanias particularly admired the people of Tanagra in central Greece because their sanctuaries were set apart from their residential quarters 'in a clean place'.

Another purely religious reason is suggested by Vitruvius, who wrote of the Romans that they believed that the sites of their protector deities 'should be located in the very highest place, the vantage from which to see the greatest possible extent of the city walls'. Probably the ancient Greeks believed the same: the homes of tutelary gods should overlook what they were meant to protect.

## Hallowed ground

'There is also a building called the Erechtheion... On the rock is the outline of a trident. Legend says that these appeared as evidence in support of Poseidon's claim to the land.'

Pausanias, Greek travel writer, 2nd century AD

In some cases the particular siting of monumental temples is hard to tie in with the cults themselves. This seems true, for instance, of western colonies where temples have been massed for visual effect in closed precincts, as in Metapontion or Selinous. Previously hallowed ground does not seem to have been a major factor in the creation of the 'temple ridge' at Akragas, where only one of the seven colonnaded temples is on the site of a predecessor.

In older parts of the Greek world, what lay beneath a temple could define a site's sanctity. In the Erechtheion (pp. 143–44), fissures in the underlying bedrock were pointed out to Pausanias as the marks of Poseidon's trident. They were so sacred that they were given special consideration in the building's

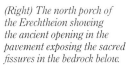

*(Right) The north porch of the Erechtheion showing the ancient opening in the pavement exposing the sacred fissures in the bedrock below.*

(Right) Foundations beneath Apollo's 6th-century temple at Eretria include those of an immediate predecessor (early 7th century BC) and a hairpin-shaped 'hut' of the 8th century BC (centre right) of debated function.

(Far right) Part of a foundation deposit from the 6th-century BC temple of Artemis at Ephesos, including these early coins of electrum, an alloy of gold and silver.

(Above) Restored view of a pre-existing shrine and altar reconstructed by the Athenians when the north hall of the Parthenon was built. The old site had been beneath the pavement on exactly the same spot.

design, which exposed them to heavenly view through a hole in the roof, as if encouraging the god to repeat his epiphany. These were places consecrated by revelations of divine power.

In other cases, what hallowed a temple-site in the first instance was the presence of earlier shrines underneath. When a temple was destroyed, for instance by fire or earthquake, the community, if it had survived itself, would normally rebuild it on the same spot. The Parthenon is now thought to have been at least the third temple on its site, the temple of Artemis at Hyampolis the fifth. Successors routinely reused material from predecessors, some-times even their foundations, and replicated their plans, including the elongated proportions of an earlier age.

Piety as well as economy seems to have shaped these practices. A particular consideration may have been preserving the placement of an older divine image, as at Kastabos (p. 214), where the statue-plinth from the old temple was reused for the same purpose in the new.

In a few cases, archaeology reveals the remains beneath a temple of much hoarier structures, believed by some to be chieftains' huts, the first repositories of the deity's sacred objects. Such finds push back into an even remoter past the ultimate origins of a site's sanctity.

## Foundation rituals

The Greeks marked the foundation of new cities with religious ceremonies, including sacrifices, omen-taking and prayers which might last a whole day. Finds suggests that, on a smaller scale, similar rituals marked the construction of temples. The evidence – never systematically collected – comes in the form of deposits of pottery, ash, coins and miscellaneous valuables deliberately buried beneath walls or the base for the chief statue inside the shrine. Among colonnaded temples conspicuous examples include the last-but-one temple of Hera on Samos (mid-6th century BC) and

Athena's temple at Priene, dedicated (?334 BC) by Alexander the Great. The practice was Near-Eastern in origin, and was aimed at ensuring the temple's future well-being.

## Orientation

'[The house] faces the fairest quarter of the day (for the fairest and loveliest is surely the beginning); it welcomes in the sun when he first peeps up; light fills it to overflowing through the wide-flung doors…'

Lucian, Greek writer, around AD 150

The ancient Greeks have more or less nothing to say about the orientation of their temples, leaving the topic wide open to modern speculation. Most Greek temples are aligned on an east–west axis, with the main entrance facing more or less east. Ancient texts indicate that Greek sanctuaries normally opened at daybreak – in part, no doubt, to take advantage of the coolest part of a Mediterranean day. The standard orientation may then have had a practical purpose (as is often assumed): to permit the light of dawn to illuminate the sacred image inside.

This effect has been observed in modern times at Bassai, although this temple is one of very few

somehow fitting the temple onto its designated site was at least as important as alignment with the heavens.

## 'Sacred landscapes'?

The beauty and power observed in the Greek landscape have long led modern observers to assume that these factors dictated the siting of ancient Greek temples. As the English antiquarian Aubrey de Vere rapturously declaimed on Delphi in 1850:

'So girt with white peaks flashing from sky chasms,
So lighted with the vast blue lamp of Heaven,
So lulled with music from the winds and waves,
The guest of Phoebus claps his hands and shouts,
"There is but one such spot: from Heaven Apollo
Beheld; – and chose it for his earthly shrine."'

In ancient Greek literature, too, the Olympian deities were closely linked to the landscape. Of Apollo, once more, it was said that 'All mountain peaks and high headlands of lofty rivers flowing

*Taken in the 1960s, this photograph shows dawn rays hitting the southwest corner of the back room at Bassai. On one view, the effect was intentional, so as to bathe in sunlight an image of Apollo standing on this spot.*

which face north, and the rays of dawn stream in through an east-facing side-opening into an interior space of uncertain ancient function. In fact, in many east-facing temples the statue may have been too tall, or too far back in the inner building, for the sun's rays to have achieved such an effect.

Adopting an approach familiar to students of Stonehenge, some scholars have speculated that Greek temples served as a form of sacred calendar. Their alignment on particular days with the sunrise or (a variant view) a star would announce days of special cultic significance such as festivals. On the other hand, archaeologists regularly explain away 'irregular' (that is, non-eastward) temple orientations by reference to the difficult lie of the land in a particular place. Insofar as this explanation is true, it suggests that, in the last analysis,

*The luminous landscape around Delphi, set on the lower slopes of Mount Parnassos.*

out to the deep and beaches sloping seawards and havens of the sea are your delight' (*Hymn to Delian Apollo*, perhaps 7th century BC).

With such passages as weapons it has been argued that Greek temples were deliberately placed so as to orientate the ancient viewer towards key features in a surrounding 'sacred landscape', especially hills and mountains, themselves understood (on this view) as manifestations of the deity in the temple. On such a reading Greek sacred sites would join others interpreted nowadays as metaphors for the cosmic thinking of the cultures which built them, such as Peru's Nazca Lines.

On the other hand these symbolic readings of temple-siting in ancient Greece have so far been based on subjective observation and can seem hazy. The difficulty is to prove the consistent application of a set of demonstrable general principles, particularly in the rugged terrain of Greece, where inadvertent alignments with natural features, especially high ground, are arguably hard to avoid.

## The temple as metaphor?

Since the notion of 'metaphor' has been raised, it needs emphasis in an ancient Greek context that the investment of material objects with metaphorical meanings is a familiar phenomenon to researchers in the social sciences. In this process the human mind may 'use the domain of the familiar in order to grasp the significance of the unfamiliar', as archaeologist Christopher Tilley has put it.

Turning to the temple itself, the ancient Greeks, who made rich use of verbal metaphor in their literature, were certainly capable of ascribing a metaphorical value to their architectural forms. In the 1st century BC Vitruvius could compare the Doric column to a male body in its 'proportions, strength and beauty', the Ionic to the 'slimness of a girl'. This Roman critique reflected an old Greek stereotyping, but was probably no earlier than the 5th century BC, when some Greek writers first presented the Ionian Greeks, subjugated by Persia, as somehow unmanly.

*Herakles stands in for the giant Atlas as supporter of the sky while Atlas fetches the golden apples of the Hesperides. This metope (for the term, see p. 62) from Zeus's temple at Olympia was placed over the front porch, just below the ceiling – which Herakles seems, as it were, to be holding up.*

In the formative period of stone temple design, around 600 BC, these cosmic arrangements may have been translated into the different attributes of a Greek temple, notably roof and gables, columns and floor.

Such an interpretation seems less far-fetched in the light of the Olympieion at Akragas, begun late in the 500s BC. Here huge male figures, with lowered heads and raised arms bent as if bearing a great burden, alternate with columns in seeming to 'support' the upper parts (see p. 29).

The idea that the gables of a Greek temple were a metaphor for the heavens is not a new one. The scholar Paul Hommel long ago suggested that this was why sculptured representations of deities and heroes were placed here in (some) Doric temples, and why gate-like openings appear in temple gables in Asia Minor from the 4th century BC, where they seem to have been used to stage (as we shall see in Chapter III) appearances of the deity's statue.

If the attic space symbolized the heavenly realm, this might also explain the frequency of monumental staircases from the temple interior into the upper parts, especially in western Greece (see pp. 88–89). It has been suggested, by archaeologist Margaret Miles, that these staircases (among other things) served in temple ritual.

To modern eyes, one of the oddities of Greek temple design is the relative frequency with which sculptured representation of gods and heroes are placed high up beneath the ceiling – too high and ill-lit for comfortable viewing by grounded humans (e.g., pp. 67, 142, 156). Was the intention to remind the ancient worshipper whose gaze was drawn to these supernatural figures, distant and only dimly visible, of the heavenly realm 'above' him?

Coming down to earth, archaeologist Erik Østby has recently suggested that the temple platform's convex curvature – one of the 'refinements' of temple design discussed later in this chapter – served as a metaphor for the curve of the earth's horizon, appreciated by the ancient Greeks whenever they took in the panorama of the sea.

Again, on its own this idea may seem implausible – but less so, perhaps, when taken with the way in which oracles housed in temples were invariably placed at a lower level than the temple-platform (e.g., Nemea [?], Delphi, Klaros, Didyma, Aizanoi) – as if the space below was also a metaphor, this time for the subterranean depths, which Greek belief traditionally linked with the power of prophecy.

The outer colonnade, which was such a distinctive feature of the Greek temple, has attracted other metaphorical readings. According to John Onians,

There may have been older, cosmic, metaphors in the overall design of the Greek temple. Metaphors of this type are familiar in the study of architecture of other societies both past and present. Notable is the case of ancient Greece's neighbour Egypt, where the 'idea of the domain of the god as a created world in microcosm' was well developed in temple-architecture (Egyptologist Richard Wilkinson). This was a land and culture which the Greeks were rediscovering just as they were working out the basics of temple design.

It is tempting to consider Greek temple design from this viewpoint not least because the cosmic thought of the ancient Greeks – evidently under the influence of the ancient Near East – conceived the universe in architectural terms. In the poems of Homer and Hesiod (8th to 7th centuries BC) the sky is kept apart from the earth by tall pillars or by Atlas, a god, who supports the weight on his head and hands. Heaven is understood as a solid roof over the world, imagined by the poets as made of iron or bronze. Heaven also has portals, guarded by the *Horai* or Seasons.

the Doric version (but not the Ionic) represented a unit of the Greek heavy-armed citizen-infantrymen (hoplites) who started to appear in the mid-7th century BC. On another view, the practical shelter to devotees provided by the temple's colonnades was a symbol of divine protection which the community sought from its tutelary deity.

How much credence, if any, should be given to these modern approaches to the Greek temple as 'solid metaphor' (Christopher Tilley)? Now that the colonnaded Greek temple is coming to look more and more like an act of conscious design, rather than the result of slow evolution, the cosmic interpretation seems cumulatively to have a certain force. But unless new evidence turns up (which seems unlikely), such speculations in the case of the Greek temple may never transmute into proven fact.

*A reassembled 'Atlas-figure' from the Olympieion at Akragas.*

# Design and Construction

## Project management

Who oversaw temple construction? Temple-building in ancient Greece was an affair of state – and a huge challenge. Communities had not only to raise the necessary funds, but also to organize and manage an operation of great complexity which might last over many years. Most of these communities were not used to regular building activity on this scale, and needed to import specialist skills and materials. Temple-building disrupted the community. But it also galvanized the economy, providing the local workforce with rare opportunities to diversify skills.

Sponsors of temple-building could be tyrants or kings. In the case of a panhellenic entity like Delphi, the commissioning body was the council of 'Dwellers around' (Amphiktyones), in fact representing much of Greece, who maintained the sanctuary and its cult. In the 4th century the councillors delegated supervision of the rebuilding of Apollo's temple to a board of 'temple-builders' (naopoioi).

Normally the sponsor was the polis community. Here the decision to build was approved by the politically active citizenry in its assembly, usually on a recommendation from the council, the body in day-to-day charge of the city.

By the 5th century BC the decision normally included the appointment of an expert (*architekton*) who produced a detailed specification (*syngraphe*), first heard of in the later 6th century BC, and who had earlier worked out the overall design. How this design was conceptualized is uncertain – drawings and models eventually came into play – but oral description and sets of figures may have been more important at first (see p. 60). A small board of citizens acted as a building committee.

The sponsor could proceed either by direct labour or – as was more usual by the 4th century BC – by

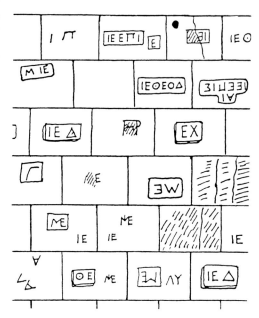

## Setting up a temple-building project in a Greek city

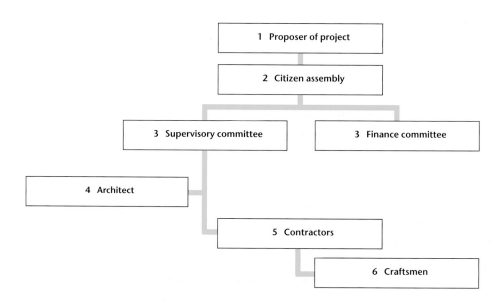

dividing the work up into different tasks which were then put out to contract. For the relatively small temple of Asklepios at Epidauros (p. 165), at least 68 different contracts were let. Finding contractors involved advertising by means of heralds, sent out to cry the details abroad.

## Labour

The names of many designers of temples are preserved, including figures famous in later antiquity such as Iktinos, Pytheos and Hermogenes. These three are among a number said to have written architectural treatises, including self-advertising works on their own temples.

Libon, who designed Zeus' temple at Olympia, was a local man familiar with local conditions. It is unlikely that smaller cities had such expertise on tap, and an expert must often have been brought in from outside. The most famous case was the Athenian Iktinos, the Parthenon architect said to have designed the temple at Bassai for tiny Phigaleia.

Detailed insight into the organization of temple-building comes from the inscribed accounts (pp. 70–71). These show that the exceptional nature of temple-building generated a workforce from many different places. The cities of the northeast Peloponnese, an early centre of temple-building, were a major force in construction, especially Argos and Corinth. In the 4th century the area was a key provider of contractors and materials for the temples of Asklepios at Epidauros and Apollo at Delphi.

Skilled artisans, in particular master-builders and masons, are likely to have travelled for their work. Archaeologists have found apparent evidence from temple masonry itself for itinerant craftsmen: in the later 4th and earlier 3rd centuries BC, for instance, the same workshop may have worked on both the temple of Artemis at Sardis and the Artemision of Ephesos.

Many lower-order skills could be provided locally, as with the Delphian quarry-workers, smiths, hauliers, carpenters, tilers, stonemasons, and plasterers who turn up in the Delphi accounts. Farmers not least stood to gain, because they seem to have been the chief source of the farm-animals used to drag the wagon-loads of building materials. On one estimate, more than 200 oxen a day were used to build the Parthenon.

*(Above left) Slab inscribed with building accounts from the Asklepieion, Epidauros.*

*(Above right) Southern Italian vase showing a craftsman adding painted decoration to a marble statue of Herakles.*

## Breakdown of trades by civic status

| | citizens | metics | slaves | unknown | Totals |
|---|---|---|---|---|---|
| architects | 2 | – | – | – | 2 |
| under-secretary | 1 | – | – | – | 1 |
| guard | – | – | – | 1 | 1 |
| masons | 9 | 12 | 16 | 7 | 44 |
| sculptors | 3 | 5 | – | 1 | 9 |
| wax modellers | – | ?2 | – | – | ?2 |
| woodcarvers | 1 | 5 | – | 1 | 7 |
| carpenters | 5 | 7 | 4 | 3 | 19 |
| sawyers | – | 1 | – | 1 | 2 |
| joiner | – | 1 | – | – | 1 |
| lathe worker | – | – | – | 1 | 1 |
| painters | – | 2 | – | 1 | 3 |
| gilder | – | 1 | – | – | 1 |
| labourers | 1 | 5 | – | 3 | 9 |
| unknown trade | 2 | 3 | – | 2 | 7 |
| *Totals* | 24 | 42 | 20 | 21 | 107 |

We know that the *architekton* was an educated man. Humbler artisans could come from mixed backgrounds. The inscribed accounts from Athens for the completion of the Erechtheion in 409–407 BC show citizens, metics (free resident foreigners), and slaves working side by side with their masters.

Here the high proportion of metics, for whom 5th-century Athens was a magnet, may have been unusual. Slaves turn out to be relatively prominent in the less specialized trades of masonry and carpentry and this may have been true generally.

Prisoners of war, finally, could provide forced labour. At Akragas, it was the many Carthaginian captives from the victory at Himera 'who quarried the stones of which… the largest temples of the gods were built' (Diodorus Siculus).

### Materials

'a temple was built [at Engyon, Sicily]… which not only excels in size but also occasions wonder by reason of the expense incurred in its construction; for since the people had no suitable stone in their own territory they brought it from their neighbours, the citizens of Agyrrion, though the poleis were nearly 100 stades [19 km/12 miles] apart…'

Diodorus Siculus, *c.* 40 BC

The choice of building stone for a temple project was a momentous decision, dictating not only the finished appearance but also the biggest single expense. For the 4th-century Ephesians embarking on their new Artemision, the matter was so weighty that (according to Vitruvius) they debated in public whether to use marble 'from Paros, Prokonnesos, Herakleia or Thasos'.

Mediterranean geology ensured that many Greek communities had access to local supplies of building stone. Favourites for early temple-building were the soft, light-coloured stones, geologically related to travertine or occasionally sandstone, which some ancient texts call *poros*.

For the delicate carving producing the decorative finish, especially in Ionic temples, the stone ideally would be hard and crisp: high-quality limestone or, best of all, marble.

Some cities had a high-grade stone readily available. Mylasa in southwestern Turkey had a mountain nearby 'where a white stone of great beauty is quarried'; 'as a result this city is superbly adorned with colonnades and temples' (Strabo). Most fortunate in this respect was Athens, with quarries of the much-admired white marble of Mount Pentelikon (Pendeli) 11 km (7 miles) from the city.

Temples in areas less blessed with good stone relied heavily on imported materials, sometimes for all the upper parts.

For economy, most temples used a mix of stones, reserving the finer materials for the most visible parts. Aphaia's colonnaded temple on Aigina confined imported marble from Paros for its roof-tiles to the row at the bottom of the roof: as has been pointed out, viewed from below, the whole roof would have seemed to be marble.

The reason for these economies, which we shall meet again, was chiefly the high cost of land transport. Partly this was a matter of poor or non-existent road surfaces. Greek building accounts point to the summer months, between July and September, as the favoured time for transporting building stone. This was the dry season, when dirt roads could support the heavy weights. The other reason was the nature of the traction: teams of lumbering oxen, hired for the most part, it seems, from local farmers in the fallow period of the agricultural year.

The second most indispensable material was wood, used for the internal support of the roof, interior ceilings and temple doors. The wood itself having perished, ancient texts provide some clues. A 5th-century inscription from Karpathos records

Fired clay (Italian *terracotta*) was the sole medium for roofing temples throughout the 6th century. Its cheapness continued to appeal even after the introduction of marble tiles around 500 BC: the 4th-century temple at 'panhellenic' Nemea, for instance, had fired-clay roof-tiles.

A temple also used a significant amount of metal. The amount of lead and iron used for the ties that bonded the masonry blocks was sufficient for decommissioned temples to be mined for this purpose.

The great doors, a focal point of temple-design, could be made from exotic woods as at Epidauros, but might be bronze, as at Olympia. Their lavish fittings, now known only from ancient descriptions, made regular use of precious metals and ivory. It was probably to protect these luxurious doors, as much as anything else, that in so many temples security grilles were fitted between the columns of the front porch (see pp. 76–77).

Apollo's 5th-century BC temple at Syracuse had doors of such costly artistry that, 400 years later, they attracted the greed of the Roman governor and notorious art-thief Gaius Verres (73–71 BC):

'Upon those doors were various scenes carved in ivory with the utmost care and perfection: Verres had all these removed. He wrenched off, and took away, a lovely gorgon's head encircled with serpents…. There were a number of massive gold knobs on these doors, all of which he carried off without hesitation…'

Cicero, Roman orator, 70 BC

*(Left) The stone for temple G at Selinous in Sicily was supplied by the ancient quarry at Cave di Cusa, 13 km (8 miles) to the northwest.*

*(Below) An unfinished column-drum, Cave di Cusa. Sixty-two unfinished column-drums like this one were abandoned when work on the temple at Selinous stopped in 409 BC.*

Athenian gratitude to these Aegean islanders, who had 'presented the cypress for the temple of Athena mistress of Athens' – the Parthenon's ridge-beam on one modern view. The temple of Asklepios at Epidauros contracted for five different kinds of wood, some of it from as far afield as Crete: they included tall conifers for roof beams, as well as elm, lotus-wood and boxwood for the doors. Delphi's 4th-century temple relied on Arkadian timber, shipped across the Corinthian gulf through Sikyon.

## Building methods

'The architect who was in charge of the work was
Chersiphron. It was a remarkable feat that he was able
to raise the epistyle blocks of such a great work.
He accomplished this with wicker baskets full of sand,
which he heaped up in a sloping ramp that reached to the
top of the column capitals, and by gradually emptying
the lower baskets the work settled into place.'

Vitruvius, Roman architect, late 1st century BC

Especially in the early days, temple building offered
a major technical challenge for ancient Greek communities. Ancient writers present temple-builders
like Chersiphron, the architect of the 6th-century
Artemision at Ephesos, as heroic figures producing
inventive solutions to the problems of stone construction. No doubt this picture was largely true.

The problems began at the quarry. Given the
simple technology possessed by the ancient Greeks,
every colonnaded temple represented a remarkable
victory by quarrymen and hauliers. It has been estimated that the Parthenon required around 1415
cubic m (50,000 cubic ft) of quarried marble. Basic
iron tools such as wedges, levers and mallets, great
skill and hour after hour of grindingly hard work at
the quarry-face underlay this statistic.

To limit weight and transport costs, quarrymen
normally roughed out the blocks before they were
transported to the building site, following measure-
ments prescribed in advance by the architect. At
first, perhaps, the blocks were delivered to the building site by means of sledges and rollers, as the
Egyptians did. But by the 5th century BC heavy
four-wheeled wagons were in use.

A nest of wooden scaffolding marked the construction site. Quite how the architects and
master-masons collaborated to realize the finished
building is not clear. But there seems to have been a
strong element of rule of thumb. There is no real
evidence to suggest the habitual use of three-dimen-
sional models or a detailed overall plan (see p. 56).
On the other hand, it is clear that some details were

worked out on site. This follows from the practice of
incising working drawings on the walls of temples
from the 6th century BC on. The most impressive
examples come from the temple of Apollo at
Didyma. Dating from the 3rd century BC, they cover
a huge area of more than 200 square m (2150 square
ft) on the walls of the inner court and of the inner
shrine. They include profiles of column-bases,
plans of ceiling coffers, and a method for calculat-
ing the contour (*entasis*) of the columns. They were
preliminary sketches only, and in some cases were
demonstrably modified in the execution.

A variety of technical models were also made
available for copying by workmen on site. For
instance, the inscribed accounts for the Erechtheion
on the Athenian Akropolis record payments for
wax models of the decorative details of the ceiling
coffers. We also hear of samples of column capitals,
of paintwork and of carved mouldings. Complex
arrangements of architectural sculpture, of which
more below, must also have normally been based on
models in wax or clay provided by the master artist.

The fact that masons finished off the blocks on
the spot explains the layer of stone chippings which
archaeologists often find on temple sites. Individual
blocks arrived from the quarry with protective
mantles, and also projections or tenons. These
sometimes were clearly meant for help in lifting. But
sometimes – at Segesta, for instance – they were
probably meant to give blocks further protection
during the repeated manipulations of the construction process. On some temples, even ones which
appear to have been completed, the protective
mantles often survive, especially at the level of the
platform, where their retention may have been for
decorative effect. With columns, to ensure a precise
correspondence, masons would add the fluting only
after a column had been assembled from its drums,
having first indicated on the bottom drum where
the flutes were to begin.

For the detailed carving and finishing off of the
stonework Greek masons worked with a variety of

*The masonry of the
unfinished 5th-century BC
temple at Rhamnous (see
p. 147) illustrates various
techniques: the thick protective
band (left, lowest course); a
shallow band on the face of
the steps, probably decorative
(left and right);* anathyrosis
*(see p. 61), use of guidelines
and unfluted drums, all to the
right.*

chisels. Compasses must have been used to engrave the mechanically applied grooves decorating the base of the cushion (*echinus*) of Doric capitals. In the 6th century BC a lathe was used to create the horizontal grooves on Ionic bases in the temples of Samian Hera.

Surviving building blocks provide many clues as to the working methods of the temple masons. It was standard practice to apply so-called *anathyrosis* to the upright side of the block: the centre was roughly hollowed with a pick except for a narrow border round the edges, which was worked smooth. This technique derived ultimately from Egypt.

The Greeks borrowed from the Egyptians a system for fastening blocks together. This reduced the risk of movement in the event of earthquakes – a constant hazard in Greek lands. Blocks were secured horizontally by metal couplings of varying shape – dovetail, double-T, and pi-shaped were among the most popular, set in lead to protect them against rust. Drums of columns were secured vertically by plugs or dowels, which could be of wood as well as metal. They too were set in lead, poured in after one drum had been placed on another by means of a shallow channel in the stone.

Which block was to go where? It was probably general practice for blocks to carry masons' marks – not necessarily carved, but painted or added in black-lead. For the most part they no longer survive, but the naked eye can still often see guidelines lightly incised in the stone, indicating the placing of the first column-drum, the staggering of the steps of the platform, and so on. By the 5th century BC, small cavities in the stone surface point to the use of levers or crowbars for the final manoeuvring into place.

At the Doric temple of Segesta in Sicily, the remains of a construction ramp confirm that this was one method which Greek builders used to raise blocks to a higher level. But blocks also retain cuttings which betray more sophisticated techniques for lifting and lowering them into place, such as U-shaped channels for the looping of ropes, or oblique holes for the insertion of metal 'crabs' (*karkinoi*) or lifting claws. Such traces prove the invention by the later 6th century BC of the pulley-operated crane. This, in turn, required smaller loads, and helps explain why the monolithic columns of the 6th century BC gave way to superimposed drums.

The masonry of a Greek temple constitutes a major part of the temple's beauty to the modern eye. It needs to be remembered that temple builders were in the habit of covering building stone of inferior quality with a coat of painted plaster (see 'Colour', pp. 67–69). In all-marble temples like the Parthenon, however, the ancients probably shared the modern aesthetic response to finely dressed stone. In mature temple-building the blocks were carefully arranged in courses of equal height, as well as having their joints harmoniously aligned in alternating courses. The dressing was so fine that joints in the best work were hair-line.

Finally, we should mention wooden carpentry: being entirely lost, this is one of the mysteries of ancient Greek temples. Their pitched roofs were supported by a system of timbers slotted into the tops of the walls below, into the gables and into the cross-walls at attic level, as in temple F at Akragas. It may be that the longest timbers – such as those from the Sila forests in southern Italy – could have spanned the roof in one go. Whether Greek temples used timber ties to support the roof (trussing) is a matter of debate.

*Some modern reconstructions of ancient lifting techniques: U-shaped channels permit the looping of ropes; by the 6th century smaller loads might be manoeuvred with a pulley-operated crane. They are based on the evidence of surviving blocks with lifting channels such as at the temple of Aphaia, Aigina (in the photograph; see pp. 148–49).*

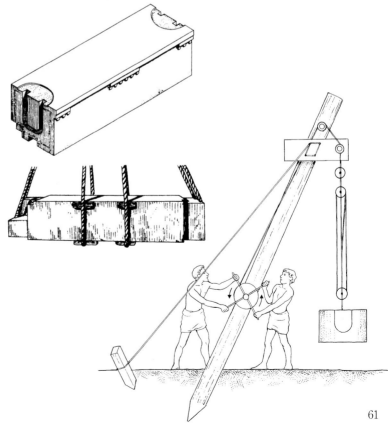

61

# Adorning the Temple

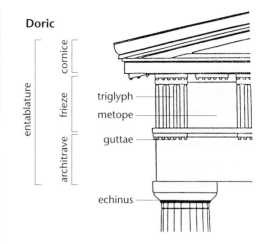

## The chief styles

The ancients called the chief styles of Greek temple-building (perhaps by the 5th century BC) 'Doric' and 'Ionic'. The style later known as 'Corinthian' was added in the 4th century BC. But 'Aeolic', referring to a distinctive type of column capital found mainly in the lands of the Aiolian Greeks in the northeast Aegean, is a modern term. The first three have been called 'orders' since the 16th century. But ancient architects were not tightly bound to a particular set of 'rules', as this modern usage implies. Pausanias (*c.* AD 150) refers more loosely to a temple's Doric 'workmanship' (*ergasia*).

Even after the basic conventions for each style had been established during the 6th century BC, succeeding generations of architects continued to innovate and experiment. Doric columns from the 6th century (chunky) and 4th century (slim), for instance, can easily be distinguished by the modern eye.

The influential idea that both styles arose from the translation into stone of a perishable architecture in wood goes back to the Roman writer Vitruvius, drawing on ancient Greek sources. Certain features seeming to echo carpentry, such as the cylindrical 'pegs' (guttae) in Doric and the 'small teeth' (dentils) in Ionic, on the face of it bear out this ancient view. The general approach could have been adopted from Egyptian architecture, where stone columns commonly copied perishable supports made from palms, papyrus plants and so on.

The origins of the decorative constituents are

*(Below) Left to right: Doric, Ionic, Corinthian and 'Aeolic'. Columns normally had concave flutes. The Doric capital comprises a cushion resembling a sea-urchin (echinus) with a square slab on top: the earlier the capital, the flatter the cushion. Ionic columns were taller and slimmer and sat on a base, not directly on the floor. The capital comprises a band with leaf decoration over which fits a horizontal element ending in pairs of scrolls. Corinthian columns were like Ionic, but their more ornate capital combined acanthus leaves with scrolls. 'Aeolic' capitals (late 7th–6th centuries BC only) were related to Ionic; their scrolls spring vertically.*

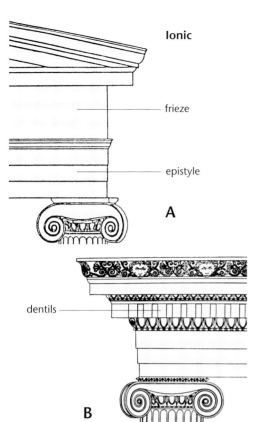

**Ionic**

frieze

epistyle

**A**

dentils

**B**

(Above) This capital from
Ramat Rahel in Palestine
(7th century BC) closely
resembles the 'Aeolic' capital.

harder to pin down. There was certainly eastern
inspiration, clearest in the 'Aeolic' capital. Other
influences may have been home-grown: the cushion
of the Doric capital, for instance, resembles Mycenaean capitals, still visible in 7th-century Greece.

What seems clear is that the nameless temple-
builders who first evolved the essentials of these
styles did not do so simply by 'petrifying' existing
architecture. For instance, structurally the arrangement of triglyphs around all four sides of a Doric
temple, if these represent ornamental cappings on
the end of wooden planks, does not make sense.
Rather they designed a variety of stylized elements
into a new architectural synthesis – one utterly
unique to ancient Greece.

(Below) The so-called Lion
Gate at Mycenae (13th
century BC). The lions flank
a column with a cushion-like
capital supporting a square
slab, reminiscent of later
Doric.

*(Above) Doric and Ionic styles.
Conventionally the superstructure above the temple columns
is called the entablature. It
normally consisted of three
superposed horizontals: the
architrave; the frieze; and the
cornice. The Greeks called the
architrave (originally a French
term) the epistylion, 'epistyle'
(Greek: 'over the pillar').
'Frieze' (another modern loan
word) describes the horizontal
decorative band that rests on
the architrave. In Ionic the
frieze can take a band of
relief sculpture (A) or a row
of dentils over decorative
mouldings (B). In Doric
temples it comprised
alternating triglyphs and
metopes. Both are authentic
Greek terms. The triglyph
(Greek: 'thrice-cloven') was a
block with three vertical faces
separated by grooves. The
metope ('between the holes')
was the recessed panel
between the triglyphs. Its face
could be carved in relief or, as
at Bassai, a sculptured panel
could be slotted in front of it.
In temple-design, the ancient
significance of these terms is
problematic: see pp. 63–64.*

*Various theories seek to explain the design of the Doric triglyph with its three vertical faces (pp. 62–63). On one view the inspiration was a common 7th-century BC religious offering, the three-legged cauldron, shown here replacing the triglyph on a Doric frieze from Samos (3rd century BC).*

The ancient names 'Doric' and 'Ionic' were ethno-geographical, formed on the names of the two chief linguistic and cultural sub-divisions of the Greek people, the Dorians and Ionians, the former concentrated in central and southern Greece, the latter in Athens and 'Ionia', the central part of the west coast of Asia Minor. If overseas colonies are factored in, the early stylistic distribution roughly correlates with the ethnic one, and probably explains the origin of the names.

On the other hand the correlation was never precise. The Ionian Athenians built what today is the most famous Doric temple, the Parthenon, and the Dorian Greeks of Syracuse began the biggest Ionic temple in the west (p. 122). Migration is sometimes used to explain these stylistic 'intrusions': could Metapontion's fine Ionic temple, for instance, reflect an influx of new colonists from Asia Minor? Cultural politics are also suspected: a fondness for Ionic in 5th-century Athens, especially in the Erechtheion, which replaced an older Doric temple, has been linked to Athenian self-promotion as the mother-city of all Ionians.

### The search for due proportion (*symmetria*)

'The final goal of an architect is to make the work well-proportioned for the perception and, as far as possible, to find counter-devices against the deceptions of the eye…'

Heron of Alexandria, Greek inventor, AD 50–100

Between the 6th and the 4th centuries BC the Doric style perceptibly loses weight. In the 6th century columns are relatively squat, but by the end of the 4th century they had gained height and slimmed down. A similar process has been observed with the entablature and the pitch of roofs: they became, respectively, lower and gentler. Finally, the whole building, at first long and thin, rapidly became more compact: already by 500 BC, at Aphaia's latest temple on Aigina (pp. 148–49), the ratio of width to length had been scaled down to 1:2.

In the Parthenon, better preserved than most temples and certainly the most closely studied in modern times, the design's precise concern with mathematics can be followed more closely. In particular, the ratio of 4:9 keeps cropping up: of width to length; of the lower diameter of the columns to the interval between them; of the height of the entablature to the temple's width, and so on.

All this concern for proportions was reflected in the technical literature put out by architects, including a general work by one Silenos 'about the proportions (*symmetriai*) of Doric buildings' (Vitruvius). Architects of Ionic temples were similarly preoccupied. In the late 3rd century one of them, Hermogenes (p. 39), pioneered a new set of proportions which emphasized high, closely spaced columns and halls which were double-width (that is, in theory roomy enough for a second surrounding colonnade). His best-known work, at Magnesia in the Maeander valley (pp. 201–2), won praise from later Greeks for its 'harmonious appearance' (Strabo, late 1st century BC).

This quest for harmony through mathematics was linked to Greek conceptions of beauty. A leading 5th-century sculptor, Polykleitos, supposedly opined that 'perfection arises from [*the meaning here is debated*] a minute calculation through many numbers'.

Originally, at any rate, this quest may have been more than purely aesthetic. The ancient Greeks are known to have ascribed a mystical quality to numbers, especially the followers of the 6th-century BC sage Pythagoras, whose largely lost teachings seem to have embraced the idea that numbers and proportion were organizing principles of the cosmos. To return to the idea of the temple as metaphor, it is conceivable – as Erik Østby has suggested – that the mathematical harmonies which have been discerned in Greek temple-building were somehow an expression of this cosmic thinking.

From the 6th century on Doric temples began to incorporate what nowadays are described as 'optical refinements': columns bulged outwards and tilted inwards; the temple platform, and with it the whole superstructure, arched upwards. Sometimes effects seen as intentional turn out to be accidental: the curvature in Poseidonia's temple 'of Poseidon' (pp. 113–14), first observed in the 19th century, has been downgraded to natural settlement caused by the impact of the collapsed upper parts. Elsewhere, as at Thebes (p. 168), the evidence for intentionality is incontrovertible. In the 4th century curvature crossed the Aegean, and architects made it a feature of the 'Ionian renascence' (pp. 38–39).

Modern opinion differs as to how easily Greek masons could have implemented these refinements and at what extra cost, and also over the methods.

One old mystery has been solved: examples of the 'unequal steps' (*scamilli impares*) for implementing curvature, which Vitruvius mentions, have now turned up at Knidos in southwest Turkey. They turn out to be bores in the stone of graded depth, used to calculate the curve.

frames; decorating the steps of ceiling coffers and so on. The Ionic style, often thought of as dainty where Doric was sturdy, made most use of them (see pp. 120, 179, 186, 202), especially the egg-and-dart. The hawk's beak, so-called from its profile, was the standard Doric moulding, usually decorated with a leaf pattern.

From the outset, imagery integrated into the architecture of colonnaded temples formed an integral part of the religious experience which these buildings offered for ancient worshippers. Stone sculpture, usually marble, took over from the early figures and painted plaques in fired clay (see p. 174) from the later 6th century BC.

Subject-matter was mostly the supernatural world of gods, heroes and the monstrous. An early favourite was the horrific gorgoneion, a full-frontal head of the female monster whose gaze turned humans to stone. But artists during the 6th century became increasingly adept at massing sculptured figures into complex compositions telling the religious stories which we call Greek 'myths'.

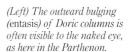

*Adorning the Temple*

*(Left) The outward bulging (entasis) of Doric columns is often visible to the naked eye, as here in the Parthenon.*

*This stone gorgon's face stared balefully at the viewer from the east gable of the temple of Artemis, Corfu (early 6th century BC). The fearsome eyes were deliberately undercut to be seen from below.*

Upward curvature itself has been found in ancient Egyptian architecture: some believe that the idea, and possibly technical instruction, passed to Greece from Egypt. As to the purpose, curvature of the platform had the practical effect of draining off rainwater. In Roman times compensation for optical illusions was offered as an explanation: curvature, on this view, stopped a temple from seeming to 'sag'. The possibility of a symbolic meaning too has already been noted. On the other hand, these 'refinements' are sometimes so delicate as to be scarcely perceptible to the human eye: how aware of them, even, were the ancient Greeks?

Writers of later antiquity, such as Heron, cited above, took it as read that it was the ancient viewer whom they were meant to please. Here we are reminded of the intense scrutiny which their builders expected temples to come under – above all, the evaluating gaze of the citizens who funded the project and over whose daily lives, so often, these temples visibly towered.

## Sculpture

The Greek temple has sometimes been likened to a work of sculpture as much as architecture. The total effect relied ultimately on stone-carving, including the refinements discussed and the masonry finish, as well as sculptural decoration as such.

This last could take essentially two forms: ornamental mouldings on the one hand, and figured work on the other. Mouldings with carved or painted decoration were an integral part of the appearance of a colonnaded temple, framing and emphasizing the different elements in the elevation. After the 6th century BC, they tend to crop up in standard positions – running under the gutter; crowning the interior walls; on lintels and door-

Often these narratives were universal favourites, especially the epic struggles in which good (the gods, the Greeks) won out over evil (amazons, giants, the monstrous horse-men or centaurs, Trojans). Then there were mythical scenes with more specific referents, showcasing the temple's deity or the local hero, or evoking the fabulous origins of a festival or a city.

A temple's exterior showed off this imagery in the best viewing conditions. On a Doric temple free-standing groups could fill the gables, and figures could be carved in relief on the metopes in the entablature. On an Ionic temple, a continuous band in relief could run round part or all of the entablature. Even skyline figures (*akroteria*) on the apex of a gable could achieve narrative complexity, as in 4th-century BC Karthaia (pp. 180–81).

More puzzlingly to us, awkward sightlines and dim lighting were not an obstacle to the display of architectural imagery inside the colonnades. In Doric temples the metopes above the front and back porches could be carved. Continuous bands of relief placed high up in the halls were a feature of Doric temples in 5th-century Athens, most famously on the Parthenon (p. 142). In Bassai, uniquely, such a band ran round the walls of the shrine just below the ceiling.

The phenomenon occurs in Ionic too. At Priene, the lofty coffer-lids of the halls had relief sculpture (see illustration, right); at Chrysa (p. 190), sculpture drums were placed just below the column capitals.

To describe all this imagery as 'decoration' is to risk missing its point. A symbolic point to the neck-craning involved in looking at sculpture on or just below the ceiling was canvassed earlier (p. 54). Early gorgon-faces were meant to frighten and – probably – to ward off evil; mythical narratives offered presentiments of divine power. Setting and composition may have been intended to encourage interactivity, moving viewers round the building or, where standing figures in the centre of the gable created a strong vertical axis, drawing their gaze down to the temple interior with its divine statuary (see the illustration pp. 152–53).

As with all religious stories, much of this fantastic imagery had an ethical sub-text: Greeks defeat non-Greek 'barbarians', men defeat women, order defeats chaos, and so on. Modern interpreters also see some of these narratives as allegories for contemporary history and politics – not unreasonably, given the intensely polis-centred context of temple-building.

On the other hand, it is well-nigh impossible to fix any of these modern readings as certainly ancient –

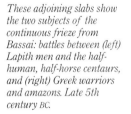

*These adjoining slabs show the two subjects of the continuous frieze from Bassai: battles between (left) Lapith men and the half-human, half-horse centaurs, and (right) Greek warriors and amazons. Late 5th century BC.*

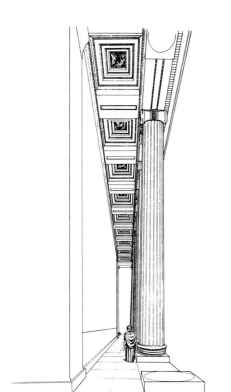

of this the endless debate about the meaning of the Parthenon frieze is a forceful reminder. The first explicit reference to the political in temple sculpture falls after the Roman conquest of Asia Minor, at Lagina (pp. 211–12).

## Colour

Colour was integral to the ancient experience of a Greek colonnaded temple. One consequence of this colour, and likely aim, would have been to make the building more visible from afar.

In some temples, the brightness of freshly quarried stonework seems to have played a prime role in colour effects. At Kyzikos Hadrian's mega-temple, whose quality of conspicuousness was praised by the Greek writer Aelius Aristides (c. AD 150), was built in white marble from Prokonnesos (pp. 188–89). On first exposure, the local marble used for the Ephesian Artemision was 'extremely white' (Vitruvius). Pentelic marble is likewise startlingly white when freshly cut.

The attraction of white stones may have been precisely their brilliance. Local stones of duller hue were often coated in plaster and painted cream or white (a finish which could also disguise a coarse texture). Sometimes contrasting stones were used to

*Adorning the Temple*

*In Athena's temple at Priene scenes from the mythical battle between the gods and the giants decorated the high-up lids of the ceiling coffers in the halls. Late 4th century BC.*

*Freshly cut blocks of Pentelic marble in the restoration of the Parthenon contrast starkly with the mellow honey-colour of the original blocks.*

create colour effects, as in a 4th-century temple at Messon (p. 186) on Lesbos.

Painted attachments in fired clay at roof level were among the glories of the early colonnaded temples. They included sheathing for the gutters and the frames of gables; also waterspouts, the attachments (antefixes) masking the ends of tiles in the lowest row, and skyline ornaments (*akroteria*). Abstract patterning was picked out in contrasting colours limited in range – since they had to survive the firing process – but not necessarily in visual impact, as with the mainly black, red and white on the roof of the 'Basilica' at Poseidonia (p. 113).

The brightest colours were those painted onto stonework (including marble) from the column-tops upwards, including sculpture. Most of this paintwork is lost, and expert opinion tends to divide between those who emphasize and those who play down its effects. But it probably was, and was meant to be, striking.

At Akragas the roof-tiles of the Doric temple D (5th century) were painted pink, blue and white. At Gela in southern Sicily another 5th-century Doric temple (C) had painted patterns in white, yellow and blue on the marble frames of the gables. The Parthenon made extensive use of painted ornament, some of it in gold leaf.

*(Right) Block from the entablature of a Doric temple at Akragas, preserving patches of the original plaster painted white and pink.*

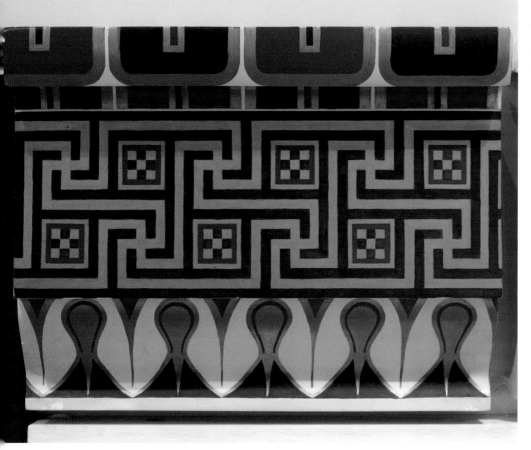

*Reconstruction of decorative paintwork on the Parthenon.*

Some of the best-preserved paintwork comes from the non-colonnaded predecessor (6th century) of Aphaia's temple on Aigina: scientific analysis reveals pigments made from chalk, red ochre, green malachite and Egyptian blue. On the Erechtheion, Ionic capitals were studded with beads of coloured glass.

Colour in ancient Greece, especially red, white and black, had religious overtones. It is possible that certain colours in temple ornamentation were favoured for these reasons, white perhaps in particular, associated with religious festivals and, more generally, good omen.

*19th-century reconstruction of the coloured glasswork on the Ionic capitals of the Erechtheion (see p. 144).*

# Finance and Repairs

### Maintenance

Colonnaded temples could be subject to earthquake and fire requiring major repairs, quite apart from routine wear and tear. In times of war or economic hardship maintenance could be neglected. Excavators have traced the history of the longest-serving temples, such as those of Olympia, the Athenian Akropolis or (a colonial example) Cyrene over many centuries, recording repeated alterations and repairs along the way.

Multiple sets of roof-tiles and guttering, sometimes confusing archaeologists as to a temple's date, are commonplace. At Olympia some of the gable figures have heads of later date. The word *ganosis*, literally 'brightening up', appears in the sacred accounts at Delos to describe the practice of 'varnishing' architectural marble. Controversially, the ochre patina observed in modern times on parts of the Parthenon is claimed by some as evidence for this kind of ancient treatment.

### Funding

The modest-sized temple of Asklepios at Epidauros is the only one for which the total cost is known: 23–24 talents. To put this sum in a larger context, it pales beside the estimated annual revenue of 5th-century Athens at the height of her power: around 400 talents. Nor would it have been entirely beyond the pocket of the richest known Greek individual of the time, the Athenian banker Pasion, who left an estate of 20 talents and 60 more in outstanding loans.

On the other hand, larger, more sumptuous temples, and ones with heavier hidden costs, would have brought in a massively larger bill. On one reasonably sane estimate, for instance, the Parthenon would have cost around 470 talents.

Apart from the gifts of kings and emperors, and the murky funding for tyrannical projects, Greek cities mainly raised finance for temple-building from their own resources. Fifth-century Athens was exceptional in using (or so ancient tradition claimed) the defence contributions of its maritime alliance to build 'the works of Perikles'.

Normally the deity, through the sacred property held in his or her name, no doubt contributed. According to Diodorus Siculus (*c.* 40 BC), Sicilian Engyon's lavish spending on a temple of the Mothers was permitted by 'the vast quantity of sacred revenues' from livestock and land. Cities must also have used their own disposable funds.

The individual contributions of citizens were important, perhaps crucial. Aristotle (4th century BC) saw expenditure on sacred buildings by the rich as an honourable outlet of personal 'magnificence'. At just this time at Kastabos (pp. 213–14) a private citizen called Phileas made a large enough donation towards Hemithea's new temple to have himself

*(Above) Herakles slaying the Nemean lion: metope from the temple of Zeus, Olympia. Most of the original is in the Olympia Museum except for the lion, now in the Louvre (right). The head and body are thought to be ancient replacements, perhaps following earthquake-damage in the 4th century BC.*

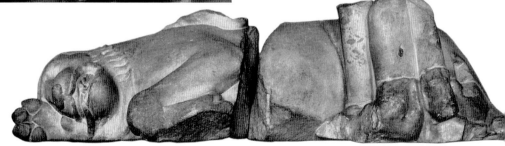

discreetly inscribed on a nearby wall – not the temple itself – as the dedicator.

Cities also opened public subscriptions (*epidoseis*). Around 285 BC, for instance, a citizen spoke in the Samian assembly 'on the subject of the restoration of the great temple, so as to complete it by means of funds collected by subscription'.

These subscriptions – a sign, by the way, of local prosperity – often seem to have been a complementary, rather than the main, funding source. One of their purposes was precisely to express the communal character of temple-building. At Tanagra in Boiotia around 200 BC, 98 women contributed sums of between 1 and 5 drachmai each to rebuild a temple of Demeter. The value of the sum raised, 473 drachmai, must have been chiefly symbolic.

## Record-keeping

A distinctive feature of ancient Greek temple-building was minutely detailed record-keeping.

From the 5th century BC records could be inscribed for public display, sometimes at such length as to constitute monuments in their own right. They are a major source of information for many aspects of Greek temple construction.

Important records of this kind survive for the 5th-century Akropolis, and the 4th-century temples at Epidauros (see p. 57) and Delphi. One motive was accountability: the officials who had handled public monies thereby put their honesty on display before the literate public. As records of the scale of the undertaking and as minute itemizations of the individuals who took part, they were also permanent testimony to a great enterprise of collective piety.

*(Above) This monumental inscription – reconstructed by Lee Ann Turner – recorded the contracts for the temple of Zeus at Lebadeia in Boiotia (3rd century BC?). A row of up to 16 slabs, each nearly 2 m (6 ft) high and inscribed with nearly 190 lines of text, was set into a base between 14 and 16 m (46–52 ft) long for display next to the temple.*

*(Left) The letters of this Latin inscription from Olympia were originally picked out in bronze. They record a repair to the front porch of the temple of Zeus sponsored by Marcus Agrippa, the son-in-law of Augustus (see p. 153).*

*(Right) Lion's-head gutter-spouts from the temple of Zeus, Olympia. The top two are original; the bottom two are ancient repairs from the 4th (left) and 1st century BC respectively.*

# The Parts of the Temple and their Uses

The Greek temple was a holy shrine, and its sacred focus beyond the great doors was the imagery of the immortal gods. Far more so than modern scholars once thought, the ancient Greeks worshipped these statues as idols, as forms which could be literally inhabited by the divinity.

Temple interiors were designed to dramatize these ancient encounters with the sacred, and priests may have staged 'appearances' of the divine statuary in the temple's doorways and gables. Oracular deities, especially Apollo, 'spoke' from the inside of their temples. Other ritual uses of the temple are only hinted at, in mysterious features such as crypts or staircases.

The sanctity of the temple acted like a magnet for other (more or less) religious activities. Temples made ideal treasuries. Along with their contents, they were increasingly sought out by religious tourists – pagan pilgrims. Their hallowed walls were repositories for official inscriptions, and statues of great men (and sometimes women) were set up in their outer colonnades or the interior itself. In such ways many colonnaded temples remained at the living heart of their communities until the close of pagan antiquity.

*The interior of the unfinished temple at Segesta, Sicily.*

III   The Living Temple

# The God in the Temple

The ancient Greek temple was the creation of a religious culture which has been dead for 16 centuries. Both have been swept away so comprehensively that a humility about the limits of modern knowledge needs to attend any generalizations about the rituals which ancient Greeks performed in temple-space and the beliefs which these embodied. No ancient writings have survived to detail the routine acts of worship inside a Greek temple. Even the best-preserved temples such as that 'of Concord' at Agrigento or the Hephaisteion in Athens have seen their interiors, the focus of ancient rites, changed out of all recognition.

## The temple as a dedication

So great were the resources, material and human, lavished on a colonnaded temple that the end-product was a gift to the divinity in its own right. Donors were said to have 'dedicated the temple'. A dedication (*anathema*) carried a specific religious meaning: the ancient Greeks worshipped their gods on the principle of gift-exchange, hoping that divine favour would reward the donor. That said, a temple was not an end in itself. It had a ritual purpose, above all as the deity's house.

## Temples and divine statues

The very specific way in which the residence of a god in his *naos* was defined by the presence of his image emerges from the inscriptions of Delos. When Apollo's statue and offerings in his sanctuary there were transferred around 280 BC from one temple to another, their former abode was downgraded from 'the temple [*naos*] of Apollo' to 'the *poros* temple' or just 'the *poros* house [*oikos*]'.

The relatively small number of colonnaded temples in the ancient Greek world can easily give a false impression that the essential function of these structures, to house and secure 'the sacred things' (*ta hiera*), was not a prerequisite of Greek worship. But this would be to ignore the far greater number of more modest structures in simpler precincts which fulfilled this same function, such as the shrine of Artemis at Messene, or the rural sanctuary of Zeus Messapeus in the hills northeast of Sparta (modern Tsakona).

Even where a public sanctuary dispensed entirely with a *naos* or any kind of 'sacred house' (*hieros oikos*), this did not mean that the cult in question was without its sacred objects in someone's safe possession. In Messene's cult of Zeus of Ithome 'a priest chosen each year keeps the divine statue in his house' (Pausanias). At Chaironeia, 'the man who acts as priest keeps the sceptre [of Zeus] in his house for the year; and sacrifices are offered to it daily…' (Plutarch, c. AD 100).

Historians of Greek religion habitually refer to the 'cult statue' to describe the deity's chief image in his temple, although the expression has no precise ancient equivalent, and in some ways limits our understanding of ancient Greek ritual. For instance, in the mid-2nd century AD Hera's temple outside Argos contained the goddess' colossus in gold and ivory by the 5th-century sculptor Polykleitos. Pausanias goes on: 'Beside her is an

ancient image of Hera on a column. But the most ancient one is made of the wild pear tree…. a seated image, not large'.

This aggregation of sacred images in a temple was not uncommon, and their degrees of holiness were not clearly demarcated in the various ancient terms for representations of deity. The most common of these were *agalma*, literally a 'delight', and (in later texts) *xoanon* ('image').

However, the design of colonnaded temples commonly emphasized a particular statue or statue-group by placing it opposite, and facing, the great door on the temple's central lengthways axis. The raised bases for statuary so positioned tended to be placed to the rear of the shrine proper, allowing for viewing by as many worshippers as possible.

*(Above) This cluttered shrine of Artemis Orthia in Messene occupies a single chamber behind a colonnade in a much larger complex. Inside against the back wall is a massive base for divine statuary. Outside the colonnade in the open air was the goddess's altar (see pp. 80–81).*

*(Right) The Hera of Polykleitos depicted on Roman-period coins of Argos.*

# The Parts of a Temple

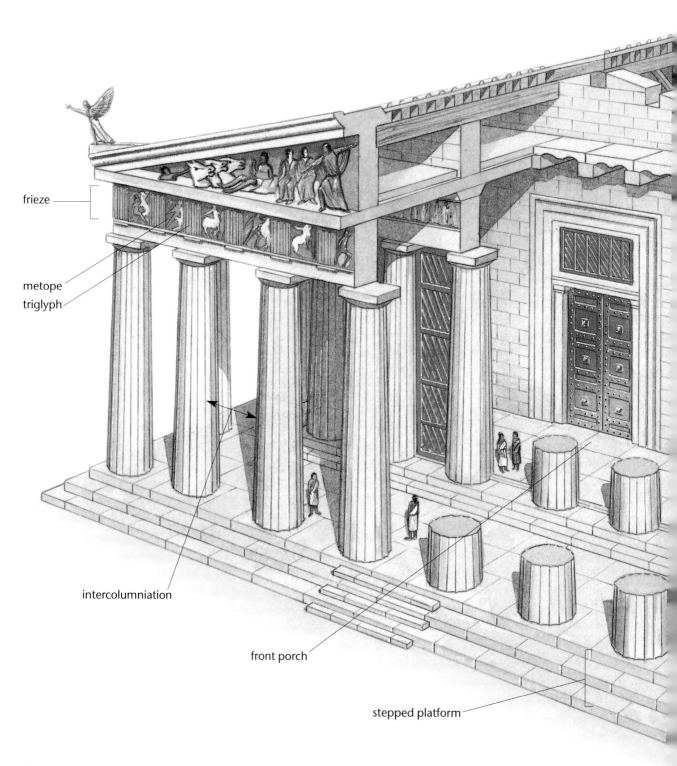

frieze

metope

triglyph

intercolumniation

front porch

stepped platform

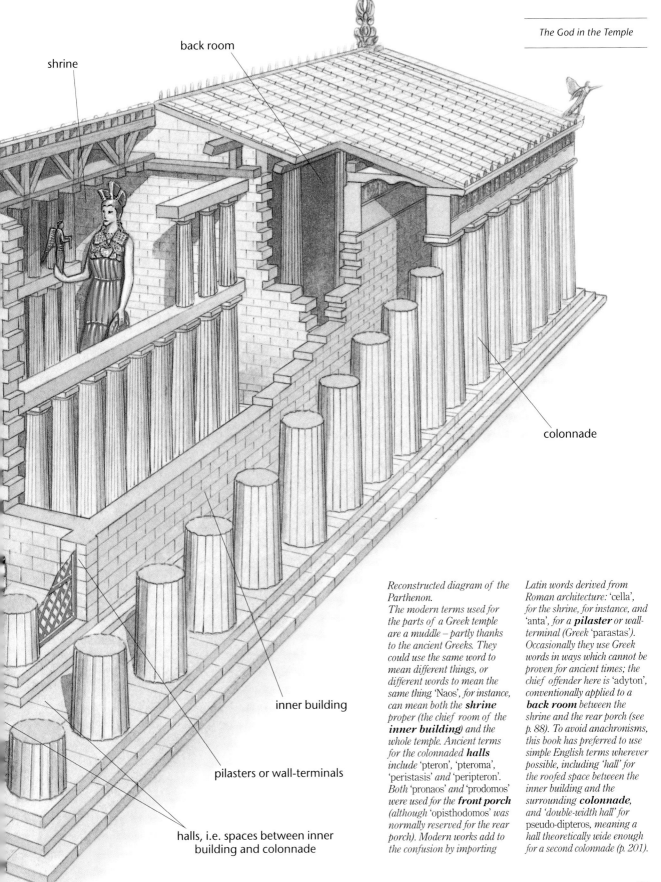

shrine

back room

colonnade

inner building

pilasters or wall-terminals

halls, i.e. spaces between inner building and colonnade

*Reconstructed diagram of the Parthenon.*

*The modern terms used for the parts of a Greek temple are a muddle – partly thanks to the ancient Greeks. They could use the same word to mean different things, or different words to mean the same thing. 'Naos', for instance, can mean both the **shrine** proper (the chief room of the **inner building**) and the whole temple. Ancient terms for the colonnaded **halls** include 'pteron', 'pteroma', 'peristasis' and 'peripteron'. Both 'pronaos' and 'prodomos' were used for the **front porch** (although 'opisthodomos' was normally reserved for the rear porch). Modern works add to the confusion by importing*

*Latin words derived from Roman architecture: 'cella', for the shrine, for instance, and 'anta', for a **pilaster** or wall-terminal (Greek 'parastas'). Occasionally they use Greek words in ways which cannot be proven for ancient times; the chief offender here is 'adyton', conventionally applied to a **back room** between the shrine and the rear porch (see p. 88). To avoid anachronisms, this book has preferred to use simple English terms wherever possible, including 'hall' for the roofed space between the inner building and the surrounding **colonnade**, and 'double-width hall' for pseudo-dipteros, meaning a hall theoretically wide enough for a second colonnade (p. 201).*

In a practice which derived ultimately from the Near East, these raised bases for statuary sometimes received foundation-offerings, as seen in Chapter II (pp. 50–51), and the installation of the statue was marked by religious ceremony, as at Magnesia-on-the-Maeander in the 2nd century BC. Here the temple-warden and priestess of the city-goddess Artemis were to celebrate the 're-establishment' of the goddess *xoanon* in her new temple 'with the most conspicuous sacrifice', and the city decided to mark the anniversary annually with a great festival, when boys were to be 'let off their lessons and slaves their labours'.

All this may not quite add up to a ritually animated 'cult statue' in the ancient Egyptian sense (below), but it justifies the notion of, say, a 'central' image and 'subsidiary' ones.

### Idolatry

'…on account of our belief in the divine all men have a strong yearning to honour and worship the deity from close at hand, approaching and laying hold of him by persuasion by offering sacrifice and crowning him with garlands.'

Dio of Prusa, Greek writer, *c.* AD 100

The Greek philosopher Stilpon of Megara was allegedly banished by the 3rd-century BC Athenians for maintaining that the great statue in the Parthenon was not the goddess herself. Stilpon's disbelief belonged to a tradition of Greek philosophical scoffing which went back to the 6th century BC. It was echoed in the attacks of Christian writers such as Clement of Rome (*c.* AD 96) on the notion that the 'divine spirit' could reside in a deity's statue.

But the persistence of the line of attack points to its pertinence. Lewis Farnell, one of the greatest historians of Greek religion, took the view that 'the nature and power of the divinity were there in the image', not just for the early Greeks, but to the end of paganism.

Ancient evidence tends to bear out this view. Like true idols (that is, animate images), the statues of the Greek gods could come alive. It is true that the ancient Greeks did not – to our knowledge – perform rituals, as the Egyptians did, magically to bring to life the statues in their temples. But ancient writers, especially from the 4th century BC, often refer to hair-raising events involving divine statues.

In the eye of the believer they could sweat, shed tears and bleed, and walk off their pedestals. Bellowings were heard from inside temples. The educated Plutarch (*c.* AD 100) conceded that statues 'may emit a noise like a moan or a groan', but he drew the line at talking statues: others, clearly, did not.

Ascribing a supernatural vitality to divine statues was encouraged by the increasing accomplishment of Greek sculptors. The oldest representations in Greek temples seemed artisti-cally crude to later Greeks: portable figures in wood or stone, or aniconic representations like the wooden 'plank' representing the goddess in the Samian Heraion.

In the 5th century BC, led by the Athenian Pheidias, sculptors perfected the technique for making colossal statues in gold and ivory (chryselephantine) built around a wooden frame attached to a mighty 'mast'. These extraordinary creations deliberately sought to recreate the appearance of the gods as traditionally conceived by the Greeks: supernaturally tall beings, shining with light, their flesh as flawless as ivory.

*Artist's impression of the colossal gold-and-ivory statue of Zeus in his temple at Olympia. The shallow basin in front was filled with olive oil in the belief that this would offset damage to the ivory from the dampness to which Olympia is prone.*

Far from reducing the images of the gods to the status of mere art-objects, as is sometimes suggested, these statues attracted particular reverence. As a poet wrote of the Pheidian Zeus at Olympia: 'Either Zeus descended to you from heaven, or you, great artist, ascended and saw the god.'

## Adoring the statue

'For her nurse… bethought herself of a plan, which was to carry the child every day to the temple of Helen at Therapna… and there to place her before the image, and beseech the goddess to take away the child's ugliness.'

Herodotus, 5th century BC

Temple images were the focus of a range of performative acts by the ancient Greeks. The relationship of the faithful to these statues was interactive, not just a matter of passive 'seeing'. The anecdote of Herodotus, true or not, shows the function of these images as a focus for individual prayer – the most common form of religious expression among the ancient Greeks. A range of movements could accompany such adoration of the image, including outspread arms, kissing and, from no later than the 4th century BC, kneeling to implore the deity.

At least in later times, adoration of the image took other forms too. In the 1st century BC the mouth and chin of the image of Herakles in his temple at Akragas were noticeably worn away from kissing by the faithful.

The Greek writer Lucian (AD 150) tells a satirical tale from his own day of a secular portrait-statue in a private house to which the superstitious attributed healing powers, decking it out in thanks with ribbons, garlands, gold leaves which they

*In this vase-painting from Athens (5th century BC) a statue of Athena appears to come alive in response to a worshipper who raises his right hand with his index finger bent – a ritual gesture of greeting reserved for the gods.*

(Right) A portable image of Artemis Orthia in the form of a pillar topped by a bust (missing) is held by an attendant of the goddess in this statue from Messene (2nd century BC?).

Knotted fillets hang from the arms of a local statue of Athena on (right) a 4th-century BC coin of Assos (see pp. 190–91) and completely cocoon the statue of a local deity (above) on a Roman-period coin from Anemourion (southwest Turkey).

placed on the chest, and coins stuck with wax to the thighs. These details may well convey the authentic flavour of idolatry in contemporary Greek temples.

Two practices which seem to have been particularly widespread were the placing of wreaths on, and the hanging of woollen strips or ribbons (*stemmata*, *tainiai*) from, divine statues. The former, noted by Dio (p. 78), meant that it was 'impossible to get a clear look at the statue in the temple' when Pausanias (2nd century AD) visited a shrine in the southern Peloponnese.

On another occasion Pausanias found his view of the base of an image of the goddess Kore completely obscured by the accumulation of ribbons – again, presumably left by devotees. This practice can be traced back at least to the 5th century BC, when Argive Hera's priestess accidentally set fire to the ribbons hanging from the goddess' statue.

As well as receiving worship from individuals, the divine statues in a temple were objects of formalized rites carried out by the priestly personnel discussed in Chapter IV. This is an area where Greek worship was influenced by the religious practices of the eastern Mediterranean. One of the divine statues in a Greek temple was often small because for certain rituals, as in ancient Egyptian temples, it had to be easy to carry.

At festival time we hear of some statues being brought out of temples and displayed in procession to the people. At Sparta in the late 1st century BC, the portable image of Poseidon was carried by a functionary called the 'bearer of the god' (*siophoros*).

At Sparta again and in neighbouring Messene, portable statues are known to have been brought out to 'watch' rituals performed at the altar in their honour.

For a colonnaded temple some of the best evidence concerns the Artemision at Ephesos. Inscriptions show that in the 1st century BC, during the festival of the Daitis, a small image of the goddess was taken to the sea, accompanied, among others, by a singer, a salt-bearer, a wild-celery-bearer, a robe-bearer and a bearer of the statue's removable decoration (*kosmos*). Perhaps exceptionally (but how would we know?), the statue was also taken once a month to the meetings of the Ephesian citizen assembly in the theatre.

As in ancient Egypt Greek temple-images received rites of bathing, dressing and feeding. Famously the 'old statue' of Athena on the Akropolis was the recipient of a new robe (*peplos*) woven by Athenian women once every four years and borne up to her temple in a great civic procession. This same statue received an annual grooming at the hands of an Athenian priestly clan, the Praxiergidai, who 'carry out these ceremonies in strict secrecy on the twenty-fifth day of the month Thargelion, when they remove the adornment and veil the statue' (Plutarch).

In the 3rd century BC the portable statue of Samian Hera was carried in procession to the sea (once more) during the festival of the Tonaia, possibly bathed, and then given a meal of barley-cakes. Offering-tables placed in front of the principal statue of a temple, as at Rhamnous, were used, among other things, for gifts of blood-less food.

(Above) Clay models of various types of ritual cake, from the sanctuary of Demeter, Corinth.

(Left) The altar of Artemis Orthia at Messene, flanked by a pillar into which the portable statue of the goddess could be slotted when she was brought out to 'witness' rites in her honour.

# Indian parallels?

(Below) Plan of the Dadabari temple, Jaipur. The black dots are Jain idols. Note the axially placed central idol, the surrounding space for circumambulation (see p. 86), and the platform sometimes used in ritual for a portable idol.

(Right) A devotee performing individual puja in an Indian temple.

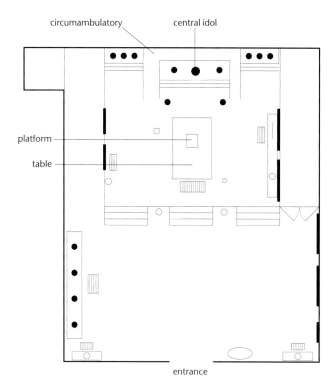

circumambulatory

central idol

platform

table

entrance

Much of this ancient Greek adoration of statues has counterparts in the polytheistic faiths of modern India, notably the ceremonial performance called *puja*, a series of ritual acts during which a temple-idol is invoked, bathed, dressed, decorated (with, among other things, garlands and silver foil), and offered food. In Hinduism the priests tend to take charge of the rite, but in the Jain religion it is performed by individuals, often daily, as an act of personal spirituality.

The significance of these similarities of ritual behaviour from a different time, place and culture can hardly be pressed. But, to evoke a fine distinction from the Christian milieu, they reinforce the case for classing the ancient Greek 'cult of statues' as fully blown worship, not just 'veneration'.

## Staging divine appearances

'I noticed in a dream a statue of me. At one moment I saw it as if it were me, and then again it seemed to be a large and beautiful statue of Asklepios.'

Aristeides, Greek orator, c. AD 160

Belief in divine epiphany, that gods could appear to their human worshippers, was an ancient strand in Greek religiosity; if anything, it may have strengthened over the centuries. Historians of Greek religion point out that popular ideas about how the gods looked on such occasions were shaped by divine statues. When the gods manifested themselves to their adorers in dreams, often it was their statues which had come to life.

Psychologically the ground for such 'appearances' (*epiphaneiai*, epiphanies) could be prepared by the way in which temple officials staged the revelation of the statue inside. In the centuries after Alexander, there is evidence for the dramatization of this moment, rather like a theatrical performance. This concern extended to the reliance on special effects, such as those described by the Greek inventor Heron of Alexandria (1st century AD), in his work *On the Making of Automata*.

It is unknown whether such devices were ever actually installed in a Greek temple: but the mere fact that Heron discussed them suggests, for later antiquity, the drama sought in the staging of sacrifices before a temple, and the crucial interplay between the ritual at the altar and the opening and closing of the temple doors.

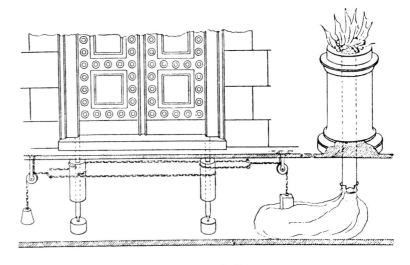

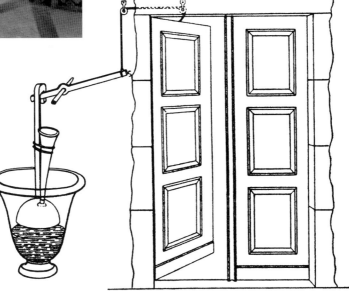

*Two automatic devices powered by compressed air, by the Greek inventor Heron of Alexandria (1st century AD): (left) designed to trigger a trumpet blast when shrine-doors are opened, and (above) to open and shut shrine doors at the start and finish of the sacrifice on the altar.*

In this South-Italian vase-painting (4th century BC) a colossal gold or gilt statue of Apollo is revealed through the open doors of his temple, while the 'real' Apollo, with his lyre, appears outside.

Aligned with the doors, usually, in the temple interior, was the god's chief image. With the doors open, the deity, through his statue, became a spectator at the sacrifices performed in his honour. This interactive relationship was stressed by the siting of the altar, normally placed in front of the temple's main facade, and, topography permitting, often on the same precise alignment as the doors and the main statue inside.

Rituals to accompany the daily opening and closing of temples are described in this Greek inscription (AD 15–37) from Teos, referring to the temple of Dionysos there (see pp. 196–7):

'…the council and people decreed that hymns in honour of the god Dionysos, protector of the city, shall be

Seated statues of divinities gaze out from their shrine to the open-air altar in front and an approaching procession of worshippers. Athenian water-jar, about 450 BC.

sung daily at the opening of the temple by the youths and the priest of the boys; and during the opening and closing of the temple by the priest of Tiberius Caesar there will be libations, incense-burning and illumination of lamps, (paid for) by the revenues of Dionysos.'

From early on it was not unknown in Doric temples, and normal in Ionic ones, to widen the spacing between the central pair of columns on the main facade: this improved sight-line benefited, not just the god-in-the-statue looking out, but also the worshippers at the altar, looking in. The successive rises in floor-level in some temple interiors (p. 86) would also have helped those outside to see the statue within.

In later temples in western Turkey, finally, large openings in the front gable are thought to have been used to stage 'appearances' of a deity's statue, brought up for this purpose by an inner staircase leading to the attic. Sets of three such openings, the central one larger, are known for the Artemision at Ephesos (see p. 35), Apollo's temple at Chrysa, and another temple of Artemis, at Magnesia-on-the-Maeander. Here the openings were represented as a door with moulded posts and a lintel. This detail seems to militate against a merely functional interpretation of these openings as measures to relieve the weight of the upper parts.

It has been argued that these openings represented the heavenly 'gates' of ancient Greek cosmology and that they were used to stage epiphanies of the deity's idol on days of festival to expectant worshippers below. The evidence is

circumstantial but becomes more compelling when taken with the ancient texts. At Ephesos, the festivals of Artemis were called her 'most manifest days' (*epiphanestati hemerai*). The Magnesians claimed that Artemis had appeared to them in the years around 220 BC. Later temple epiphanies perhaps commemorated this momentous event.

As with so much in Greek religious rites, the idea of the deity appearing in the temple may have come ultimately from the ancient Near East. But the theatricality of these epiphanies, like the opening of a temple's doors, also evokes the Greek stage, where special effects for engineering epiphanies were already employed in the 5th century BC, and trios of doors for the actors from at least the 4th century BC. Greek drama originated in religious ritual way back in the 7th century BC. By the 4th and 3rd centuries BC, the influence may have been in the opposite direction.

*Remains of an opening in the gable of the temple of Artemis, Magnesia-on-the-Maeander.*

*Reconstruction of the main facade of the temple of Artemis, Magnesia-on-the-Maeander, showing the three gable-openings.*

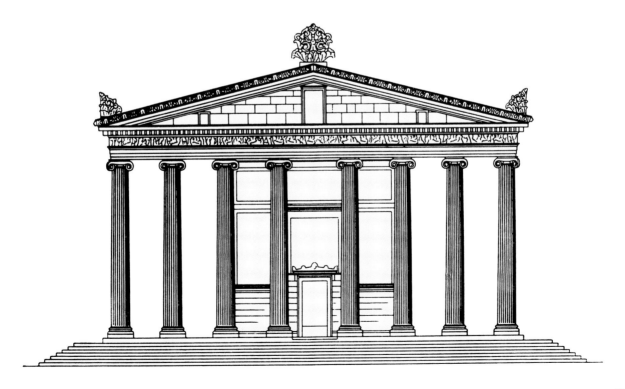

# A Focus for Ritual

## Experiencing the temple interior

Temple architecture did its best to rise to the momentousness of the encounter between ancient worshippers and the idols inside. In progressing from the outer colonnade into the interior, the worshipper would often experience successive rises in floor-level before finding him- or herself before a central statue, which in some temples might be placed in an inner statue-house or, especially in the western colonies, in a back room (below).

Often a double row of columns in the shrine turned the internal approach into a processional way – this intention is particularly clear in temple G at Selinous. At the Ephesian Artemision it was the outer approach through the front porch which was treated in this way (see the plans on p. 28).

It is unknown whether circumambulation of the statue was an ancient Greek ritual (see p. 82). But in the design of some interiors walking around the central statue was certainly a possibility – as in the Parthenon, where the colossus of the goddess was framed on three sides by an open colonnade with a walkway behind (see the plan on p. 142).

Lighting effects were a crucial part of this experience of the interior. As well as natural light, attracted by lofty temple doors and, from the 5th century BC at the latest, windows in the wall between the interior and the front porch, the interior itself was lit by oil-lamps. These sometimes provided round-the-clock lighting – as in the Erechtheion, where an elaborate gold lamp is said to have burnt 24 hours a day. Lamps are a frequent find in Greek sanctuaries, and marble lamps are found in temple interiors – the Artemision of Ephesos, for instance.

Aromatic smells, finally, played their part in enhancing mood inside the temple. The burning of incense, especially myrrh and frankincense from Arabia, is well attested in ancient Greek religion. The ancient inventories of the treasure inside the Parthenon list at least sixteen precious incense-burners (*thymiaterion*, singular), some of them silver, others gilt. Their use in ceremonies marking the opening and closing of temple doors is specifically attested at Teos in Asia Minor (pp. 84–85).

## Access to the interior

'…neither iron nor bronze is to be brought into the temple except coin, nor footwear nor any other kind of hide; nor can a woman enter the temple except the priestess and the prophetess.'

Greek inscription from Lesbos, 2nd century BC

The question of how accessible Greek temples were is crucial to our understanding of their place in the religious culture of their time. Unlike, say, Egyptian temples, Greek temples generally speaking were open to the community as a whole, subject to Greek rules about religious pollution.

These routinely forbade entry into the larger sacred precinct – let alone the temple – to persons considered impure as a result of contact with birth and death or sexual activity, as well as from more serious infractions such as (female) adultery, male prostitution and killing. It is likely that the placing outside the temple's entrance of a stoop of purificatory water for the use of worshippers was common, even if archaeology has provided only one certain instance, from the first temple of Poseidon at Isthmia (see below).

As the inscription cited above shows, in some temples the curious workings of religious taboo restricted access to one sex only. In others entry could be refused to members of a particular ethnic sub-group of the Greeks – as on the Akropolis in 508 BC, when the priestess of Athena sought to prevent entry to a Spartan king on the grounds that he was a Dorian Greek (the Athenians were Ionians; he entered anyway). Some or all temples in the community could close on inauspicious days, and (at least in later times) on days of collective mourning for a local grandee.

*(Right) Plan of temple G at Selinous showing the pair of internal colonnades flanking the approach to the statue-house, the floor of which formed the fourth and final rise in floor-level, starting with the initial flight of steps up onto the platform.*

*(Far right) An elaborate marble stoop (perirrhanterion) found in situ outside the front porch of the 7th-century BC temple of Poseidon at Isthmia. Its rim shows wear and polish from years of constant handling by people entering the temple.*

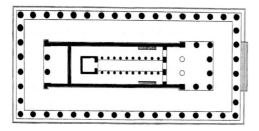

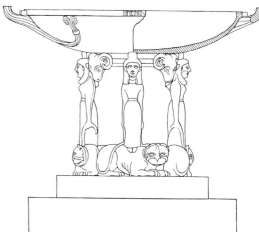

A more fundamental question is the general accessibility of temples. From their beginnings in the 8th century BC they had provided storage for costly offerings, and it is unlikely that they were ever open at all times to all comers. Their great doors had locks (p. 102).

In later times at least, many minor temples opened only on the feast-day of their divinity. On the other hand, there was probably always a distinction between these and the major temples. Greeks reserved colonnaded temples for their most important cults, whether in the urban centre or the rural territory, and these are more likely to have been kept open by day as a matter of course than smaller, less important, shrines.

The temple of Dionysos at Teos, with its daily ceremonies of opening and closing (p. 84–85), is a case in point; so is the earliest temple of Poseidon at Isthmia, its water-stoop worn away from its constant handling by visitors. Then again, oath-takers in the agora needed ready access to nearby temples at least during the hours of business. Temples of the healing god Asklepios seem also to have been opened daily. The offertory boxes (see pp. 92–93) inside some temples to receive payment for sacrifices on the altar outside imply frequent comings and goings.

Priestesses, if not priests, may have been in the habit of opening up their temples and remaining on the premises, whether seated by the doors, as with Athena's priestess on the Akropolis in 508 BC, or falling asleep inside, as with Argive Hera's unfortunate priestess in 423 BC, whose lamp then set the temple on fire (one thinks of an afternoon nap in the building's darkened shrine). Both were colonnaded temples.

The question of accessibility is linked in a larger sense to the nature of ancient Greek religious ritual. This centred on sacrifices on an outside altar, with nothing comparable to the regular religious services of a mosque or a church, requiring roofed accommodation for group worship. Although there

*(Above right) An open-air sacrifice depicted on a cup (6th century BC). The masonry altar is on the right and is approached by a procession escorting the victim, an ox, to the piping of a flautist.*

*(Right) In this conventional reconstruction of temple-rituals, the chief image of the deity looks on from the shrine as a group of worshippers perform rites at the axially aligned altar outside.*

*Reconstruction of the shrine inside the temple of Athena Alea at Tegea (4th century BC). In archaeologist Peter Corbett's words, this was 'a large unencumbered hall… well suited to the assembly of a considerable number of people'.*

*The unusually well-preserved attic of the temple of 'Concord' at Akragas in Sicily was divided into three chambers by two cross-walls over the porches, each pierced by a triangular opening (one of them visible here) for human circulation.*

certainly were formal ceremonies from time to time on the temple platform, Greek temples were not used for communal liturgy.

But another pattern of use is possible, in which, once the doors were open, individual worshippers drifted in and out in ones or twos or larger groups, as in the temples of modern India.

How many people an ancient temple interior could comfortably accommodate would of course vary considerably from temple to temple. But architects showed a concern for making room for people. A long narrow shrine without internal columns was a feature of temples in the colonial west, where the penchant for a back room, in some cases demonstrably used for divine images, may have further freed up interior space for worshippers.

Temple design in the Aegean area reflected similar concerns. Rows of large single columns in shrines gave way to rows of smaller super-posed columns, reducing bottom diameters and freeing up space. On Richard Tomlinson's estimate, there may have been room for up to 500 in the Parthenon's shrine. By the 4th century BC there is a trend towards enlarging shrines by, for instance, omitting interior columns entirely, and by reducing the size of the rear porch, or omitting this too.

Then there were the mega-temples. Was their huge size never linked to a desire to create roomier buildings for worshippers? It certainly would have had this effect, as a glance at the plan of the Samian Heraion (p. 28) or temple G at Selinous (p. 86) shows.

Once inside, how free was the visitor to move around the interior? In ancient writings there is a clear tradition about temple areas that were, literally, 'not to be entered' (*adyton*), but these restricted spaces are hard to pin down archaeologically, and seem to be a particular feature of oracles (p. 91).

Otherwise there are few obvious signs that access to major temples was restricted once the doors had been opened. Given the pious propensity to touch the sacred statues, however, it was not unusual to place protective screens in front of a major image, especially if it was famous and costly, as at Olympia, or even to put it in a separate statue-house, as at Kastabos (p. 214), a healing sanctuary where touching the goddess may have been considered therapeutic.

## Mysterious attics

'…when the men of Elis were repairing the dilapidated roof of the Heraion, the wounded corpse of a foot-soldier was found between the ceiling and the roof…'

Pausanias, 2nd century AD

This anecdote is the only explicit ancient reference to the fact that in many temples there was access to an attic. It confirms that attics could be used for roof-repairs, and suggests that in this case, Hera's temple at Olympia, the attic was rarely visited.

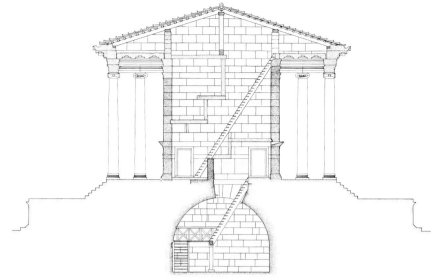

*(Left) Lateral cross-section through the rear of the temple of Zeus at Aizanoi, showing two wooden staircases, one to the oracular crypt, the other to the roof-space. The two monumental access-doors (shown here) from the rear porch indicate that the staircases had a ritual significance.*

*(Below) One of the pair of monumental stair-wells on either side of the shrine-entrance in the temple of 'Concord' at Akragas, each with its own portal.*

But this is by no means the full picture. Staircases into the upper parts of temples are well attested archaeologically in the Greek world. Sometimes they received monumental treatment of a kind difficult to reconcile with the mere needs of maintenance. Didyma and Aizanoi are examples in Asia Minor. In the western colonies, stone staircases were built into masonry 'towers' and came in pairs flanking the doors. These arrangements imply a need for frequent access and possibly, as noted in Chapter II, a ritual use for the attic (p. 54).

Light in attics was provided by openings called *opai*. Special roof tiles have been found at Bassai for this purpose. At least one *ope*, on Apollo's 4th-century temple at Cyrene (pp. 226–27), was something much more elaborate, since a group of citizens is recorded as clubbing together to pay for it.

In 279/8 BC, when Delphi was under attack from marauding Celts, the priests and priestesses shouted that they had seen 'the god jumping into the temple through the open top of the roof': the reference must be to a sizeable *ope*. The striking manner of entry, by the way, favours the idea that the Greeks saw the temple roof as a metaphor for the heavens (p. 54).

## Rituals elsewhere on the temple platform

On one modern view the colonnades framing the inner building of the Greek temple were no more than glorified baldachins, or ornamental frames, for the statuary within. This seems unlikely. For the Roman writer Vitruvius, the double-width halls associated with Hermogenes (p. 64) were not just for architectural effect (although he admits this aspect): they offered people 'a wide and unobstructed space' as protection against the weather.

Modern scholars have gone further, suggesting that the halls were used for religious processions at festival time, and that the architectural sculpture

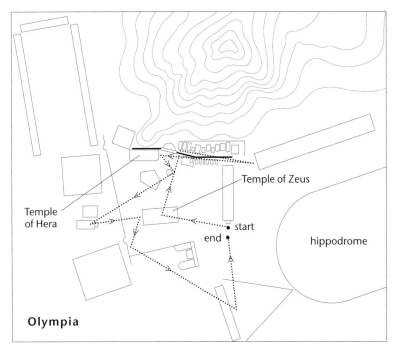

Olympia

Temple of Zeus

Temple of Hera

start
end

hippodrome

*Reconstruction of the route taken by the monthly sacrificial procession at Roman Olympia in which a priest offered sacrifices of frankincense and cakes (see p. 81) on the different altars, including the one inside the Temple of Zeus.*

modated a monumental open crypt of mysterious purpose, to which worshippers descended by a grand staircase.

In Selinous' temple F the spaces between the outer columns (intercolumniations) were later blocked up with masonry screens to a height of 4.7 m (15½ ft). The intention, probably, was to restrict the view of rites performed in the halls. The same explanation may account for the substitution of continuous walls in temple BII at Metapontion (pp. 119–20) and the Olympieion at Akragas (pp. 127–28). At Magnesia (pp. 201–2) in western Turkey, the screening off of the side-intercolumniations of the two porches suggests that the concern to shield ritual performances in the outer parts of a temple was not confined to the western Greeks.

In two colonnaded temples in the central Peloponnese, Bassai and Tegea, there was additional access to the shrine from one of the long halls. In the case of Tegea (pp. 159–60), an imposing side door in the north hall had its own monumental ramp, implying stately movements of some kind.

This ramp at Tegea was one of two – the other led up to the main entrance. Masonry ramps in this position – a feature of Egyptian temples – are well attested in mainland Greece. They have also turned up in southern Italy (Foce del Sele) and Asia Minor (Letoon).

The need for processions to move in and out of a temple with appropriate dignity – not least if a portable idol was involved – helps to explain the presence of grand ramps of this type, which solved the problem of how to negotiate the high steps of the platform. The alternative, a sensible flight of steps, is a well attested addition to older Greek temples in Roman times (e.g., pp. 113, 184).

The only temple ramp whose use can be documented from ancient literature is that of Zeus'

sometimes set high up in the halls and porches (see p. 66) may identify ritually significant parts of the temple where concentrations of worshippers were anticipated. Comparative evidence from modern India (see p. 82) suggests how the halls could have been used in ritual circumambulation of the divine statuary in the inner sanctum.

Staying with the archaeological facts, in two cases the use of these halls for particular localized ritual can be demonstrated. The Parthenon's north hall turns out to have housed its own subsidiary statue-house and altar. In Cyrene's 4th-century temple of Apollo (pp. 226–27), the east hall accom-

*The east side of the temple of Apollo, Bassai. The opening in the north wall of the inner building – just visible – was originally barred with a grille, not a door as used to be thought (pp. 156–58).*

temple at Olympia. It did indeed serve processional needs, although here the purpose was sacrificial. According to Pausanias (c. AD 150), 'a priest, holding office for one month, soothsayers and libation-bearers, and also a guide, a flute player and a woodman', once a month sacrificed on the altars at Olympia, in the case of Zeus 'going to the altar inside the temple'. Interior altars for burnt sacrifice were exceptional, although another famous temple, Apollo's at Delphi, had one too.

## Oath-taking

Individuals habitually entered Greek temples to swear the formal oaths, with the gods as witness, which were part of the fabric of ancient Greek social life, required in such routine transactions as marriages and contracts. To do so in front of a divine statue, while not a prerequisite, strengthened the oath. Thus the law code of Gortyn in Crete around 450 BC permits a woman to swear an oath 'before the statue of the Archer [i.e., Artemis]'.

Oath-taking was integral to business deals in ancient Greece, and the agora was the business centre of the Greek city. This helps to explain the proximity of colonnaded temples to the civic centre or agora, as at Metapontion (p. 119) or Priene (pp. 202–3), and the Persian king Cyrus' dismissive comment about the Greeks: 'I have never yet been afraid of men who have an agora in the centre of their city, where they swear this and that and cheat each other' (Herodotus).

## Temple asylum

'[Aristodikos] went all round the outside of the temple, and took from their nests the sparrows and other birds which had built there; and the story goes that while he was doing it he heard a voice from the *adyton*, saying: "Impious wretch, how dare you do this wicked thing? Would you destroy those who have come to my temple for protection?"'

Herodotus, 5th century BC

This tale, set in Didyma in the mid-500s BC, reflects the age-old Greek belief that sacred space was inviolable and afforded living creatures the god's protection. As a direct result, Greek sanctuaries could be sought out by people on the run. Such a person was called a suppliant (*hiketes*), who could seek asylum at the divine image within the temple.

In the period after Alexander cities increasingly sought external guarantees of 'inviolability' for their major sanctuaries. Since suppliants could turn a temple into 'a walled shelter for robbers', as the Artemision of Ephesos was described by the Greek writer Philostratos (early 3rd century AD), the authorities sought to limit and control asylum-rights by careful delimitation of the sacred space around the temple. At the Artemision once more:

'…the boundaries of the inviolability have often been changed. Alexander increased them by a stade.

Mithradates shot an arrow from the corner of the roof [of the temple] and reckoned that it had gone somewhat beyond that stade. Antony doubled this and thus encompassed in the right of inviolability a part of the city; but this was deemed harmful, making the city over to wrongdoers, and Augustus Caesar revoked it.'

Strabo, late 1st century BC

## Oracles

A minority of preserved colonnaded temples formed a class apart in ritual terms, since they housed an oracle (*manteion*). In Delphi on the Greek mainland, Didyma in western Turkey and Klaros, further north on the same coast, inspired mediums uttered the words of Apollo, Greek god of prophecy par excellence. Aizanoi, in western Turkey's interior, spoke for the local Zeus.

Physical arrangements for the rite of consultation, insofar as they are understood at all, are described in the individual entries for these temples in Chapter V. In all of them the experience involved some degree of physical descent (*katabasis*) into a lower area, the *adyton* ('not to be entered') in Delphi and Didyma.

At Klaros and Aizanoi, this lower zone took the eery form of an underground masonry crypt with vaulted roof, probably intended to evoke the sacred caves which the Greeks associated with entry to the underworld. At Klaros the approach was through a disorientating labyrinth of underground passages; at Aizanoi by wooden ladder.

This contrived experience was designed to be traumatizing. At the oracle of Trophonios at Lebadeia in central Greece, with no colonnaded temple but where underground arrangements were similar, a consultant newly returned to the surface was 'still possessed with terror and hardly knows himself or anything around him' (Pausanias, 2nd century AD).

*Athenian vase-painting (5th century BC) showing the Pythia or prophetess seated on her ritual tripod in the temple of Apollo at Delphi.*

# Other Temple Activities

### Treasuries

'The following are in a leather bag: objects of
silver, bronze, overlaid wood, gilt, and silver overlay;
weight: 1650 drachmai. Sealed with the public seal.'

Inscribed inventory of the Parthenon, 4th century BC

A 'doorless' (*athuros*) temple was unusual. Doors
were needed, not just because they played their
part in religious drama, but because temples
doubled, in effect, as treasuries. The 'sacred things'
which temples housed by definition included
valuable offerings, not least the divine statues and
their ornamentation (*kosmos*).

Physical evidence for the attachment of
dedications to the walls of temple interiors has
been noted both at Bassai and in the Parthenon.
Over the generations more and more gifts from the
faithful only increased the quantity of treasures
needing protection. Like venerable churches today,
Greek temples faced the dilemma of being both
places of worship and heritage sites.

A number of colonnaded temples, especially in
the west, have small back rooms, entered from the
preceding shrine. Finds of bases within show that
sometimes they housed a divine statue. In the
deepest interior of the shrine, they probably also
served as treasuries. Metal grilles were regularly
fitted between the columns of the front porch.

These protected the great doors, treasures in
themselves, but also precious offerings, as in the
Parthenon (see pp. 76–77).

We know about the Parthenon's service as a
treasury because the democratic Athenians
required a minute accounting of these valuables
from the officials who cared for them (see Chapter
II). In the 5th and 4th centuries BC these inventories
were 'published' on stone, as with the extract
above. They allow a detailed reconstruction of the
rear chamber's function as a closed treasury.
Cuttings show that its great doors from the rear
porch were reinforced on the inside with vertical
iron bars hidden in the wood.

Many temples featured what ancient texts call
'treasuries' (*thesauroi*), fitted with locks. Their
remnants can be identified with the masonry floor-
cavities and 'boxes' found in some temples inside

*Reconstruction of the rear
chamber of the Parthenon
as a treasury, with most
valuables stored on shelves or
suspended from the walls.*

the area secured by the doors. Inscriptions show that they served to collect offerings of small coin (*pelanos* or *aparche*) from worshippers, often as a charge for sacrificing on the deity's altar.

Temples, finally, were used as secure places to deposit valuables, whether owned by the state or privately. Around 500 BC the philosopher Herakleitos chose to deposit his book of philosophy in the temple of Artemis in Ephesos, his home-city. But literal treasure was more often in question. At Priene Athena's temple was the recipient of a sum of money from a Cappadocian prince, and the conversion of the rear porch into a closed room may have been to provide for its secure storage.

It was then but a short step to a deity becoming a banker, as at Rhamnous (p. 147), where an inscription of around 450 BC records 'Of Nemesis's monies the total in the hands of the 200-drachma borrowers: 37,000 [drachmai]'. In the mid-2nd century AD, the Artemision of Ephesos could be described as 'the treasury of Asia'.

The role of some temples as banks indicates their economic importance in the day-to-day life of the host community. Their treasures also offered a tempting crisis fund, most famously in the case of Athena's statue in the Parthenon.

In an address to the Athenians on the eve of the Peloponnesian War (431 BC) their leader Perikles reminded them:

'If they were reduced to the last extremity, they could even take off the plates of gold with which the statue of the goddess was overlaid; these, as he pointed out, weighed 40 talents, and were of refined gold, which was all removable. They might use these treasures as self-defence, but they were bound to replace what they had taken.'

Thucydides, 5th century BC

*Ionic temple at Lokroi (South Italy). The upright blocks (centre left) belong to the sides of a square masonry cavity 1.20 × 1.20 × 1.49 m (4 × 4 × 4.90 ft) for a treasury (thesauros) under the original floor-level of the shrine in the temple.*

*A marble Hermes carrying the baby Dionysos, wrongly attributed by Pausanias to the famous 4th-century BC sculptor Praxiteles. In the 2nd century AD he saw this statue displayed in the temple of Hera at Olympia, where it was rediscovered in the 19th century.*

## Temples of culture

*Kynno*: 'But it is daytime and the shoving is getting greater, so stop there! for the door is thrown open and there is access to the shrine.'

*Kokkale*: 'Only look, dear Kynno, what works are those there! See these, you would say, were chiselled by Athena herself – all hail, Mistress! Look, this naked boy, he will bleed, will he not, if I scratch him, Kynno; for the flesh seems to pulse warmly as it lies on him in the painting...'

Herodas, Greek poet, 3rd century BC

This fictional exchange set in an unidentified temple of Asklepios dates to the 3rd century BC. Since the 6th century BC at least the ancient Greeks had recognized the pleasure to be had from travelling to other cities and seeing the sights. The treasures housed in sanctuaries and temples were prime destinations for these ancient 'lovers of sights' (*philotheamones*), whose modern-seeming tourism is best understood as a form of pilgrimage. Pausanias, a constant companion in these pages, is the best known exemplar of the type, writing up his *Description of Greece* in the 2nd century AD.

Apart from ritual performances, these sacred sights chiefly comprised, as in the quote above, manmade offerings, especially sculpture and paintings: what we would call works of art. In the late 1st century BC the Greek writer Strabo could describe Hera's great temple on Samos as a 'picture-gallery' (*pinakotheke*). Ancient writers often refer to the display of religious paintings in colonnaded temples: locations included the porches and the walls of the long halls (see pp. 46–47).

In the Samian case, there may have been a deliberate decision to concentrate in the one temple some of the 'things worth viewing' (*axiotheata*) in this famous sanctuary. This certainly happened at Olympia. In the mid-2nd century AD Hera's temple there housed a miscellaneous collection including some 21 pieces of statuary, as well as antique furniture (see pp. 150–51).

Some of these items had been transferred from elsewhere in the sanctuary, as we know from Pausanias. He was fascinated by what he saw here in the 2nd century AD, describing one item (an inlaid wooden chest) at the same length as his account of the neighbouring temple of Zeus.

As well as objects to view, finally, there might be cultured voices to hear. An ancient tradition claimed that the 5th-century BC historian Herodotus 'waited for a packed audience to assemble' at the Olympics before giving a reading of his *Histories* in the rear porch of Zeus' temple. This use of a back-porch for recitals is found much later (*c.* AD 100) in Poseidon's temple at Isthmia, used by Greek show-orators to declaim in public.

## Writing on temples

'...Artemidoros Papas, son of Demetrios, one of the generals of the city, oversaw the restoration of the *grammateion* of the sacred documents about the gods...'

Greek inscription from Nysa, 1 BC

This *grammateion* or 'surface for writing' was probably a wall in the temple of the god Pluto in Nysa (p. 201) in western Turkey. The custom of inscribing official documents onto the walls of Greek temples can be traced back to the 7th

century BC. It may ultimately have been inspired by ancient Egypt.

As the evidence stands, the practice was much more common in Asia Minor. But one of the largest assemblages could be found on the Greek mainland – at least 70 documents on the wall in the south hall of Apollo's temple at Delphi, inscribed over four centuries starting in the late 2nd century BC.

Typically the subject-matter of these documents would be the granting and definition of the rights and privileges of the sanctuary, or of its host community. The Prienians used Athena's temple to inscribe a dossier of official communications from Graeco-Macedonian kings (beginning with Alexander the Great), and, later, the Roman senate. This type of display underlines the role of the temple as a marker of communal identity.

Because a major temple was such a communal focus, it also guaranteed an inscription's visibility. Free-standing inscriptions were placed in the front porch or immediate environs for the same reason. As an inscription from Teos puts it: 'so that everyone may see the decisions of the people, this decree is to be inscribed on a stone slab… and set up beside the temple of Dionysos'.

The ancient Greeks literate enough to read these texts were always a minority. The purpose of these inscribed collections was partly symbolic. Their monumentalization in stone gave their content a quasi-magical guarantee of permanence, all the more so since they were under the god's direct protection and shared in the inviolability of his *naos*.

For the same reason, archives of perishable documents could be kept in temples, as at Selinous, or the temple of the Maiden at Neapolis in northern Greece (p. 179) with its 'archive of public debtors' (*chreophylakion*).

Legibility for humans, however, was also a factor. Where the exact setting is known, these documents were always inscribed on outer walls where they could be viewed even if the temple doors were locked: either in the long halls or in the front porch, including its two pilasters or wall-terminals, viewable even when the grilles of the front porch had been secured. At Delphi the documents were placed at eye-height on the lowest course of the wall; at Priene larger letters were used for texts placed higher up (see p. 37).

The other most common type of authorized inscription on colonnaded temples memorialized the name of a rich donor. Sometimes these texts were placed on the particular part of the structure paid for: most often a column, as at Euromos (pp. 208–9).

This practice is most commonly found in Asia Minor, where it can be traced back to King Kroisos of Lydia, who donated columns for the 6th-century Artemision at Ephesos. The most imposing inscriptions carried the name of a principal donor in large letters above the columns of the main facade.

But these are exceptional before the 1st century BC, Labraynda (p. 209) being the only certain example. Although Priene permitted Alexander to inscribe his name as dedicator on the temple of Athena, the text was tucked away at the top of a pilaster or wall-terminal in the front porch (see pp. 36–37).

Only from the 1st century BC do donors' names appear on the main facade of colonnaded temples. Names of individual donors who built or restored Greek temples, not least the Roman emperors, were now not uncommonly placed in this position, their visibility sometimes enhanced from the reign of Augustus on by the use of gilt-bronze lettering, as at Ilion (p. 189).

Unofficial inscriptions or graffiti from ancient times (as opposed to recently) seem to be rare on Greek colonnaded temples. Their scarcity seems to reflect the awe in which the ancient Greeks held the gods' 'sacred stones' (see Introduction).

## Worldly honours

In later times, when the fortunes of Greek cities increasingly lay in the hands of external rulers and local oligarchs, there was a growing temptation for cities to exploit the prestige and conspicuousness of their colonnaded temples as the setting for worldly honours – as at Klaros, where the Kolophonians placed a statue of a royal prince inside Apollo's colonnade (p. 197). Under Roman rule, Greek cities might honour local worthies, women as well as men, by voting them an honorific statue to be set up 'beside' the deity's chief image in the temple interior.

Where rulers were concerned such honours were allied, but by no means equivalent, to divine worship. This phenomenon is considered in the next chapter.

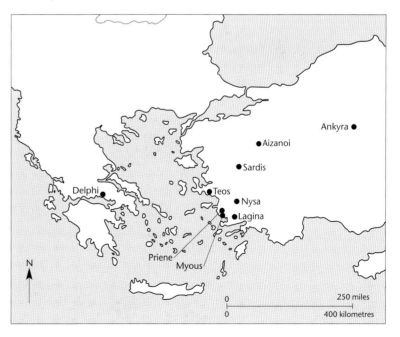

*Distribution of colonnaded temples where official documents are known to have been inscribed on the walls. Possibly inspired by ancient Egypt, the practice in Greek temples can be traced back as far as the 7th century BC.*

# The Temple in its Sacred Setting

The ancient Greeks reserved the colonnaded temple, supreme expression of their religious architecture, first and foremost for a surprisingly small group of heavenly gods led by Apollo and Athena. The widespread building of colonnaded temples to these same few deities emphasizes the unity of Greek religion. A variety of other deities, sometimes of purely local significance, also received this type of temple. But new colonnaded temples built solely for the worship of temporal rulers were extremely rare.

Greek communities entrusted their temples to the charge of local priests and priestesses. A temple was the centrepiece of a larger sacred space or sanctuary, each with its own special festivals, when the temple doors were flung open and divine imagery might be carried out in procession.

Christianity's triumph spelt the end of the old pagan temples. In an unexpected epilogue, Western architects in more recent centuries have revived the forms of the Greek colonnaded temple to showcase the public buildings of great cities in Europe and the USA. That they have done so is a testimony to the lasting appeal of a building type which constitutes one of the supreme aesthetic achievements of the ancient Greeks – a poem in stone.

*The temple of 'Concord' at Akragas (Agrigento), Sicily.*

IV    Encounters with the Gods

# A Place of Worship

including indigenous deities with a Greek gloss (the Maiden at Neapolis, Leto in Lykia) and, in one case (Messene in Messene), a figure whom most Greeks would have considered somewhere between mortal and deity, rather than a fully blown goddess. The list is a reminder of the wide embrace of ancient Greek polytheism, and of the highly localized prominence of many Greek cults.

## The deities worshipped

The cult in over a quarter of colonnaded temples (around 60) is unknown. Of those where the deity can be more or less firmly identified (around 142), an astonishing 90 or so (over 60 per cent) turn out to be dedicated to the same five Olympian deities: Apollo, Athena, Zeus, Hera and Artemis, with the first two significantly ahead of the rest.

In spite of the incomplete data, this picture seems far from random, since the top five deities are known to have presided over the closest concerns of the Greek public domain. Apollo took a special interest in the social formation of youths, in giving political advice through his oracles, and in the founding of colonies. Athena was an armed goddess perceived as 'polis-protecting'; so was Hera, another warrior goddess, who was also close to women's concerns, as, even more so, was Artemis, sister of Apollo. Zeus finally was the king of the gods, particularly responsible for justice and right.

Excepting Roman emperors, the remaining 'top ten' were all traditional Greek deities, even if Asklepios, god of healing, was a relative latecomer. After these, the numerous other figures who can be identified as recipients of colonnaded temples range from central (Demeter, Herakles) to fringe (Hekate) Greek deities, with others of very obviously local significance (the Aiolian Goddess, Diktynna, Aphaia),

## Worshipping rulers

'…[the Rhodians] dedicated a four-cornered sanctuary in the city, equipped on all four sides with stade-length colonnades, which they called Ptolemaion.'

Diodorus Siculus, *c.* 40 BC

The Greek worship of powerful human rulers as manifestations of divinity began seriously with Alexander the Great. However, on the present evidence it seems to have been extremely rare for a colonnaded temple to be purpose-built for the worship of a Graeco-Macedonian king, with one probable example only, at Hermopolis Magna in the Nile valley, heartland of the Ptolemaic monarchy (pp. 224–25). Structures like the Philippeion at Olympia (see below) or the so-called Ptolemaion in Lykian Limyra, imposing though they were, clearly avoided the traditional forms of Greek temple architecture.

Where colonnaded temples were used for the worship of Graeco-Macedonian royalty, it was more likely to result from 'temple-sharing'. This practice is well attested by inscriptions, as with a decree of Teos in western Turkey (204/3 BC) ordaining that Antiochos III and Laodike his queen were to 'share in the temple' with Dionysos, the city's patron deity (pp. 196–97), and have their 'divine statues' (*agalmata*) installed next to his.

## Temples and their Deities

The top ten deities worshipped in colonnaded temples, ranked by the number of temples in which they were the sole or chief deity:

| | | |
|---|---|---|
| 1 | Apollo | 29 |
| 2 | Athena | 24 |
| 3 | Zeus | 16 |
| 4 | Hera | 10 |
| 5 | Artemis | 11 |
| 6 | Roman emperors | 10 * |
| | (*6 are with other deities) | |
| 7 | Asklepios | 4 |
| 8 | Dionysos | 3 |
| 9 | Aphrodite | 3 |
| 10 | Poseidon | 3 |

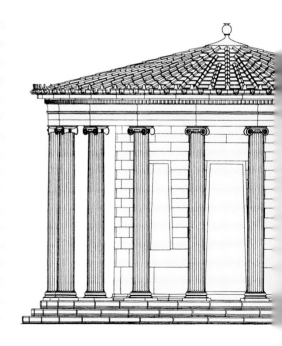

*Block from the facade of Athena's temple in Priene recording in Greek the rededication of the temple by 'The People to Athena Polias and Caesar Augustus the God, Son of a God.'*

Only with the advent of the universal Roman monarchy under the first emperor Augustus did Greek cities build new colonnaded temples in any numbers for cults of the ruler and his family. Even so, no such temple is certainly attested for exclusive service in emperor-worship.

Where there is explicit evidence, the dedication associated the emperor with a traditional god, notably Zeus (Pergamon) or Apollo (Sagalassos). In only one case is the emperor (Antoninus Pius, also at Sagalassos) named first in the dedication, as if the senior partner in the temple-cult.

Hadrian was probably associated with Zeus in the god's great new temples at Athens and Kyzikos. In terms of the symbolics of power, it was particularly fitting for the Roman emperor to 'temple-share' with the Greek king of the gods.

Significantly, where it is the goddess Roma who is

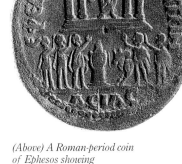

*(Above) A Roman-period coin of Ephesos showing worshippers before an image of a Roman emperor in a temple.*

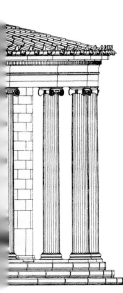

*(Left) Restored view of the so-called Philippeion at Olympia, commissioned by the Macedonian king Philip II in 338/7 BC to house a gold-and-ivory statue group of him and his family, including the future king Alexander.*

*(Right) The Roman emperor Vespasian (ruled AD 69–79), one of the collection of imperial statues found in the temple of the Mother or Metroon at Olympia (p. 154).*

worshipped alongside the emperor, and not an Olympian deity, the colonnaded temple takes a non-traditional form, as in Athens (p. 144) or Mylasa (pp. 210–11). What this picture suggests is a Greek reluctance, even in Roman-imperial times, to decouple the colonnaded temple from the worship of the traditional pantheon.

With pre-existing temples the story is similar. Imperial statues now followed royal ones into their interiors, and sometimes cities rededicated these temples, as at Priene, or Rhamnous, where the temple of Nemesis was reconsecrated to Livia, consort of Augustus. Only at Olympia is a colonnaded temple known to have been divested of its original cult, that of the Mother (p. 154), whose statue was removed, and made over entirely to emperor-worship.

# Priests and Festivals

*Statue of a richly dressed priestess from Priene. The inscribed base reads: 'Nikeso, daughter of Hipposthenes, wife of Eukritos, priestess of Demeter and Kore.' Around 300–250 BC.*

## Priests and priestesses

'…the priest is to open the temple every day…'

Greek inscription from Chalkedon (Istanbul), *c.* 200 BC

Every colonnaded temple lay in a sacred precinct or sanctuary and was in the charge of the deity's priest (*hiereus*) or priestess (*hiereia*). This was one of the ways in which Greek religion, unlike other aspects of Greek public life, gave prominence to females. Normally a god was assigned a priest, a goddess a priestess. But there certainly were exceptions: Athena Alea at Tegea, for instance, had a priest, Poseidon at Kalaureia a priestess. It was rare for a temple to be served by both a priest and priestess, as on the Athenian Akropolis, where the various deities housed in the Erechtheion were served by both a priest (of Poseidon) and a priestess (of Athena). Especially in later times, the same priest or priestess could look after several cults in different sanctuaries.

State priests and priestesses were figures of consequence in the community, entitled to profitable perks and honorific marks of status, such as front-row seats at public spectacles. But there was no priestly caste in ancient Greece, and Greek priests

*(Right) In the theatre of Dionysos at Athens public priests and priestesses enjoyed a view from the front-row on special thrones inscribed with their priestly titles.*

did not constitute a powerful interest-group as they did in ancient Egypt. That said, some priests and priestesses in Asia Minor presided over major religious centres with a life of their own, such as the Artemision of Ephesos or the Hekateion of Stratonikeia. These places may have been rich and important enough to be almost independent of the cities which hosted them.

State priesthoods were bestowed on citizens by a bewildering variety of methods, including election, selection by lot, heredity and purchase. Age requirements likewise varied, although maturity seems to have been commonly associated with priesthood.

Looks mattered, as did family background: in the 2nd century AD the priest of Ismenian Apollo at Thebes (p. 168) had to be a 'strong, handsome youth from a distinguished family'. But Greek priesthood generally was not a vocation and required no special training or skill. Unlike the office of king, says the Athenian writer Isokrates (4th century BC), that of priest is 'one which any man can fill'. In later times, however, an ability to support the costs of the cult from personal wealth became increasingly important.

Although a daily liturgy in Greek temples does not seem to have been the rule, priests and priestesses took the lead in the rituals of sanctuary life. The Greek writer Plutarch, a priest of Apollo at Delphi (around AD 100), described his duties as sacrificing, marching in processions and dancing. Ancient definitions of priesthood stress in particular the priest's role as 'he who addresses the blood-sacrifices to the god', and that of priests and

(Above) In this Boiotian vase-painting (4th century BC), a mythological priestess (right of the altar) drops her temple-key while fleeing from the scene.

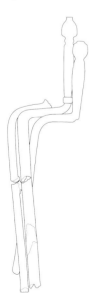

(Below) A bunch of iron keys, one inscribed 'Belonging to Apollo', found at the ancient city of Halieis in the eastern Peloponnese. The best-preserved is nearly 55 cm (22 in) long. About 475–450 BC.

priestesses together as those 'who offer prayers to the gods on our behalf'.

As seen in Chapter III, much of this activity was centred on the outside altar, often under the gaze of the deity within. Priestly duties included officiating at regular animal-sacrifices on behalf of the community. Prayers would be said, and often the priest himself seems to have wielded the sacrificial knife. Equally priestesses, and priests, could, and did, delegate this bloody duty to a professional, the *mageiros*, a ritual cook-cum-butcher.

As to the temple itself, priests here had a fundamental duty of care, as is shown by their stewardship of the temple keys. In Greek literature, the post of priestess was near-synonymous with 'having charge of the key' (*kleidouchos*). Above all these were the keys to the great doors, but also to the lockable treasuries inside.

It follows that the priesthood was responsible for the security of the temple and its contents. In this it was supported by lesser figures, including security guards and sometimes fierce dogs, as at the Cretan Diktynnaion (p. 182).

Times of danger for the sanctuary put priestly personnel on their mettle. In 492 BC, after his city's defeat by Gela's tyrant Hippokrates, the Syracusan priest of Olympian Zeus was found, Diodorus Siculus relates, 'in the act of taking down the gold dedications and removing in particular the robe of Zeus, made with a great deal of gold', presumably to safeguard them. In 480 BC, when the Athenians abandoned their city to the approaching Persians, the priestesses of the Akropolis (in one ancient

tradition) were ordered to stay behind and protect the sacred property.

More routinely, priests and priestesses had a general responsibility (often, in practice, delegated to a subaltern, the *neokoros* or 'temple-warden') to keep the inside of the temple clean and tidy, 'to give thought for the care and fitting adornment of the divine statues', as one inscription puts it, to make sure that visitors behaved decorously, and to keep out unauthorized people.

Athenian dramatists offer glimpses of these sub-alterns, as in Euripides' play *Ion* (410 BC). Here the seemingly humble temple-warden (in fact the god's son) is on daily and day-long duty at the doors of Apollo's temple at Delphi. His tasks included sweeping and watering the floor; firing arrows at birds nestling in the gables; keeping watch generally; and advising worshippers on the ritual.

Stone thrones (*thronoi*), from which seated priests and priestesses could survey their domain, were a feature of Athenian temples. In Apollo's temple at Cape Zoster (pp. 144–45) one was placed in the shrine right next to the divine statues and offering tables. At Rhamnous, two flanked the door into the shrine of the smaller temple, their position recalling the story in Herodotus of the priestess of Athena on the Akropolis sitting on her throne in the temple's front-porch (pp. 86–87).

The general care exercised by priests and priestesses over sacred property involved them in the cult's administration. But in major sanctuaries there were likely to be state-appointed officials who took care of sacred treasure and revenues and dealt with major building works. In later times priests and

priestesses themselves might contribute to the upkeep of the sacred edifices in their case, as at Cape Zoster.

To our knowledge priests and priestesses were not distinguished sartorially much before the 5th century BC. Even then, it has been suggested, Athenian priestly dress amounted to little more than 'Sunday best', although male priests in general by then grew their hair long, and normally wore a garland or wreath on the head. By the 2nd century BC dress could be more elaborate, as with the 'purple garment [*chiton*] and gold rings', prescribed for a priest on Kos when in his sanctuary (2nd century BC).

How much time the priest or priestess spent in the temple varied greatly. As we saw earlier (pp. 86–87), anecdotes suggest that priestesses in particular might habitually be on the temple premises. Some certainly must have had time on their hands, like the 88-year-old priestess of Athena honoured by the Athenians (*c.* 400 BC) for 64 years of service.

Permanent residence in the sanctuary is sometimes attested, as with the boy-priest of Athena Kranaia outside Elateia (p. 169), who lived in the colonnades near the temple. Adult male priests, with other obligations, family and civic, were perhaps more likely to come and go. Generally ancient Greek priesthood was a responsibility more than a full-time profession.

## Temples and festivals

Greek temples were shown at their best for the deity's festival. This could happen annually, or every two or four years, and a major sanctuary

*A relief on an altar from Delphi showing women arranging garlands.*

could expect to welcome huge numbers of people. An inscription relates that at Kastabos (pp. 213–14) in southwest Turkey, around 150 BC, the sacred precinct was no longer large enough to contain the festival crowds.

Temples on these occasions were decked out. In the Erechtheion decorations were hung from either side of the columns, secured by bronze pins set into small holes drilled into either side of the Ionic capitals. At Ephesos a priestess of Artemis, Vipsania Olympias, is said to have 'placed wreaths on the temple' at festival-time.

As we saw earlier, festival-time seems often to have been the occasion for special rituals around divine statues, which might receive new adornments, or (if the portable kind) be carried out of the temple for processions or other rituals. This was the preferred time for *theoria*, or religious tourism, and the most likely time for parts of the temple to be given over to fringe cultural activities like the readings of Herodotus (p. 94).

Many sanctuaries, not just panhellenic ones (pp. 30–31), included competitions (*agones*) as highlights of their festivals. At Olympia, agonistic equipment was kept there: the bronze shields used for the men's race in armour in Zeus' temple, and the ancient table of ivory and gold 'where they put the wreaths for the winners' in Hera's temple.

*(Left) Reconstruction of a pair of marble thrones flanking a temple doorway at Rhamnous. Found in situ in 1813, they now survive only in fragments.*

# The Context of the Temple

## The sanctuary setting

Colonnaded temples were set into sacred precincts of varying size and complexity. By definition they served only the more important cults of the community, and they usually formed part of a larger architectural entity. A panhellenic sanctuary like Delphi or Olympia, or a major state precinct such as the Athenian Akropolis or the Samian Heraion, was constituted by a continuing aggregation of new structures and votive monuments over many centuries.

Other elements included a processional approach, in Roman times normally paved, and a monumental entrance into the sacred space, marked out by a continuous wall or by boundary stones.

Within the precinct, apart from other temples, shrines and altars, common features included colonnades (*stoai*) for use by pilgrims and to display offerings, dining rooms for the consumption of sacrificial meat, and a water supply. Votive and honorific monuments in all shapes and sizes were standard, often concentrated in the most conspicu-

*Athenian coin of Roman times with a unique ancient depiction of the Akropolis as an ensemble of monuments, including (left to right): the processional approach; the Propylaia (monumental gateway); the colossal open-air statue of Athena; and the Parthenon (compare the illustration on p. 33).*

*A masonry-lined well in the Asklepieion at Epidauros.*

ous position, around the temple, as at Epidauros or Delphi (see pp. 46–47).

From the 4th century BC there is slight evidence for the landscaping of the temple's immediate surrounds, as at Nemea, where cypress trees were planted, or the Hephaisteion at Athens, surrounded by rows of shrubs in the 3rd century BC. In neither case can the provision of shade have been the aim, which may have been aesthetic.

## Relationships with other structures

The special significance of the temple with its altar meant that normally both were placed in the central area of the sanctuary, with less important structures pushed to the periphery. Before Alexander, significant relations between the colonnaded temple and other structures in the sanctuary can sometimes be observed, above all the tendency to place the deity's altar directly in front, and preferably on an axial alignment, as noted in Chapter III. But there were clearly exceptions here, such as Zeus' temple at Olympia, or the Parthenon.

Where there was more than one temple, there was a tendency towards simple massing, at Meta009-tion for example (pp. 119–20). Sometimes this was done with mathematical accuracy, as with the carefully aligned pair at Poseidonia (p. 113), or, three centuries later, the trio at the Letoon in Lykia (pp. 214–16).

To what extent more subtle effects were aimed for is debated. For instance, on the Akropolis, the Parthenon and the contemporary gateway or Propylaia are within three degrees of sharing the same axial alignment. But the rising ground and other structures meant that the visitor would only get a full view of the Parthenon after leaving the gateway well behind. What optical effect, if any, was being aimed for here, is unclear (see p. 33, illustration of Athenian Akropolis).

Another modern observation points out that gateways and approaches could be so sited that visitors would have always had their first close-up view of the temple from an angle, revealing at once two of the four sides and thus emphasizing the temple's three-dimensionality. Again, how far such effects were planned, let alone the extent to which a broadly applied principle might have operated, remains to be established.

Only from the late 4th century BC do new principles clearly emerge in the planning of Greek sanctuaries. These aimed at tying the temple into a dramatic architectural vista. The chief instrument was the colonnade, which Greek architects now started using in more or less rectilinear units to frame an open court with the temple somewhere in the centre.

Occasionally these new courtyard settings exploited a hilltop to interact with an impressive

*(Left) The paved processional road linking the city of Samos to the nearby sanctuary of the Heraion.*

*(Below) This model of the akropolis at Pergamon shows a series of building-complexes all facing in the same direction in a 'fan' arrangement. The spatial centrepiece was the sanctuary of Athena (see p. 192), framed by two-storey colonnades.*

*Restored view of the temple of Zeus at Aizanoi within its colonnaded court and with axially aligned altar and gateway.*

*Restored view of the sanctuary of Asklepios on Kos, with the temple on the highest level of a series of artificial terraces.*

natural panorama, as at Pergamon or Kos. Elsewhere, however, the enclosing colonnades severed the optical link with the surrounding environment.

Sometimes, as at Messene (p. 155) or Aizanoi (pp. 218–20), temple, altar and gateway were set on a single axis, leading the visitor's eye directly to the temple facade. At Teos (pp. 196–97), the temple reared up behind the altar on rising ground, and the two were joined by a paved platform flanked by rock-cut viewing areas.

To take up a point made in the last chapter (p. 85), it may well be that the architectural aesthetic in all this was essentially theatrical. The sacred precinct was now a stage, the temple front a scene-building, and the drama was provided by the ritual perform-ances enacted on the temple-platform and around the altar in front, including the door ceremonies and staged epiphanies already discussed.

The taste for these architectural effects, once introduced, never went away for as long as the ancient Greeks built temples, and they were taken over enthusiastically by the Romans. Older sanctuaries were regularly upgraded to accommodate them – examples include Messene (2nd century BC) and Isthmia (2nd century AD).

## Conclusion

'…in order that… the rites in the sanctuary may be conducted with greater magnificence on completion of the temple…'

Greek inscription from Kos, 3rd century BC

Colonnaded temples were the supreme expression of the 'magnificence' with which ancient Greek communities aspired to embellish the dwellings built for their patron deities. Although the building-type by definition placed great emphasis on the exterior, architects took pains too, as we have seen, with the interior space, where a range of human activity took place, not all of it strictly religious.

For two or three centuries after they first began to be built, the monumentality of all-stone colon-naded temples would have stood in stark contrast to other public buildings of much simpler design and construction, let alone the modest private houses of the citizens. This point needs emphasis:

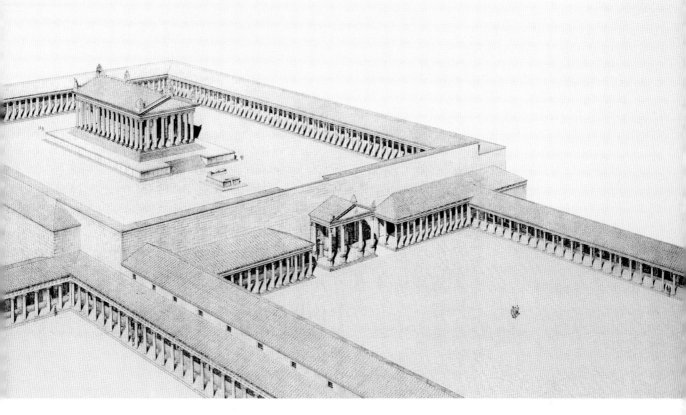

monumental architecture in the Greek world before the 4th century BC meant temples, and it was these which the 5th-century BC Athenian historian Thucydides, in a famous passage noted in Chapter I (p. 33), assumed would be admired by future ages.

From the 4th century BC the colonnaded temple began to lose some of its unique architectural grandeur as Greek cities increasingly invested in other types of all-stone public buildings of growing elaborateness: theatres, colonnades, council-houses and so on, not to mention the finely dressed city walls which aimed in part to please the eye. At the same time the wealthy began to build more elaborate private houses.

This trend continued under the Roman peace, when a colonnaded temple in a Greek city might be just one of a variety of imposing masonry buildings incorporating (but, in these other structures, never entirely framed by) rows of Doric, Ionic or Corinthian columns.

At the same time the quality of workmanship on temples is said to have declined. This is the conventional modern view, which inclines to see high-quality masonry and carving as characteristic of the period before Alexander, and less painstaking work as symptomatic of later times.

Even if one accepts that this view has some basis (and exceptions can certainly be found), there is no hint that the ancients themselves shared it. Certainly temple-building remained a challenge to Greek architects and a stimulus to their theorizing at least until the time of Hermogenes (late 3rd century BC; see p. 64) and probably later. The Menesthenes named by Vitruvius as the architect of Apollo's famous temple at Alabanda seems to have worked in the late 2nd or early 1st century BC.

Nonetheless, that there was an important evolution of attitudes from the 4th century BC onwards seems clear: monumental architecture, once an expression of the unrivalled power of the gods, had become increasingly available as a more general statement of civic and private wealth and status.

But the colonnaded temple never lost its function as either a symbol of identity or a working religious space for the political community which built it. This is shown by the case of Aizanoi (pp. 218–20), a Greek city of recent creation in the Anatolian interior. Here, in the 2nd century AD, building a major temple in the conservative Ionic tradition of Hermogenes offered the local notables who probably funded it the means of asserting the claim of this remote community of Anatolian 'Greeks' to membership of the wider world of the Greek city, and of Greek culture. But, as its cavernous crypt reminds us, Aizanoi was not just a cultural statement, but also a functioning Greek temple.

*'Hellas is everywhere where Greeks live.'*
Dio of Prusa, *c.* AD 100

# Seven Journeys Through Greek Lands

This section catalogues Greek colonnaded temples known from their archaeological remains, no matter how poorly preserved they are. Where successive temples occupied the same site, the focus of the entry is on the latest. In defining 'Greek lands' I follow the Greek writer Dio (*c.* AD 100), from Prusa (modern Bursa) in what is now Northwest Turkey: 'Hellas [Greece] is everywhere where Greeks live.' I have included colonnaded temples in the Greek architectural tradition built under Roman rule, with the exception of those of Roman Syria, a numerous class which in some ways is more Roman (and Syrian) than Greek.

The catalogue is arranged in a broadly geographical way, starting with the Western Greeks of Southern Italy and Sicily, then moving eastwards through Greece and Turkey, before heading clockwise round Syria and North Africa. The geographical order adopted here also has a (rough) chronological dimension too. The best-preserved early temples (6th century BC) are mainly to be found in Southern Italy and Sicily; the most celebrated temples of the following century are in mainland Greece, Athens above all; and the best-preserved temples of later date cluster in Asia Minor (modern Turkey).

*Temple of Poseidon, Sounion, near Athens*

**V   Temples of the Gods**

# Italy and Sicily

Pompeii: Doric temple.
By the 2nd century BC,
when a smaller temple was
superposed on the platform,
the original structure had
been destroyed. A date in
the late 6th century BC is
likely on style.

Contact between ancient Italy and Greek lands was always close. In the early Iron Age Greeks sailed west to trade, especially for metals. These pre-historic contacts help to explain later legends of Rome's Greek origins. From the 8th to the 5th centuries BC, Greeks settled in southern Italy and Sicily, attracted especially by the fertile coastal plains. 'Greater Greece' was how the ancients described this populous western enclave, where Greek civilization flowered in its own right, especially in the 6th and 5th centuries BC. During this time the richest western colonies, places like Poseidonia (Roman Paestum) or Akragas (mod. Agrigento), rivalled and even outstripped the Greek mainland in the scale of their temple-building.

From the 4th century BC, regional prosperity declined in the face of incessant conflict, until finally the Romans conquered the whole region by 200 BC. Many former colonies were now resettled as Roman towns. Sometimes the Greek temples were already ruined before the Christian era. Others remained in use long enough to be converted into churches in the 6th and 7th centuries AD. The cathedral of modern Syracuse, an extraordinary sight for Greek temple-lovers, is the only Greek temple to remain hallowed ground today.

The colonnaded Greek temples of Italy are described in anti-clockwise direction starting from Pompeii, those of Sicily clockwise, beginning with Syracuse.

## ITALY

## Pompeii

The most famous of all Roman towns after Rome itself, Pompeii developed from a local settlement strongly influenced in the 6th century BC by the surrounding Greek colonies on the bay of Naples. This explains why, nestling among the Roman streets, a small Doric temple can be found. The scanty remains occupy the centre of a triangular ancient precinct on the southwest edge of the lava plateau on which Pompeii sits. The original platform remains in situ, shorter than the Greek norm, suggesting indigenous influence. Limestone Doric capitals survive, and a colonnade of 11 x 6 or 7 m (36 x 20 ft) is likely. By the 2nd century BC, when a smaller temple was superposed on the platform, the

*(Below) Pompeii: Doric temple (highlighted) – restored plan of the Forum Triangulare.*

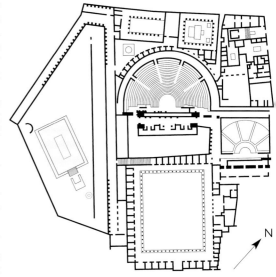

original structure had been destroyed. A date in the late 6th century BC is likely on style.

## Poseidonia (Roman Paestum)

Some 80 km (50 miles) southeast of Naples, the ruins of Poseidonia sit on a low eminence surrounded by the fertile plain of the river Silaris (mod. Sele). The city was founded about 600 BC by Greeks from Sybaris, an older colony on Italy's instep.

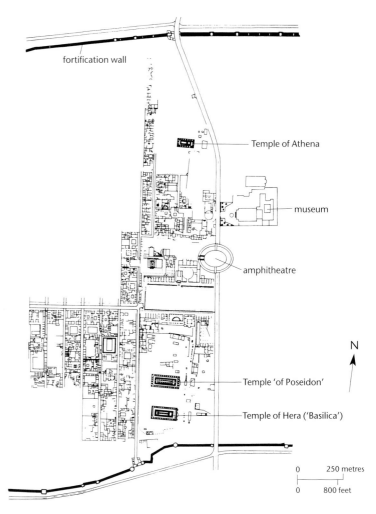

fortification wall

Temple of Athena

museum

amphitheatre

N

Temple 'of Poseidon'

Temple of Hera ('Basilica')

| 0 | | 250 metres |
| 0 | | 800 feet |

Although the new city never achieved a wider renown in ancient times, its colonial farmers grew extremely rich. Their civic pride is reflected in the three standing temples, which are the best-preserved in the entire Greek world. The originality of the older two testifies to the cultural flair of the western Greeks. In 273 BC the city became a Roman colony, renamed Paestum.

*(Above) Poseidonia (Roman Paestum): the town plan in Roman times.*

*(Left) Poseidonia: the temples of Hera (nearest to the viewer) and 'Poseidon', with the Temple of Athena visible in the distance.*

111

*(Above) Temple of Hera ('Basilica') shown from the northwest corner. Note the dumpy proportions of the columns.*

*(Right) Temple of Hera ('Basilica'): plan of the temple as completed, showing the central colonnade of the shrine, a rather old-fashioned feature for this date (around 550–520 BC).*

*(Far right) Temple of Hera ('Basilica') – detail of the top of a fluted shaft, showing the cushion-like capital – sign of an early date.*

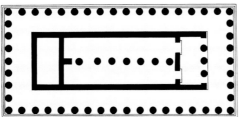

### Temple of Hera ('Basilica')

This is one of the oldest Greek temples with a stone colonnade, as shown by the pronounced bulging of the columns and the cushion-like Doric capitals. Work began around 550 BC to judge from pottery and other finds, finishing around 530–520 BC. The temple stands in the southern sanctuary of the ancient urban centre, and finds point to Hera as the deity.

Built in limestone with sandstone touches, the temple measures 24.5 x 54.3 m (80 x 178 ft) on the top step. An elongated colonnade of 9 by 18 columns encloses an inner building comprising a back room where originally a rear porch had been planned, a shrine proper, and a front porch. The central row of columns, already a bit old-fashioned, may reflect colonial nostalgia for homeland traditions.

However, the temple features novel decoration. The columns are adorned around the neck by a collar of projecting leaves, with an extra collar of great delicacy on five of the columns on the back, or west, end. Distinctive, too, are the small side scrolls (volutes) decorating the capitals of the pilasters terminating the walls of the front porch, a motif probably originating in the Peloponnese. The

temple once had a fired-clay roofing system mainly in black, red and white. At first the Roman colonists maintained the temple, adding a crescent-shaped step, flanked by statue-bases, on the east side. By the 1st century BC the temple was abandoned and used as a quarry.

## Temple 'of Poseidon'

This, the largest of Poseidonia's temples, is exceptionally well-preserved, although missing its roof. It is carefully aligned with the neighbouring 'Basilica', as if the two were linked, and may have been a rebuilding of a (hypothetical) older temple of Zeus, Hera's husband, or even a second temple to Hera. The temple has 6 by 14 columns and a raised shrine flanked by porches and approached by steps. Dimensions are 59.93 x 24.31 m (196 x 80 ft) on the top step, the date (on style) probably somewhere between about 474 and 450 BC. Materials are local limestone and sandstone. Mainland touches include the two rows of doubled-up Doric columns inside the shrine, but typically Greek-Italian are the stair-wells for access to the attic which flank the shrine-entrance.

Since the 18th century the temple has been admired for its harmony and sturdy majesty. The German archaeologist Friedrich Krauss, who died

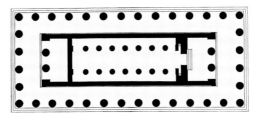

*(Above left and right) Terracotta decorative sheathing from the level of the eaves, including water spouts, from the temple of Hera ('Basilica') at Poseidonia (Paestum).*

*(Below and left) Temple of 'Poseidon', with restored plan showing the staircases on either side of the entrance into the shrine.*

in 1978 after a lifetime's study of Poseidonia's temples, considered it without peer as a purely Doric temple (which the Parthenon, with its Ionic elements, is not).

### Temple of Athena ('of Ceres')

This highly original temple in a sanctuary at the northern end of the urban centre has preserved its colonnade and most of its two gables, but the interior superstructure is largely lost. The cult's identity is inferred from finds. Much smaller than its southern neighbours, it sits on the highest point of the low limestone outcrop on which the city was built. Measuring 14.52 x 32.88 m (48 x 108 ft) on the top step, it has 6 by 13 Doric columns, a porch fronting a shrine, stone staircases flanking the shrine-entrance, and a ramp to the first step of the front platform. The material is local limestone, with sandstone touches. On style the date is about 500 BC.

The Doric and Ionic styles are combined here for the first time in all Greek architecture. While the colonnade is Doric, the inside porch was fronted by eight Ionic columns, by way of emphasizing the approach to the shrine. The treatment of the short facades is without parallel, especially the coffers (sunken panels) which decorate the underside of the eaves and the omission of the projecting course which normally defined the base of the gable.

Later in antiquity the temple was damaged by a fire, falling timbers badly blackening the paving of the porch. Weathering-patterns show that only the shrine was re-roofed, probably for service as a church, to judge from the seven Christian graves found in the halls. At the time (1805) of the first modern restoration, the intercolumniations had been walled up and the temple served as a stall for farm animals.

*(Below) General view of the temple of Athena at Poseidonia (Paestum) showing the east facade with its unusual gable design.*

*(Right) Plan of the temple of Athena, showing the successive rises in floor-level on the way into the shrine.*

*(Far right) Restored Ionic capital from the temple of Athena.*

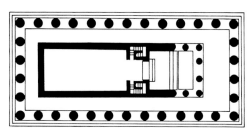

## Foce del Sele

Some 8.5 km (6 miles) north of Poseidonia, near the mouth of the river Silaris (Sele), stood Poseidonia's chief rural sanctuary, dedicated to Hera. Surrounded by flat farmland, the scant remains are little visited today. An important colonnaded Doric temple in limestone and sandstone was built here about 500 BC on the same alignment as an earlier, non-colonnaded, neighbour some 14 m (46 ft) to the north. Measuring 18.61 x 38.95 m (61 x 128 ft), the Doric temple had 8 by 17 columns, a back room, shrine and front porch faced by Ionic columns, a pair of stairwells flanking the shrine entrance, and a monumental ramp up to the east platform. Eight sandstone metopes survive with relief sculpture.

Gravely damaged by fire about 400–350 BC, the temple may then have gone out of use, although a 4th-century BC metope may point to a restoration. The sanctuary itself survived into the 2nd century AD.

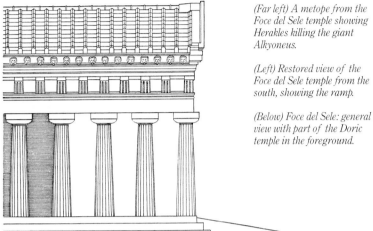

*(Far left) A metope from the Foce del Sele temple showing Herakles killing the giant Alkyoneus.*

*(Left) Restored view of the Foce del Sele temple from the south, showing the ramp.*

*(Below) Foce del Sele: general view with part of the Doric temple in the foreground.*

## Eleia (mod. Castellamare)

Eleia is about 60 km (37 miles) south of Poseidonia, its focus a lofty akropolis commanding expansive views both inland and to the shore. The Greek colony was founded around 540 BC by Phokaians from Asia Minor fleeing the approaching armies of Persia. Atop the akropolis, facing northeast, the platform survives of what must have been Eleia's chief temple, including the moulded profile of the bottom of an interior wall, giving a date on style around 500–475 BC. The temple had a rear porch, unusual in Greek Italy at this date, and probably a colonnade of uncertain style.

## Hipponion (mod. Vibo Valenzia)

Hipponion, on the west coast of Italy's toe, was founded about 600 BC by Greeks from the western colony of Lokroi Epizephyrioi, becoming a Roman colony renamed Vibo Valentia in 192 BC. Buried beneath the sizeable modern town of Vibo, the ancient city has left few visible remains outside the archaeological museum. Foundations of a major colonnaded temple have been found on the Telegrafo or Belvedere terrace, which commands a stunning coastal panorama. Dimensions were 37.45 x 20.5 m (123 x 67 ft), the style probably Doric, and the date late 6th century BC to judge from the fired-clay roofing. Slight remains of an Ionic temple, its upper parts in limestone, stuccoed and painted, have been found on the Cófino hill, with views out to the Apennines. Dimensions were 27.5 x 18.1 m (90 x 59 ft), and there was a colonnade. The Roman colonists seem to have used the temple as a quarry.

## Lokroi Epizephyrioi

This major colony of Lokrians from central Greece was founded towards 700 BC on the east coast of Italy's toe, just south of modern Gerace (Calabria). It developed into one of the most powerful colonial centres of Greek Italy, forming alliances as far afield as Sparta, before succumbing to the Roman general Scipio Africanus in 205 BC. The modest remains of Lokroi's one-time greatness are scattered among fields and hamlets between an inland ridge and the busy corniche road flanking the beach.

## Ionic temple at Marasà

Although ruinous, this remains the best preserved of the few Ionic temples in Greek Italy. Dated on style around 500–450 BC, it replaced on a different southeasterly alignment a wood and mudbrick predecessor begun about 600 BC. With old-fashioned dimensions of 43.7 x 17.3 m (143 x 57 ft) on the top step, the new temple was built in fine white limestone imported from Syracuse, with 6 by 17 columns, one now restored. A masonry cavity, much debated in recent years, seems to be a treasury (*thesauros*), originally sunk into the floor of the shrine (see pp. 92–93). A marble group of the Dioskouroi, a sky-line decoration or maybe from a gable, dates about 420 BC on style and was an addition. The deity is uncertain.

## Doric temple in the Contrada Casa Marafioti

Traces of foundations for a Doric temple measuring roughly 20 x 36–40 m (66 x 118–31 ft) have been found near the modern Casa Marafioti, on a natural

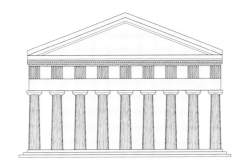

*(Above left) Remains of the Marasà temple, its altar in the far background.*

*(Above) Remains of the Marasà temple: partly restored stump of an Ionic column from the colonnade.*

*(Left) The Doric temple: reconstruction of the main facade, its top-heavy appearance reflecting the early (6th-century BC) date.*

*(Far left) The marble group of the divine twins Kastor and Polydeukes (Dioskouroi) from the Ionic temple at Marasà.*

*(Left) Fired-clay skyline group of a sphinx supporting a horseman, from the Doric temple. This and the Dioskouroi group are both now in the museum at Reggio di Calabria.*

terrace commanding superb views of the coastline. The deity was probably Olympian Zeus, subject of an archive of documents on bronze (350–250 BC) buried in situ about 120 m (394 ft) to the southeast. A colonnade is thought likely, and finds included a rare 'pentaglyph' – i.e., a triglyph (see p. 62) with five vertical faces instead of the usual three. Fired-clay decorations include a group of a sphinx supporting a mounted horseman, dated on style *c.* 430–410 BC and evidently belonging to an ancient restoration.

## Kaulonia

This colony of Achaian Greeks from the northwest Peloponnese was founded in the late 8th century BC on a coastal site north of Lokroi on Italy's toe, near modern Punto Stilo (Calabria). A chance reference by the Greek historian Thucydides (5th century BC) reveals the Kaulonians as major harvesters of timber from the nearby Sila forests. The city was destroyed in 389 BC by Dionysos I of Syracuse. The last of the great temples of Greek Italy was built here on rising ground behind what is the beach today. Now just foundations, it is restored with a colonnade of 6 by 14 Doric columns, a back room rather than a rear porch, shrine with stairwells and front porch. A solitary Doric capital helps date the temple to about 430–420 BC. It was built in limestone apart from the luxury of a marble roof, shipped out from the Cycladic island of Paros.

## Lakinion

*Lakinion: the solitary standing column from the 5th-century BC temple of Hera.*

Kroton (mod. Crotone) was founded about 710 BC by Achaian Greeks on the east coast of Italy's toe,

north of Kaulonia. Its extra-mural sanctuary of Hera, some 9 km (16 miles) southeast on the promontory of Lakinion (Capo Colonna), developed into a panhellenic centre (see pp. 30–31) and was famed for its rich dedications. A solitary column still stands from the east facade of the temple of Hera, on foundations reusing blocks from a predecessor. Details recalling the temple of Apollo at Syracuse, including upward curvature of the platform, suggest a date about 470 BC. Marble statuary probably comes from the front gable. Clay roof decorations survive as well as marble tiles. Half of these were sacrilegiously shipped off to Rome in 173 BC. Although later returned, 'no workman could devise a plan for replacing them' (according to the Roman historian Livy). It was once thought that the temple was now abandoned. Roman brickwork in an interior wall, now destroyed, proves a restoration of the temple, perhaps under Augustus. The colonnade survived until the early 16th century.

## Krimis(s)a

Krimis(s)a, on the coast of Italy's toe north of Lakinion, gave its name to a small city of indigenous (Italic) people and a nearby promontory (mod. Punta Alice) where remains have been found of the only colonnaded Doric temple of 3rd-century BC date in the Greek west. The site once commanded seaward views, now obstructed by sand dunes. The temple was an ambitious rebuilding in stone of a much older structure of wood and mudbrick which measured 46 x 19 m (151 x 62 ft) and dated around 550 BC. The new colonnade had 8 by 19 Doric columns enclosing a reconstruction of the original inner building on the same elongated plan with

*(Right) Krimis(s)a, reconstructed facade of the 3rd-century BC temple (above) and plan (below) of its predecessor, showing the back room which may have held the offerings buried here during the 3rd-century BC rebuild.*

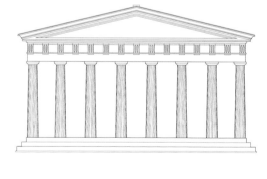

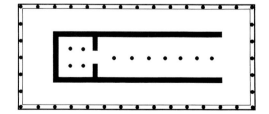

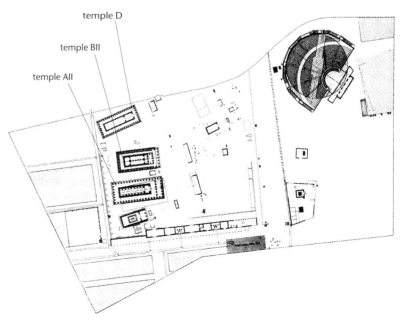

*(Far left) A marble head, perhaps of Apollo, from the sealed deposit in the temple at Krimis(s)a. Hair and eyes were added in different materials; the body was probably a cheap local limestone. About 450 BC on style.*

*(Left) Monolithic half-column from Temple BII, Metapontion. It formed part of a continuous screen-wall instead of the usual colonnade in this Doric temple.*

shrine and back room, where the new floor sealed older offerings carefully buried below, giving a construction date about 300–275 BC. An inscription confirms the deity as Apollo Alaios, a local god. The absence of Roman coins implies a final catastrophe during the wars of the later 3rd century BC.

## Metapontion

High on the arch of Italy's foot, the site of Metapontion lies near the mouth of the River Basento, surrounded by an extensive agricultural plain. Founded from the nearby colony of Sybaris along the coast to the west, the colony prospered in the 6th–5th centuries BC, but declined with the advent of Rome. 'Today nothing is left of Metapontion, but the theatre and the circuit of the walls' (Pausanias, about AD 160). The colony's central sanctuary to the west of the agora, dedicated to Apollo, was dominated by a row of three major colonnaded temples. Now largely vanished, they were already dilapidated by the early 3rd century BC.

### Temple AII

Inscriptions show that this, the largest of the temples, honoured Apollo Lykaios (not Hera, as on the site-labelling). Begun around 540 BC, it overlay the foundation trenches for an abandoned earlier temple (AI) on a more northerly alignment, changed to match the urban grid. The elongated Doric colonnade of 8 by 17 columns rests on a platform measuring 20.5 x 49.13 m (67 x 161 ft) on the top step. The most interesting find is a block from the east facade inscribed in early Greek lettering 10–15 cm (4–6 in) high with the words 'for himself and his family'. The original text, much longer, may have named the donor, conjectured to be a local tyrant and his kin.

### Temple BII

Stamped roof tiles show that this temple belonged to Hera. It too had an abandoned initial phase (BI), begun about 560–550 BC, on a plan aligned to the new urban grid. When work resumed after the mid-century, the earlier plan was retained but extended at the front, apparently so as to accommodate a colonnaded porch standing forward from the side walls, as in the temple of Athena at Poseidonia (p. 114), but here in the Doric style. Here the most striking feature is the continuous wall punctuated by monolithic half-columns which, according to the archaeologist Dieter Mertens, replaced the usual

*(Below) Plan of the sanctuary in the urban centre of Metapontion, showing the cluster of three colonnaded temples and their outside altars.*

temple D

temple BII

temple AII

*The Doric temple of Hera at Tavole Palatine on a riverside eminence outside the urban centre of ancient Metapontion.*

outer colonnade on all sides except the front, resulting in added privacy and an exceptionally dark interior. The fired-clay roof decorations from the two temples, known since 1828, were among the first proofs of the use of colour in Greek architecture (see pp. 67–69).

### Temple D

A third colonnaded temple was built about 470 BC, this time in the Ionic style. The inner building, narrow and long, was framed by a colonnade of 8 by 20 columns enclosing double-width halls. On site the plan has been restored on the ground and the facade partly reconstructed from casts.

*Metapontion, temple D: reconstruction of the superstructure showing the intricate carved ornamentation in the Ionic style.*

### Tavole Palatine

The fifteen surviving columns from this Doric temple of Hera, dated about 520–510 BC, stand 3 km (2 miles) northeast of the ancient city on a small hill by the Bradano river which may have marked the early colony's northern boundary (see p. 27). The colonnade of 6 by 12 columns, on a platform measuring 16.06 x 33.3 m (53 x 109 ft) on the top step, framed a lost inner building made up of a shrine and two porches. Reroofed in the 5th century BC, the temple was in ruins by Roman times, when quarrying was already under way.

## *Taras (mod. Taranto)*

Metapontion's eastern neighbour was the Spartan colony of Taras, occupying the best natural harbours on what is now the Gulf of Taranto. Founded in 706 BC, Taras was one of the richest cities in Greek Italy, surviving as the Roman colony of Tarentum Neptunia. On the ancient akropolis (modern Piazza Castello), two complete Doric columns, heavily restored, are survivors from the north colonnade of one of the oldest stone temples in Greek Italy, their style suggesting an early 6th-century BC date. The common attribution to Poseidon is pure guesswork. The podium of the church of St Domenico at the other (west) end of the ancient akropolis includes masonry from the foundations of another colonnaded temple of 6th-century date, also Doric.

## Rome

By 30 BC the Romans ruled an empire including most of the ancient Greek world. Their capital Rome was so profoundly influenced by Greek culture that in many respects it was, in effect, a Greek city. But the temple of Venus and Roma, largest of imperial Rome's temples, was the only one built to a specifically Greek plan. The philhellene emperor Hadrian (AD 117–38), an amateur architect, was said to have designed it, and in scale it resembles his giant temples in Athens and Kyzikos (see p. 41). The prominent site lay to the east of the Forum, by the Colosseum, and building probably began about 125–26, and may have continued after Hadrian's death. Burnt in 306, the temple was rebuilt by the emperor Maxentius, whose restored work is mainly what you see today. The concrete podium is the chief survivor of the Hadrianic temple, which was built in marble from Prokonnesos in the Sea of Marmara, with two rows of 22 Corinthian columns on the long sides and three of ten on the short sides. This marble forest sat on a high platform of seven steps which measured 48.22 x 105.73 m (158 x 347 ft) between the axes of the corner columns. The inner building, inspired by certain 'double temples' in Greece, comprised two back-to-back shrines separated by a straight wall. By 847–53 the temple was in ruins, probably felled by earthquake.

*Rome, temple of Venus and Roma: artist's impression (right) of the temple as completed, plan (left) of the (reconstructed) 4th-century temple, showing the new back-to-back apses in the shrine, and as it looks today (below).*

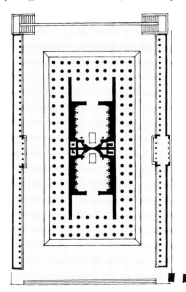

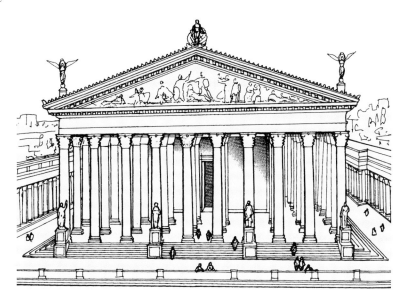

## *Syracuse*

Based on a fine natural harbour on Sicily's east coast, Syracuse was founded by Corinthians in 733 BC. It grew into the wealthiest and most powerful of all the colonies in Greater Greece.

### Temple of Apollo

On a site commanding the mainland approach to the ancient akropolis on Ortygia, this extensive ruin, including two standing columns, may well be the oldest of all the Doric temples in the Greek west. An early date (*c.* 565 BC?) is indicated by the mono-lithic columns, their weight estimated at 35 tons apiece, their unusually close spacing suggesting the concerns of the inexperienced builders. The elon-gated plan measures 21.5 x 55.3 m (71 x 181 ft) on the top step, with a colonnade of 6 by 17 columns,

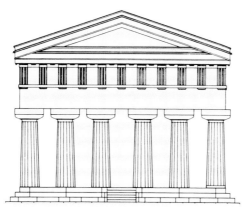

*Reconstruction of the front of the temple of Apollo, its top-heavy appearance indicating its early date.*

doubled across the front, where the central inter-columniations are slightly wider, emphasizing the view into and from the inner building. This features an early example of the back room, staple of temple-plans in the Greek west. There was a large gorgon figure in one of the gables. The deity is named in a worn early-Greek inscription running for 8 m (26 ft) along the face of the uppermost front step (see p. 122). Apollo's statue had gold hair, 'shorn off' by the local tyrant Dionysios I (early 4th century BC). The smaller flight of steps to the entrance is an ancient addition. The ruin was converted into a Norman church, when an arched opening (actually a door) was pierced in the north wall.

### Ionic temple

On the highest point of Ortygia rock-cuttings and fragments of limestone columns reveal the site of a major Ionic temple, with general dimensions of roughly 51 x 21.4 m (167 x 70 ft), underneath the 16th-century Palazzo Vermixio. Inspired by the Ionic temples of the eastern Aegean, it dates on style about 525–500 BC, and was never finished.

### Temple of Athena

Closely aligned with the Ionic temple was Syra-cuse's most famous temple in antiquity, now the local cathedral. Constructed in local limestone, probably around 475 BC, it seems to have had a non-colonnaded predecessor. With general dimensions of 55 x 23.3 m (180 x 76 ft), it closely resembles the Doric temple of Himera and is usually seen as a work of the Syracusan tyrant Gelon, said to have used his share of Carthaginian booty to build new temples. Among shared features both temples have 6 by 14 columns, the same overall proportions, and

Syracuse

- Greek theatre
- Great altar
- Roman amphitheatre
- former coastline
- Temple of Apollo
- ORTYGIA
- Temple of Athena
- GREAT HARBOUR
- N
- 0        500 m
- 0        1500 ft
- Temple of Olympian Zeus

(Left) Ruins of the temple of Apollo, Syracuse, showing the north wall forming part of a later Norman church.

(Right) Exterior of the cathedral, Syracuse, incorporating the south colonnade from the temple of Athena.

rear porches instead of back rooms. In a further move away from Sicilian temple-building traditions, the Athena temple used imported marble, not fired clay, for the roofing system. A shield displayed above the columns later served as a beacon for ships, and the temple became famed for its artworks, including a gallery of 27 panel-portraits of Sicilian kings and tyrants on the inside walls, plundered by the Roman governor Verres (73–71 BC) along with the ornate doors (p. 59). The temple's prompt conversion into a Christian church of the Holy Virgin had already happened by about AD 600, when the future bishop Zosimos of Syracuse was ordained here.

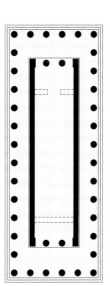

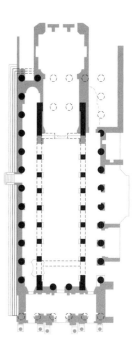

(Left) Interior of the cathedral, Syracuse, showing the north colonnade of the ancient temple of Athena.

(Below) Plans of the temple (left) and the cathedral (with surviving parts of the temple of Athena shown in black).

123

## Temple of Olympian Zeus

Only two columns still stand of this early 6th-century BC temple, built on a low hill about 3 km (2 miles) outside the ancient city, overlooking the Great Harbour and Ortygia. It measures about 22.4 x 62 m (74 x 203 ft) on the top step and, judging from similarities in design and execution, notably its 6 by 17 columns, also monoliths, and the double colonnade on the front, the temple should be close in date to Apollo's on Ortygia. The temple had rich offerings, including a statue of Zeus whose gold did not survive the greed of Dionysios I.

## *Akrai*

This colony of Syracuse, founded in 664–663 BC on a prominent hill-top 30 km (20 miles) to the west, has produced traces of a colonnaded Doric temple, measuring 16.24 x 39.52 m (53 x 130 ft) with 6 by 13 columns doubled on the west. The plan is a

*(Right) Restored plan of the temple of Aphrodite, Akrai, showing the unusual anteroom between shrine and porch.*

*(Opposite left) Drawing of a carved triglyph found at Akrai.*

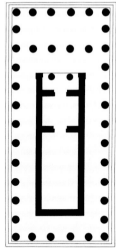

*(Right) Reconstructed facade of the temple of Olympian Zeus, Syracuse.*

*(Below) General view of the remains of the temple of Olympian Zeus, Syracuse.*

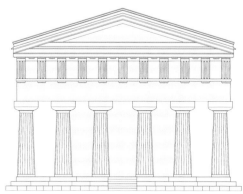

more regularly proportioned version of the mother-city's early 6th-century temples, except for an unusual ante-room between shrine and porch. Doric capitals and triglyphs were softened with carved decoration, dated on style around 525–500 BC. Finds identify Aphrodite, Akrai's chief divinity, as the goddess here. Quarrying had already begun in later antiquity.

## Gela

On the south coast, Gela was founded from Crete and Rhodes in 688 BC, was briefly the seat of a powerful tyranny, but was destroyed by Carthage in 405 BC. Traces of two colonnaded temples exist on the akropolis, both in the sanctuary of Gela's chief deity, Athena Lindia. Temple B, the earlier, on the site of a predecessor, measured 35.22 x 17.75 m (116 x 58 ft) with 6 by 12 Doric columns and had a gorgon face in the centre of the front gable. The fired-clay ornaments give a date in the early 6th century BC. One column has been reerected belonging to a second, larger, temple built further east in 500–450 BC. It had rough dimensions of 21 x 52 m (69 x 171 ft) and a plan of 6 by 14 Doric columns, as in the Syracusan Athenaion. The upper parts were limestone stuccoed white, except for Cycladic marble for the roofing and other details, painted with rich patterns in white, yellow and blue.

*(Left) Restored drawing of the fired-clay guttering, Gela, temple B.*

*(Below left) Gela, temple B: reconstructed elevation of the main front*

Quarrying seems to have begun in earnest only with the Normans.

## Akragas (mod. Agrigento)

On Sicily's central southern coast, Akragas was founded from Gela and Rhodes in 580 BC on a naturally fortified site not far from the sea. The products of its fertile territory included high-quality wine and olives, these last finding a market at Carthage

*(Below) Plan of Akragas, showing distribution of the temples along the 'temple ridge'.*

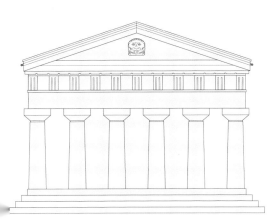

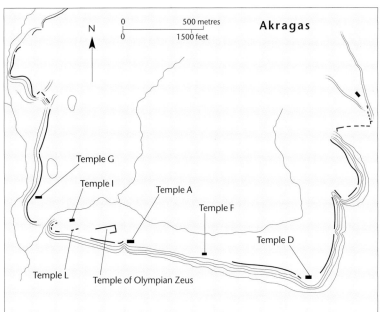

in north Africa. The colony became famous for its wealth and fine public works, especially temples, which the Carthaginians went out of their way to destroy, even mutilating their sculpture, when they razed the city in 405 BC. Later rehabilitated, the city was called Agrigentum under Roman rule, when its patched-up temples attracted the cupidity of Verres, governor and art-thief (73–71 BC; see p. 59). The city holds the record for the largest known assemblage of colonnaded temples (eight including the Olympieion) in the Greek world. Most were placed as near as possible to the city wall, especially the rocky ridge defining the city's southern limits and clearly visible from both within the walls and the ancient approach from the sea (see map, p. 125). Here rose seven colonnaded temples in the later 6th and 5th centuries BC, giving Akragas one of the most impressive skylines of all Greek cities. All built in the local shell limestone, they are presented in clockwise order, starting on the akropolis.

### Temple E

Inside the modern town centre, on a ridge probably belonging to the ancient akropolis, the church of Santa Maria dei Greci partly overlies the remains of a colonnaded Doric temple with columns embedded in the interior walls, and part of the temple-platform preserved outside. The temple had 6 columns on the short sides, but its original length is unknown. On style the date is about 500–450 BC.

### Temple D ('of Hera Lacinia')

On a manmade platform and raised up on four steps instead of the usual three to enhance visibility, this

Doric temple to an unknown deity is eye-catchingly sited on the lofty summit forming the southeast corner of the walled city. Much of the colonnade, partly restored, still stands. Measuring 38.15 x 16.9 m (125 x 55 ft) on the top step, the temple has 6 by 13 columns, porches and shrine, with stone staircases flanking the doors. A fine white stucco coated the stonework, and the marble roof-tiles were painted pink, blue and white. Later the halls received a marble paving and the flight of steps on the east side. According to archaeologist Dieter Mertens, the temple dates around 460–450 BC on style. The deity is unknown.

### Temple F ('of Concord')

Halfway between temples D and A, and once partially screened from external view by the city-wall, this is easily the best-preserved Greek temple in the Greek west, saved by its conversion into a church. Apart from the adaptation of the inner building, only the ceiling and roof are missing. Its Doric plan follows the earlier temple D, with 8 by 13 columns again, the same interior layout, and similar dimensions of 38.15 x 16.9 m (125 x 55 ft) on the top step. Uniquely there is evidence here for the original arrangement of the attic, as well as for the staircases, the best preserved of their kind. On style the date is around 450–440 BC. Before conversion into a church Gregory, the local bishop, is said to have had to 'chase away the demons who were there, hiding in the idol of Ebert and Raps', names shedding no light, however, on the identity of the pagan cult. The building has been stripped back to its antique core, presumably in the Bourbon restoration of 1788 recorded on the facade.

### Temple A ('of Herakles')

The earliest of the city's colonnaded temples, dated by style around 500 BC, was prominently sited on a knoll just east of the chief city gate leading to the agora. The south colonnade was partly reerected in 1924. Measuring 67 x 25.34 m (220 x 83 ft) on the top step, this is the second largest temple at Akragas, with 6 by 15 columns, with an innovatory plan in Sicilian terms featuring a back as well as front porch and stone staircases flanking the shrine doorway, the earliest known on the island. A fire badly damaged the temple in antiquity and there were refurbishments, probably Roman, including the addition of a row of three small cult-rooms at the far end of the shrine, one of them producing

*(Below) Akragas, general view of temple D (so-called temple of Hera Lacinia) perched on the high ground of the temple ridge.*

*(Below right) Plan of temple A (so-called temple of Herakles), showing the three cult-rooms in the shrine which were added in Roman times, when the temple was still in use.*

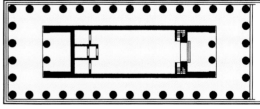

(Right) Akragas: temple A, general view, and (below) remains of the inner building.

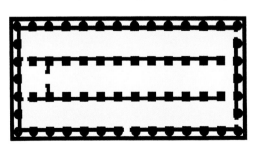

an under-lifesize statue of Asklepios. The cult remains uncertain.

## Temple of Olympian Zeus

Unfinished, and now completely collapsed, this was one of ancient Sicily's most famous temples, 'in plan and size second to no other in Hellas' (Polybius, mid-2nd century BC). Intended as the chief temple of Akragas, the site was a knoll not far from the agora and close to the southern city wall. At 110.09 by 52.74 m (361 x 173 ft), the temple just outstrips (in width) the massive temple G at neighbouring Selinous, which no doubt it was meant to rival (see p. 29), with an implied date for the start of work in the late 6th century BC. Building continued during the

5th century and probably only broke off with the disaster of 405. Naked male Atlas figures, 7.65 m (25 ft) high and of varied dates between 480 and 450 BC, are the most striking feature of a revolutionary plan replacing the outer colonnade by a screen wall,

(Right) Akragas, temple of Olympian Zeus: restored head of one of the Atlas figures.

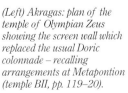

(Left) Akragas: plan of the temple of Olympian Zeus showing the screen wall which replaced the usual Doric colonnade – recalling arrangements at Metapontion (temple BII, pp. 119–20).

punctuated on the outside by huge Doric half-columns (7 by 14), with the Atlases somehow built into the intercolumniations, as if supporting the temple's weight (see pp. 29, 54). Two parallel walls, broken up by square piers to support roofing, divided the inside into three aisles. The inflated scale explains why individual elements (capitals and so on) were assembled from many smaller blocks – on one estimate, 17,000 just for the screen wall. Tiles show that at some stage there was at least a partial roof, although the central aisle may have been intentionally left open to the sky. Scrappy fragments of sculpture in high relief from the gables date stylistically around 450–440 BC. The patriotic historian Diodorus Siculus (about 40 BC) boasted: 'And being as it is the largest temple in Sicily, it may not unreasonably be compared, so far as the magnitude of its substructure is concerned, with the temples outside Sicily.'

### Temples I, L and G

At the extreme west of the temple ridge, inside the so-called sanctuary of the underworld deities, the poorly preserved Doric temple (I), originally with 6 by 13 columns, is chiefly of note for the picturesque reconstruction (1836–71) of the northwest corner, much of it in modern masonry, artfully 'aged'. The original temple dates to 450–400 BC. Sometimes claimed for the Dioskouroi, the cult is unknown. Just to the south, a scattering of column drums marks the site of a colonnaded Doric temple (L, 'of Juno Lacinia'), probably somewhat earlier than temple D. In the southwest angle of the city wall, finally, two stumps of unfinished columns belong to temple G ('of Vulcan' or 'Hephaistos'), originally with 6 by (?) 13 columns and begun, to judge from the style, around 430–425 BC. It is interesting for being the city's only colonnaded temple with a known predecessor on the same site.

## Selinous (mod. Selinunte)

On Sicily's southwest coast, commanding a large and fertile hinterland, Selinous was colonized from the older Sicilian colony of Megara Hyblaia probably around 650 BC. Its wealth is spectacularly

*(Below) Akragas, temple I: general view showing the 19th-century restorations.*

*(Right) Selinous: the temple of Hera in the distance, viewed from the akropolis through the columns of temple C.*

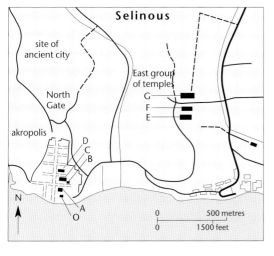

Selinous

site of
ancient city

North
Gate

akropolis

East group
of temples

G
F
E

D
C
B

A
O

N

0        500 metres
0      1500 feet

reflected in the seven colonnaded temples erected in local stone on the akropolis and a hill to the east, both overlooking the sea. All have been flattened by earthquake, although temples C and E have been partly rebuilt. The Carthaginians sacked Selinous in 409 BC and destroyed it for good in 250 BC.

## Temples C and D

The northernmost temples on the akropolis, C and D, are the oldest at Selinous, with C dated by pottery to 600–550 BC. The deity is unknown. Measuring 23.8 x 63.75 m (78 x 209 ft) on the top step, C had 6 by 17 Doric columns, doubled on the front in the Syracusan manner, monoliths yielding to drums as work progressed slowly westwards. Ascending a monumental staircase at the front, the visitor experienced further rises of level on entering both the porch and then the shrine proper, which led to a back room. An elaborate pair of triple-leaved folding doors, the earliest known of their kind from antiquity, closed the porch, and the shrine has a raised area of paving which may have been for a central offering table. Decoration included a fired-clay gorgon face (2.75 m/9 ft high) in the front gable, and sculptured metopes both to front and rear, their date disputed. At the end of its life the temple

*Selinous, view of the partly reconstructed temple C on the akropolis.*

*(Above) Selinous: a metope from temple C showing the chariot of Apollo.*

*(Above right) Selinous, temple F: remains of an intercolumnar screen in the north colonnade.*

housed an official archive, as shown by the discovery inside the south colonnade of several hundred clay stamps. The north colonnade has been partly reconstructed.

Just north, on the same easterly axis, a second and smaller Doric temple (D) was built perhaps a generation later on grounds of style. Measuring 23.6 x 55.6 m (77 x 182 ft) on the top step, it had 6 by 13 columns, all drummed, and stone roof-tiles. The inner building shares the same tripartite plan with a rise in level from porch to shrine. It was already disused in the 3rd century BC, when the near vicinity was used for burials.

## Temples O and A

An ancient transverse street, its date disputed, now separates temples C and D from this later pair to their south, of near-matching size and (it seems) plan. The southernmost, O, with only its foundations preserved, may never have been finished. Its companion, dated by style around 450 BC, measures 40.31 x 16.13 m (132 x 53 ft) on the top step, with 6 by 14 columns framing porches and a shrine curtailed in size to fit in a back room and a pair of staircases (spiral ones, uniquely). Inside the back room are floor cuttings for a lost base and statue.

## Temple F

The middle and oldest of the three temples on the eastern hill, F is dated by style to the late 6th

century BC. Measuring 61.84 x 24.43 m (203 x 80 ft) on the top step, it once had 6 by 14 columns, and in plan closely resembles temple C, with a double colonnade at the front, a long, thin inner building divided into porch and shrine, each on a higher level, and back room. Remains of two limestone metopes from the east facade show deities fighting giants. Traces are clearly visible of a curious feature in the form of masonry screens, originally some 4.7 m (15 ft) high, between the outer intercolumniations, and shown by their concealment of older plasterwork on adjoining columns to be later additions. Since they would not have completely closed the gaps, they look less like security measures than a device for masking unauthorized sight of religious rituals taking place in the halls, while still allowing the entry of natural light.

## Temple of Apollo (G)

To the north lies the earthquake-shattered pile known locally as the Pillars of the Giants. This was by far the largest of the Selinountine temples, and one of the largest of all Greek temples (see p. 28), measuring 50 x 110 m (164 x 361 ft) on the top step, with architrave blocks weighing about 40 tons, and some of the column drums, over 50 tons. Begun in the later 6th century BC, the temple was never finished, although its colonnade of 8 by 17 columns had been erected before work was finally abandoned in 409 BC. A second colonnade may have been planned in what now seem exceptionally spacious halls (see the plan on p. 86). On a higher level, the huge shrine was probably unroofed. Its two colonnades, clearly a processional way, led to a free-standing back room which surely was meant to house divine statuary. Its importance in ritual is suggested by the placing of an official inscription on the doorway recording the gift by the men of Selinous of a gold offering valued at 60 talents in

*Selinous: plan of temple F. The screen wall recalls similar arrangements at Metapontion (temple BII, pp. 119–20) and Akragas (temple of Olympian Zeus, pp. 126–27) although here the walling-up of the intercolumniations was an afterthought.*

thanks for victory in a local war. Dated around 480–470 BC on letter forms, the text shows that the 'Apollonion' (as it calls the temple) was already consecrated at this date, even though still under construction. Work stopped for good in 409 BC.

## Temple of Hera (E)

To the south the third temple on the east hill was also the most recent. Partly rebuilt, it is dated by style to the early 5th century BC. The deity is known to have been Hera from a Greek inscription in the back room of 1st-century BC date, showing that memory of the cult lingered on well after the final

destruction of Selinous. With 6 by 15 columns and dimensions on the top step of 67.82 x 25.32 m (223 x 83 ft), the temple is the second largest at Selinous. It had porches on mainland Greek lines from which come five limestone metopes depicting mythical

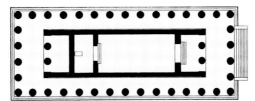

(Left) Selinous, plan of the temple of Hera, showing the successive changes in ground level on the approach to the back room with its axially aligned base for a divine statue (agalma).

(Below) Selinous, temple of Hera: view of the restored east front of the temple.

(Above) Selinous, metope from the temple of Hera showing a seated Zeus and his standing consort, Hera.

couples (including Hera, with Zeus), with imported marble reserved for female flesh. The visitor ascended through three changes of level on entering the porch, then the shrine, its entrance flanked by stone staircases, and finally the back room, where remains survive of a large statue-base, once framed by a balustrade or baldachin. On top of the base a much smaller altar, patched up with mortar, shows cultic use of the back room in Roman times.

## Segesta

(Below) Segesta, Contrada 'Mango' temple: a Doric capital and part of the precinct wall.

On an inland site southwest of Palermo, this centre of the indigenous Elymoi people had adopted Greek culture by the 5th century BC, as these two colonnaded Doric temples eloquently show. The first, in the Contrada 'Mango' outside the ancient city on the south slope of the akropolis, is known from limestone fragments of capitals and other parts, although the site itself is not located. On style

archaeologist Dieter Mertens suggests a date about 460–450 BC.

Well over a generation later, the Segestans started to build the temple for which the site is nowadays famous. This temple was also suburban, facing the ancient settlement on a knoll. Measuring 23.12 x 58.03 m (76 x 190 ft) on the top step with 6 by 14 Doric columns, it was unfinished as shown by unfluted columns and the lifting bosses left on the steps. An inner building was at least begun, the proportions suggesting provision for double staircases. The architect seems to have been aware of the mathematical emphasis in Athenian temple-building of the later 5th century, as reflected in the 9:4 proportions of the facade's width to the height of its columns. On style the date is about 420–410 BC. The intended cult is unknown.

## Himera

On the north coast of Sicily, Himera was founded in 648 BC from Zankle (mod. Messina) and Syracuse. In 480 BC the Sicilian Greeks won a great victory here over the Carthaginians, who avenged themselves by destroying the city (409 BC). Remains of a colon-

Segesta: general view of the unfinished Doric temple. The columns remain unfluted.

naded Doric temple just north of the modern road and railway at Buonfornello are usually identified as one of two which Carthage had to build as indemnities in 480 BC. The dimensions of 22.45 x 55.95 m (74 x 184 ft) on the top step closely resemble the roughly contemporary Athenaion at Syracuse (pp. 122–23) as does the plan 6 by 14 columns, shrine with two porches and staircases. Of the upper parts little is preserved except a series of stone lion's head waterspouts. The cult is uncertain.

(Below) Himera: general view of the temple site (middle foreground).

# Athens, Attike and the Saronic Gulf

*(Right) Restored lateral cross-section through the temple of Olympian Zeus, assuming that the roofing system left the shrine open to the sky.*

An offshoot of the Aegean Sea, the Saronic Gulf is bounded on its east by Attike, a triangular promontory which in ancient times formed the city-state territory of Athens. The gulf's north coast carried (as it still does) the chief land route from Athens to Corinth, passing through the land of ancient Megara, Athens' westerly neighbour. Of the various Saronic islands, by far the largest and historically the most important was Aigina, easily visible from Athens.

The Saronic area forms a natural unit, and in ancient times the sea promoted close contacts (see Kalaureia, p. 160) and rivalries among its communities. Aigina, said the Athenian statesman Themistokles (around 481 BC), was 'the eyesore of the Piraeus', the great natural harbour of Athens on the Gulf's northeast coast. Temple-building was one expression of these rivalries, with some sites, such as Sounion or Aphaia (see pp. 148–49), probably developed in part with an eye to their regional visibility.

From the 6th century BC until the end of antiquity the area was dominated by Athens. Here unusual levels of wealth and creativity combined with civic pride in the 5th century BC to produce the greatest wave of temple-building in the whole Greek world.

The following entries start with Athens and then work anti-clockwise around Attike, ending with the Saronic sites of Aigina and Megara.

## Athens

Centred on the famous Akropolis, a natural rock outcrop commanding a spacious plain opening onto the Saronic Gulf to the west, ancient Athens by the 9th century BC had become the political centre of a united Attic promontory. The city's heyday fell in the 5th century BC, when it headed a maritime alliance of Greek cities – the so-called Delian League – and controlled Greek waters by means of a formidable fleet of war galleys (the famous triremes). In later centuries the city's political importance declined but its prestige as a cultural centre endured to the close of antiquity. Nine colonnaded temples bear witness to the atypical success of Athens among the ancient Greek citizen-states as an imperial and cultural power.

In the description which follows the temples of the southeast quarter of the ancient city are described first, then those of the Agora (civic centre) to the north of the Akropolis, and finally those of the Akropolis itself.

### Temple of Olympian Zeus (Olympieion)

In ancient times 'old Athens', where the most venerable shrines were to be found, lay to the southeast of the Akropolis, in an area of the modern inner city dominated by the 16 still-standing columns of the temple of Olympian Zeus. This was the last grand temple to be built in Athens, only finished off by the emperor Hadrian. But the cult here was already old when the local Peisistratid tyrants in the 6th century BC began the construction of a huge Doric temple. Their political disgrace (510 BC) prompted the abandonment of the project. Their temple stood unfinished until the reign of Antiochos IV (175–164 BC), a king of the Macedonian Seleukid dynasty based in Syria who saw here an opportunity to

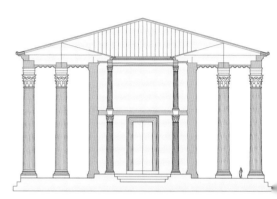

advertise his Greek credentials to a larger world. Hiring a new architect called Cossutius, a Roman from a Greek milieu, Antiochos started again. The new temple was to replicate its predecessor's dimensions and plan and used the same platform, but was to be built in fine-grained white Pentelic marble from Mount Pentelikon in Attike, and in the more up-to-date Corinthian style. The temple measures 107.86 x 41.6 m (354 x 135 ft) on the top step with 8 by 20 columns, doubled on the long and tripled on the short sides. Work stopped when Antiochos died, but the unfinished structure was already impressive enough to garner admiration from Vitruvius,

the Roman architectural writer (late 1st century BC). The project was resumed by the Emperor Hadrian, who finally completed the temple and attended the great dedication ceremony in person (AD 131/2), along with representatives from Greek cities all over the eastern Mediterranean. Hadrian was playing religious politics: as Zeus' earthly counterpart he was worshipped here as well; he seems to have had his own altar in the imposing precinct, which he also built. Exactly how much he had to do to finish the temple is disputed: a recent study, for instance, has assigned all but one of the surviving columns to the initial phase under Antiochos. Vitruvius says that the temple was open to the sky, meaning perhaps only the shrine proper, with the back room roofed to house Hadrian's gift of the chief statue, a gold and ivory colossus of Zeus harking back to the great works of the Athenian master-artist Pheidias for the Parthenon and Olympia. The precinct was full of statues of Hadrian, and the bases for some of them were still visible in the precinct. By the 5th–6th centuries, when ceiling coffers from the temple were being recycled for a nearby church, the worship of Zeus here had long ceased. Quarrying continued into the mid-18th century.

*(Above) Temple of Olympian Zeus: fallen Corinthian column.*

*(Left) Temple of Olympian Zeus: general view showing the best-preserved cluster of surviving columns in the southeast corner and the relationship to the Akropolis in the background, to the northwest.*

## Temples south of the Olympieion

The modern visitor who looks south from the Olympieion sees a large and unprepossessing zone of archaeological bits and pieces bounded by busy highways. The area is more interesting than it looks at first sight, containing traces of two colonnaded temples, both demolished to build a new city wall in AD 253–60. Immediately south stood the temple of Apollo Delphinios. Foundations measure 33.27 x 15.9 m (109 x 52 ft) and are dated around 450 BC from finds, also identifying the cult. A plan of 6 by 13 Doric columns is restored, with roofing in Parian marble. Doric capitals and drums destined for the upper parts, but apparently rejected as substandard, were found in a retaining wall. About 55 m (180 ft) away are foundations for a smaller temple

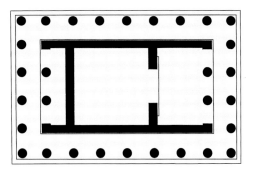

## Temple of Ares

The modern visitor can hardly avoid the sprawling
remnants of a concert hall (*odeion*) built by Augustus' son-in-law Agrippa right in the middle of the
old plaza. Just north are the limestone foundations
for a marble temple of the Greek war god Ares. The
scrappy remains hardly prepare the visitor for the
extraordinary story disclosed by archaeologists, of
a temple whose upper parts came mostly from a dismantled Doric temple of 5th-century date brought
into the Agora block by block and reassembled on
this spot, with the additional incorporation of a
reused marble gutter from a second Doric temple of
the same date, this time Poseidon's at Sounion (pp.
144–45). The chief clues are the masons' letters in
the Augustan style which can be seen on some of
the blocks still on site. It used to be thought that the
main fabric came from a (hypothetical) temple of
Ares at Acharnai (modern Menidi) to the northeast
of Athens; now the increasingly favoured alternative is a vanished temple for which foundations of
the right size and date have been found at Pallene in
Attike (p. 144). The hybrid temple in the Agora
measured 16.76 x 36.25 m (55 x 118.9 ft) on the top
step and had 6 by 13 Doric columns on the outside.
The surprising glorification of war in this now
provincial city-centre suggests that Ares here
stands for Mars, the Roman warrior god favoured
by the Emperor Augustus. The whole operation
was a (costly) gesture of Athenian loyalty to the
new regime, couched in the architectural language

of roughly 15.63 x 10.08 m (51 x 33 ft), once comprising a Roman-style podium supporting a traditional
Doric temple with 9 by 6 columns, porches and a
shrine, dated to the 2nd century AD by building
techniques. An early Christian church was later
built on the foundations. Ancient texts identify the
deities as Kronos and Rhea.

### THE AGORA

The Agora to the north of the Akropolis, an open
area increasingly hemmed in by buildings, was
the civic heart of Athens in her democratic
and imperial heyday, with government offices
and archives, law courts, shrines, memorials to
local worthies and, somewhat chaotically, a market
as well. Redevelopment continued throughout
antiquity, including major changes marking the
advent of Roman rule.

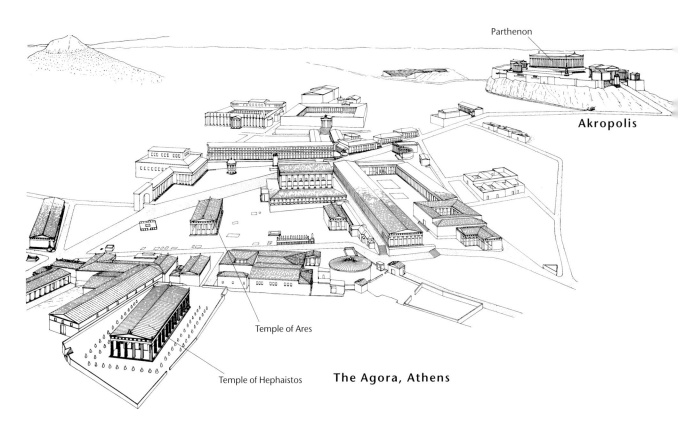

Parthenon

Akropolis

Temple of Ares

Temple of Hephaistos

**The Agora, Athens**

of Athens' own political heyday back in the 5th century BC. Fragments found in the new city wall nearby which the Athenians built about AD 280 show that by then the temple had been demolished. This sober archaeological fact sadly discounts a Byzantine author's claim that some gilt-bronze elephants displayed in medieval Constantinople were brought by emperor Theodosius II (AD 408–50) from 'the temple of Ares at Athens'.

## Temple of Hephaistos (Hephaisteion)

This is the best-preserved of all Greek temples, and for long was misidentified as the Theseion or shrine of the Athenian hero Theseus mentioned by the Greek writer Pausanias (mid-2nd century AD). It stands aloof from the Agora proper on a low hill behind and overlooking the west range of buildings, a position which may help to explain why Pausanias – to whom we owe the identification of the cult – appears to have overlooked the temple as he explored the Agora's west side, only noticing it much later when he looked back from higher ground. The first on its site, the temple lay in an ancient metalworkers' quarter – fittingly for a cult of the god of the forge. It measures 13.7 x 31.77 m (45 x 104 ft) on the top step, with 6 by 13 Doric columns, shrine and porches, with grilles in the front porch. The upper parts are Pentelic marble, with mainly Cycladic marble for the sculpture, comprising gable groups (now mainly lost), friezes over both porches, and 14 sculptured metopes, most at

the east end. The metopes are concentrated on the east end overlooking the Agora and show the Labours of the pan-Greek hero Herakles juxtaposed with those of Theseus, the local Athenian hero. The friezes are still in place and show mythical battle scenes. Inside, a doubled-up Doric colonnade framed the statues of Athena and Hephaistos, which an inscription dates to 421–415 BC, although on style and sherd-evidence the temple was begun in the mid-5th century BC. Work must have been protracted. In the 3rd century BC the surrounds were

*Ceiling coffers and frieze in the east porch of the Hephaisteion.*

*General view of the Hephaisteion from the southwest, showing the main (east) facade overlooking the Athenian Agora.*

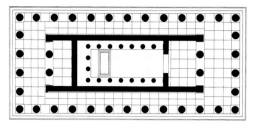

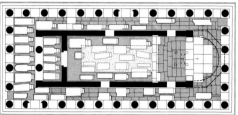

*(Right) Restored plan of the
Hephaisteion showing the
original interior
arrangements before
alteration into a church –
notably the axially aligned
base for the statue-group and
the internal colonnade which
framed it.*

*(Below right) Plan of the
Hephaisteion as a church,
showing the Christian burials
in the interior and the halls.*

landscaped with rows of plants. A monumental staircase was added in the mid-1st century AD from the Agora below. The temple was converted into a church of St George by opening up a door in the rear porch and adding an apse at the east, perhaps in the 7th century AD, with the current barrel vault dating from a more modest rebuilding (12th or 13th century?), following some disaster. By this time at the latest, the internal colonnade and original roof had disappeared. The halls and interior were still used for Christian burials at the end of Ottoman rule, after which the church was deconsecrated (1834) and became a museum. In 1937 the Christian additions were mostly destroyed, including the tombs.

## The Akropolis

This was a major bronze-age centre to judge from the still-visible traces of 13th-century BC fortification walls. In historical times it was the chief sanctuary of the Athenians, approached by a ceremonial way through a magnificent all-marble gateway (the Propylaia) which gave onto the fortified summit, a holy precinct increasingly crammed with temples, shrines and votive monuments. This was above all the home of Athena, the city's patron goddess, although she shared her sacred space with a congeries of other sacred figures, and was herself worshipped in no fewer than three separate temples. In the 5th century BC the Akropolis was transformed by the so-called works of Perikles (p. 33), of which the two most acclaimed triumphs were the Propylaia, just mentioned, and the Parthenon. Thereafter the Athenians seemed disinclined to intervene significantly in this sublime architectural heritage. Real change only came in the 3rd century AD when uncertain times caused the Akropolis to revert to its primitive role as a fortress. The cult of Athena survived here into the 5th century AD. In what follows, the temples are taken in their chronological order.

## 'Old' temple of Athena

Between the Erechtheion and the north side of the Parthenon are foundations which deserve more contemplation than they usually receive from visitors, since these are the remains of the earliest known colonnaded temple on the Akropolis. The temple was dedicated to City Athena (Athena Polias) and destroyed by the Persians in 480 BC when they occupied Athens. As is clear to the naked eye, the inner and outer foundations are worked differently, and this is the basis for the reasonable view that the outer colonnade was a later addition. The upper parts in two different types of stone, limestone and marble, are known from many fragments, which on style give a date in the late 6th century BC. This was a time of political upheaval, with the ousting of the local tyrant Hippias and the installation of a new type of popular government in 508/7 BC. Athena's impressively upgraded new temple was a monument to one or other regime – we cannot be sure which. The temple measured 43.15 x 21.3 m (142 x 70 ft) and is restored in plan with 12 by 6 Doric columns and an inner building with a colonnaded shrine to

*Foundations of the 'old' temple of Athena, re-exposed in the 19th century and partly overlain by the south porch of the Erechtheion.*

*Doric capitals from the 'old' temple of Athena burnt down by the Persians in 480 BC.*

the east and three rooms entered from the west, perhaps for minor cults. The arrangement is unusual, and has been thought to prefigure the even odder plan of the Erechtheion, which replaced, and partly overlay, the 'old' temple. Inside, presumably, stood the famous olive-wood statuette of Athena, so old that it was said to have 'fallen from heaven' and which the Athenians saved from the Persians in 480 BC to survive for a further 700 years at least. Island marble was used for the gable sculpture. This featured a battle between the gods and giants with a central Athena – the finely carved figure now on view in the Akropolis Museum. After the Athenians had beaten back the Persians in 479 BC some of the scorched upper parts of the burnt temple were built into the new fortification wall on the north side of the Akropolis, where they can still be seen. The marble sculpture was buried in a tidying-up operation. There is modern speculation that the ruined temple was partly patched up as a temporary shrine until the completion of the Erechtheion. On another view, the site was levelled to hold the crowds attending the sacrifices on Athena's altar to the east.

(Right) The west front of the
Parthenon, showing some of
the surviving metopes and
gable-sculpture. This was the
view of the great temple which
ancient worshippers had when
they arrived at the great
gateway (Propylaia) into the
Akropolis (see p. 33).

## The Parthenon

The temple of Maiden Athena (Athena Parthenos) in artistry and execution is the greatest of all Greek temples. It is also the most controversial. The building dates to 447–432 BC and was the jewel in an ambitious building programme inspired by the Athenian leader Perikles. At the outset the building provoked political debate – there were those who argued that Perikles was wrong to use money paid over by Athenian allies in order to 'deck the city out like a whore'. And Thucydides, the contemporary Athenian historian, is curiously silent about the Parthenon. The temple is only mentioned for the lavish helpings of gold on the statue of Athena: these, Thucydides makes Perikles tell his fellow citizens at the start of the Peloponnesian war (431 BC), could always be wrenched off and melted down if the going got really tough (see p. 93).

Even so, the Parthenon was surely not, as is sometimes claimed, just a glorified treasury. This seems clear from the complex history of the site. The temple gives the illusion of being built on level ground. In fact the natural rock slopes sharply away in this part of the Akropolis, and a massive manmade platform underpins the temple, ensuring visibility from a great distance, including the Saronic Gulf. This impressive piece of engineering, it turns out, was not for the benefit of the Parthenon but for a predecessor, destroyed by the Persians in 480 BC while still under construction (pp. 32–33). This unfinished Doric temple itself probably had at least one forerunner. The worship of Maiden Athena in this part of the Akropolis was already ancient when the Periklean project was conceived.

This recent history of the site meant that the builders of the Parthenon could economize by reusing the pre-existing platform and also many ready-worked blocks. We know the names of the architects, Iktinos and Kallikrates, who were overseen by the master-artist Pheidias, also an Athenian. The Periklean project called for greater size and magnificence, as befitted the new position of the Athenians as an imperial power. Accordingly the older platform was extended northwards to accommodate a wider temple, with 8 instead of the usual 6 Doric columns across the facades (see reconstruction, pp. 76–77). This greater width in turn allowed for a more spacious interior in which to fit the extraordinary creation of Pheidias: a gold-and-ivory (chryselephantine) statue of a standing, armed, Athena, some 11.5 m (38 ft) high. Chryselephantine statue-making on this scale was new, and probably pioneered by Pheidias himself. The Parthenon was a conscious showcase for the latest artistic technology. The statue is gone, of course, but inside the floor-cutting survives for the wooden 'mast' which rooted it.

Measuring 69.53 x 72.31 m. (228 x 237 ft) on the top step, with 17 columns on the long sides, the Parthenon also claimed exceptionality as the largest temple on the Greek mainland at the time (only the Olympieion, also in Athens, would outstrip it in size). The inner building comprised two shallow porches, both fitted with security grilles to protect the costly pairs of huge doors into two back-to-back chambers separated by a solid wall. To the east the larger of the two was the shrine proper. Here the Pheidian colossus was framed on three sides by a doubled-up Doric colonnade. This room is now known to have been illuminated by a pair of windows in its east wall, which also incorporated a staircase to the attic. For added security the doors of the rear chamber were reinforced with iron bars. Although the Parthenon was a Doric temple, here the interior columns, since they rose directly to the ceiling, were in slender Ionic. The ancient names for

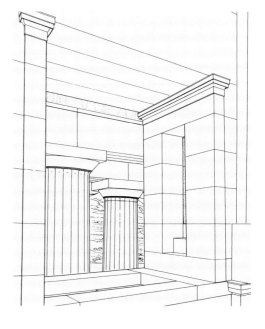

Reconstruction of the
Parthenon from the interior
of the intra-mural staircase,
showing one of the windows
in the east wall of the shrine,
looking out to the front porch.

Greek temple – to the extent that most of the architectural lines which seem straight in fact bulge.

The unparalleled splendour of the Parthenon's decoration now takes an effort of the imagination to appreciate. Built entirely in white marble from Mount Pentelikon, with mouldings and other carved features above the columns picked out in bright paintwork (see p. 69), the temple was also saturated with sculpture, most of it of a high quality. No other Greek temple was so richly decorated, before or after. Visiting in the mid-2nd century AD when the temple was intact, Pausanias recorded the two gable groups: the birth of Athena at the east end and her contest with Poseidon for possession of Attike at the west (see p. 42). We must be grateful to him: two thousand years later, the ancient stories told by the battered remnants of these groups, mostly in the British Museum today, are less than obvious. Additionally, every one of the 92 exterior metopes was carved with

*(Above) Part of the east gable of the Parthenon, showing sculpture (now replaced by casts) left behind by Lord Elgin.*

*Artist's impression of the 5th-century BC Akropolis on a day of festival. The little non-colonnaded temple in the right foreground belonged to Athena Nike ('of Victory').*

the parts of the Parthenon are controversial, but this chamber seems the obvious candidate for identification as the 'room behind' or *opisthodomos* in which King Demetrios I took up brief residence (307 BC). Inscribed inventories show that from the outset both chambers, as well as the front porch, were crowded with valuable offerings (see p. 92).

The Parthenon's masons worked with extreme care, so that the joints were originally all but invisible in places. Proportions and so-called refinements were also used to make the building exceptional. The chief dimensions, executed with minute precision, are proportional, mostly to the ratio of 4:9 (e.g., breadth to length). Then there are 'the delicate deviations from ordinary perpendicular and level construction' (Francis Penrose; see p. 44). These refinements are present in the Parthenon to a greater degree than in any other surviving

*The mysterious robe (peplos) scene on the east side of the Parthenon frieze.*

scenes of mythic struggle – amazons against Greeks, Greeks against Trojans, gods against giants, and half-horse, half-human centaurs against the Lapiths of Thessaly, whose king's wedding they viciously broke up.

Then there are the mysterious friezes, which Pausanias fails to comment on. The celebrated frieze which ran round the outside of the inner building at a distinctly uncomfortable viewing height of 12.2 m (40 ft) was 160 m long (525 ft). Sculpturally it is a tour de force, cleverly designed and superbly carved. On architectural grounds it was evidently an afterthought, one not allowed for in the original design. The real mystery is what the frieze depicts. Chatting gods at the east end have their backs turned to a religious procession approaching from both long sides, and also to a puzzling scene, placed centrally above the front porch, featuring a child and a folded cloth. On one daring theory, the child is the daughter of a mythical Athenian king, being prepared for her own sacrifice to assure Athens' victory against Thracian invaders; but if so, where is the sacrificial knife? More traditionally, others see here a scene involving the new robe (*peplos*) woven every four years by Athenian women for the

goddess, and the procession then becomes part of the Great Panathenaia, Athena's four-yearly festival. Even so, we are not out of the woods: why put on the Parthenon a scene of ritual which relates to the old olive-wood statuette kept, not in this temple, but next door in the shrine of City-Athena (the Erechtheion)? Recent discoveries by Greek archaeologists have further muddied the waters. A second, smaller, frieze is now known to have run round the front porch, again at ceiling height. Its subject matter is not yet clear, although women are present.

The Athenians maintained the temple as a shrine for Athena into the 5th century AD. But the Parthenon did not escape the imprint of the weakened city's obeisance to foreign powers. Alexander the Great took it upon himself to use the outside to show off shields captured from his Persian campaign, probably in 334 BC. The circular impression left by 14 of them can still be seen on the east front, below the metopes. The eye can also see, between these shield-impressions, groups of holes. These once secured large gilt-bronze letters – no fewer than 345 of them – proclaiming Athenian honours for the Roman emperor Nero (AD 61/2). There were Roman-period repairs too, enabling the Parthenon to survive virtually intact until a catastrophic fire of (probably) AD 267. The temple was never fully rebuilt. Instead a new roof of clay tiles (no longer marble) spanned the shrine only. Inside, a makeshift replacement for the original double colonnade was rigged up and a new statue installed, still in place after AD 450. More alterations to the original fabric, including the removal of the interior cross-wall, were required when the temple was converted into a church of the Virgin Mary, perhaps in the 7th century. In turn the church was made into a mosque by the Turks around 1460, when a minaret was added in the southwest corner. Even so, the outer colonnade and the four walls of the inner building, together with the architectural sculpture, had thus far survived largely intact. Not so after 1687: the Ottoman Turks, fighting the Venetians, had stored powder in the mosque, which took a direct hit from a cannonball, blowing out the centre of the whole building. Only now did the Parthenon start to take on its modern appearance (see p. 42), aided by a Scottish peer, the 7th Lord Elgin, whose generous interpretation of a permit from the sultan resulted in the removal (1801–5) of most of the surviving sculpture for shipment to London, where it was eventually bought by the nation for the British Museum.

The Greeks began restoration of the temple in 1841, removing as far as possible the Christian and Islamic alterations. There were further restorations before and after the First World War. Since the 1980s Greek archaeologists have spearheaded an exciting programme of conservation and restoration, uncovering along the way new evidence for the Parthenon's original appearance.

*Plan of the Parthenon showing the position of the second frieze and also the staircase and the two windows in the east wall of the shrine.*

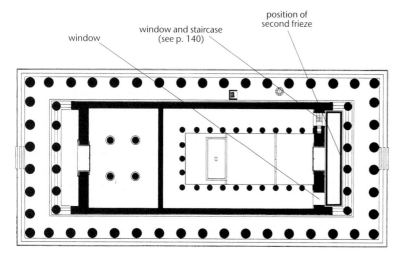

window

window and staircase (see p. 140)

position of second frieze

## The Temple of Athena Polias (Erechtheion)

To the north of the Parthenon, the two separated by the foundations of Athena's 'old' temple, this irregular Ionic temple is of outstanding interest, both for its ingenious, if ultimately baffling, plan and for the superb quality of its execution. Its plan comprises a building fronted to the east by a colonnaded porch, with total dimensions of 24.07 x 13 m (79 x 43 ft). The west end is formed by a wall with windows instead of a colonnade and porticoes on either side, prompting the Roman writer Vitruvius to include the temple among those where 'all that we regularly find in the front of others is in these transferred to the sides'. This strange plan is explained in terms of the need to include in one building various sites of great religious significance. The unprecedented portico to the south, in fact more like a balcony, is supported by six female figures, the famous 'women of Karyai' or Karyatids, as Vitruvius incorrectly called them. In the building accounts they are simply 'maidens' (*korai*), and their original symbolic significance, if any, is unknown.

An oddity in the pavement of the north porch is the ancient hole left in one corner to disclose a group of fissures in the natural rock below (see pp. 49–50). Above is a corresponding opening in the roof of the portico, as if 'it was intended that the fissures should remain, at least technically, under the open heaven' (James Morton Paton). This feature is a good example of cosmological factors influencing Greek temple-design. The explanation for the evident sanctity of the fissures is their ancient interpretation as marks left by a trident, the attribute of Poseidon.

Reconstruction of the interior, on rising ground higher to the east by 3.24 m (10½ ft), is bedevilled by the drastic changes to the building since antiquity. Traces of a cross-wall show that it was in two parts, the east chamber on the higher level. The west chamber is, frankly, a mess. If the scant evidence for its originally tripartite division is accepted,

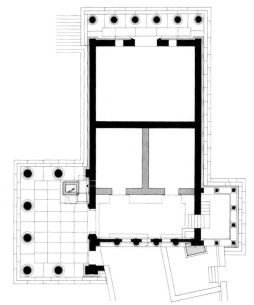

*(Above left) The Erechtheion viewed from the west, showing the north porch (left) and the Karyatid porch (right).*

*(Above) Detail of the elegantly carved Ionic columns in the north porch.*

*(Left) Reconstructed plan of the Erechtheion. Note the north porch (left) with its opening in the pavement to reveal the marks of Poseidon's trident (pp. 49–50). The tripartite restoration of the west chamber of the interior is partly conjectural.*

*(Right) Erechtheion: the so-called Karyatid porch. In the interests of conservation the maiden-figures have now been replaced by replicas and the originals withdrawn to the Akropolis Museum.*

the shrine building overall seems designed to replicate the interior of the adjacent 'old' temple, its predecessor (pp. 138–39). Most scholars place the ancient statue of Athena and her golden lamp, seen by Pausanias in 'the temple of Polias', in the east chamber, and identify the west chamber with his 'building called the Erechtheion', housing minor cults of Poseidon and the Athenian heroes Boutes and Erechtheus.

The temple is Pentelic marble. Its chief decoration, apart from the 'maidens', was a continuous outer frieze of white marble figures attached to a dark limestone background; also its Ionic mouldings, which are of stunning virtuosity, especially in the north porch. The capitals here were additionally adorned with gilded bronze (the eyes of the volutes) and beads of coloured glass (set into the guilloche band), including blue, red, yellow and purple, some still in place in the 1840s (see p. 69).

An inscription shows that the temple was being finished in the year 409–406/5 BC; it could have been planned much earlier. Early in the reign of Augustus, especially at the west end, there was extensive rebuilding after fire-damage, which had destroyed the original roof. In the AD 190s the Athenians installed a divine image of the Roman empress Julia Domna next to that of Athena Polias. The building was preserved through its conversion into a church, probably in the 7th century. In 1676 it was the residence of a Turkish household and harem (see p. 43). In 1801 Lord Elgin removed a 'maiden', now in the British Museum. By 1833 quarrying for stone and metals had badly damaged the structure. It was heavily restored in 1903–9, and again in 1979–87.

### Temple of Roma and Augustus

In front of the Parthenon's main (east) front are a rectangular set of foundations and scattered blocks in Pentelic marble from the upper parts of a rotunda. Most scholars would place the rotunda on top of these foundations, which in Roman fashion are almost axially aligned with the Parthenon. The rotunda is restored as an Ionic colonnade of nine columns sitting on a top step with a diameter of 8.6 m (28 ft). The columns are sloppy replicas of those of the nearby Erechtheion – a back-handed reminder of the consummate craftsmanship of the age of Perikles. An inscription above the

colonnades, still on site, records that the building was an Athenian dedication to Roma, the Greek deification of Roman power, and to Augustus, the first Roman emperor, and dates it to 27 BC or later. Statues of the two deities would have stood inside the open colonnade and there should have been a sacrificial altar nearby. Athens had been friendly with Mark Antony, the erstwhile enemy of Augustus, and the city's relations with Antony's victor were tricky – not helped by a statue of Athena on the Akropolis said to have spat blood in the direction of Rome at around this time. The rotunda, it has been suggested, was an Athenian peace offering. In that sense it was an exceptional building, the only significant addition to the prestigious 5th- and 4th-century BC architectural assemblage on the Akropolis. The hack imitation of the Erechtheion suggests an Athenian attempt to make this intrusive structure blend in with these august surroundings.

## Pallene

To the southeast of the ancient city, foundations for a large colonnaded temple have been found on a low hill near modern Stavro, ancient Pallene. Similar in design and date to the Hephaisteion, this may be the temple of Athena Pallenis. The upper parts may have been transposed to the Agora under Augustus to become the temple of Ares (pp. 136–37).

## Cape Zoster

On the small isthmus linking ancient Cape Zoster (Mikro Kavouri) with modern Vouliagmeni in southwest Attike are the remains of a colonnaded

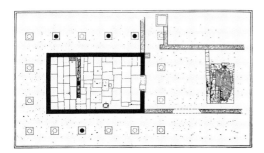

temple with an unusually well preserved shrine. Belonging to the ancient administrative district of Halai Aixonides, it was dedicated to Apollo Zoster. The inner building of 6th-century date measures 10.8 x 6 m (35 x 20 ft) and comprises a back room and shrine, where three bases for divine statues were found still in place: Apollo flanked by Artemis and Leto. Two are inscribed in lettering of about 500 BC, as dedications by 'the men of Halai'. Still in place in front is a marble offerings-table inscribed with a decree (4th century BC) praising a priest who had 'repaired the sanctuary and adorned the divine statues'. Against the nearby wall was found a marble priest's throne. Around 350–300 BC a makeshift colonnade of 4 by 6 unfluted limestone columns was added, possibly without normal capitals. The walls were extensively repaired, perhaps in Roman times.

## Sounion

Still a romantic spot today in spite of the coachloads of tourists, windswept Cape Sounion is the southernmost cape of the Attic landmass with commanding views over the Aegean. In ancient times Sounion gave its name to the most southerly of the Athenian administrative districts, and there were two important sanctuaries on the cape itself. The temple of Poseidon, its 16 standing columns partly restored, stands on the cape's summit, supported by a massive platform commissioned for an unfinished limestone predecessor of similar dimensions, never finished and evidently destroyed by the Persians in 480 BC. The position, 73 m (240 ft) above the sea, is exceptionally eye-catching. The temple measures 31.15 x 13.4 m (102 x 44 ft) on the top step,

*(Left) Plan of the temple at Cape Zoster, Attike. Inside the shrine the priest's throne against the south wall can be made out along with the (rather indistinct) row of three bases nearby.*

*(Below) Sunset at the temple of Poseidon on the Sounion headland on Attike's southern tip.*

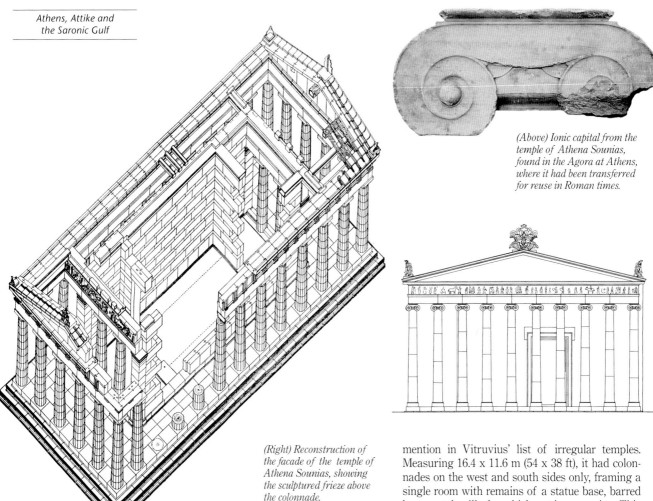

(Above) Ionic capital from the
temple of Athena Sounias,
found in the Agora at Athens,
where it had been transferred
for reuse in Roman times.

(Right) Reconstruction of
the facade of the temple of
Athena Sounias, showing
the sculptured frieze above
the colonnade.

(Above) Axonometric
reconstruction of the temple
of Poseidon, Sounion. The
entrance facade is to the left.

with 6 by 13 columns, two porches and a shrine.
The brittle local marble accounts for the 16 shallow
flutes of the columns, instead of the usual 20. There
was painted ornament, a figured frieze in Parian
marble lining the front hall, and gable sculpture.
The date on style is in the 440s BC. Under Augustus
the gutter was available for reuse in the temple of
Ares in the Athens Agora (pp. 136–37), and the
temple may have been among those destroyed by
Philip V of Macedon in 200 BC.

At Chatsworth in Derbyshire, in the north of
England, an open-air bust of the 6th Duke of
Devonshire rests on four column-drums from the
temple, obligingly removed by the British fleet in
the 1820s.

### Temple of Athena Sounias

On a lower knoll some 400 m (1310 ft) northeast of
the Poseidon sanctuary are the foundations of
Athena's Ionic temple, its odd plan meriting a

mention in Vitruvius' list of irregular temples.
Measuring 16.4 x 11.6 m (54 x 38 ft), it had colonnades on the west and south sides only, framing a
single room with remains of a statue base, barred
by a metal grille for which cuttings survive. This
temple, too, may have suffered at the hands of
Philip V and then been abandoned. In the 1st or 2nd
century AD, six columns were relocated for use in
the Athens Agora.

## Thorikos

On the southeast coast of Attike, Thorikos was the
name of an Athenian administrative district and
the centre of Athens's silver-mining industry,
most of it conducted in the pine-clad hills of the
hinterland. In the open ground south of the
ancient akropolis, now 150 m (about 500 ft) from
the sea, but in antiquity on the shore, are remains
of a rectangular Doric building orientated southwest–northeast, with its entrance breaching the
centre of one of the two long colonnades. It may
have belonged to a cult of Demeter attested in this
vicinity. The unfluted columns in local marble,
dated around 425–400 BC on style, show that
the structure was never finished. Under Roman rule
six columns were shipped off for reuse in the Agora
at Athens.

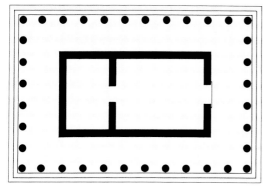

(Left) Restored plan of
the temple of Artemis
Tauropolos, Loutsa.

## Loutsa

This bustling seaside town on Attike's east coast was once the centre of the Athenian administrative district of Halai Araphenides. Foundations have been found here of a limestone Doric temple measuring 19.44 x 12.56 m (64 x 41 ft) on the top step, with 6 by 9 or 13 or 8 by 12 columns, a shrine and back room. The temple is dated variously from the late 6th to the 4th centuries BC. In Athenian myth the hero Orestes founded this cult of Artemis Tauropolos after bringing her image from the Crimea (Tauris).

## Rhamnous

On the northeast coast of Attike, Rhamnous today is a still unspoilt corner of the Athenian countryside. In ancient times it was the most outlying of the administrative districts (demes) of ancient Athens, a populous and prosperous place with a mini-urban centre of its own, complete with theatre and gymnasium. The chief deity here was Nemesis. Her sanctuary, on high ground visible from the straits of Euboia, featured a pair of temples, less than 8 cm (3 in) apart at one point, and both now claimed for Nemesis.

The larger of the two, which was colonnaded, was begun just after 450 BC, as finds show. It measured 21.3 x 10.1 m (70 x 33 ft) on the top step, with 6 by 12 Doric columns, a shrine and two porches. It was built mainly in white marble from Ayia Marina just up the coast, with Pentelic marble roof tiles and a local blue marble for parts of the platform. In the shrine stood an over-lifesize Parian-marble statue of the goddess by Agorakritos, pupil of Pheidias, its hundreds of fragments allowing part-reconstruction, along with its sculptured base. The temple is unfinished, as shown by the unfluted columns for example (p. 60). Roman-period repairs accompanied a posthumous rededication around AD 42 to Livia, widow of Augustus, announced by an inscription on the main facade.

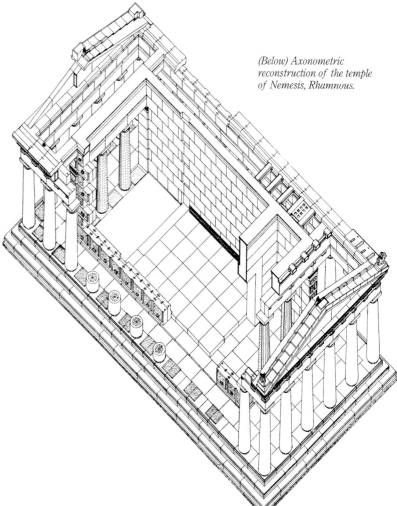

(Below) Axonometric
reconstruction of the temple
of Nemesis, Rhamnous.

Temple and statue were deliberately destroyed in late antiquity.

## Aigina

The early prosperity of this island citizen-state in the Saronic Gulf, based on a powerful fleet, is reflected in its two colonnaded temples.

### Temple of Apollo

A limestone monolith 6.8 m (22 ft) high still stands from the rear porch of this major Doric temple of Aigina's patron deity, raised high on a massive masonry platform on the coastal akropolis of the ancient city (mod. Cape Colonna), 'in the most conspicuous place', just as an inscription says. Built around 520–510 BC on style, it replaced a colonnaded predecessor. With dimensions of 16.67 x 31.86 m (55 x 105 ft), it had 6 by 11 columns, a shrine and porches. Decoration included painted stucco, white for columns and red for the inside floor, and gable sculpture, Greeks versus amazons in the west, a horse theme in the east. Destruction for its stone took place in the middle ages. The substructure was robbed in the 19th century to build the harbour jetty in modern Aigina town.

## Temple of Aphaia (and Athena)

This temple, one of the best-preserved and most interesting in Greece, is conspicuously sited on a rocky ridge in the island's mountainous northeast corner, and on a clear day would have been visible to the Athenians, bitter rivals of the Aiginetans (see p. 134) when the temple was being built (about 510 until possibly as late as 480 BC). Replacing a non-colonnaded predecessor destroyed by fire, it measures 13.8 x 28.8 m (46 x 95 ft) on the top step and has 6 by 12 Doric columns, mostly monoliths of local limestone, framing a shrine and two porches. A ramp linked the temple to its altar on

*The east (main) facade of the temple of Aphaia, Aigina. The ramp is clearly visible. See also p. 61.*

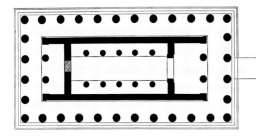

the east. In the front porch an inscription (late 5th century BC) inventorized wooden objects kept inside the shrine, where two superposed rows of Doric

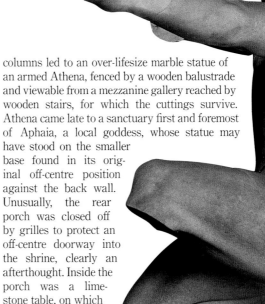

columns led to an over-lifesize marble statue of an armed Athena, fenced by a wooden balustrade and viewable from a mezzanine gallery reached by wooden stairs, for which the cuttings survive. Athena came late to a sanctuary first and foremost of Aphaia, a local goddess, whose statue may have stood on the smaller base found in its original off-centre position against the back wall. Unusually, the rear porch was closed off by grilles to protect an off-centre doorway into the shrine, clearly an afterthought. Inside the porch was a limestone table, on which a broken Athenian red-figure jar was found in 1811. This rear porch may have served as a cult-room with its own altar or a treasury (or both).

Apart from painted stucco, the temple was adorned with gable sculpture of Parian marble (also painted). Four sets are attested, an earlier pair replaced by a second. These both show the sack of Troy with a central Athena. Possible explanations for these unique arrangements are hotly debated.

Pottery indicates that the temple remained in use at least until the 1st century BC. The metope slabs, all missing, may have been removed as art objects in Roman times. Much of the temple later collapsed, thanks in part to the metal-robbers who stole its clamps. The interior has been heavily restored.

*(Above left) Plan of the temple of Aphaia, showing the off-centre doorway between the shrine and the rear porch.*

*(Above) Herakles as archer from the second (later) set of sculptures in the east gable, temple of Aphaia, Aigina. The figures were all originally painted, with additional metal attachments.*

## Megara

Megara's heyday, such as it was, fell in the 7th and 6th centuries BC. Scant remains of two temples are known, one on the westerly of the city's two akropoleis, probably that of Athena seen here by Pausanias. It was Doric, colonnaded and dated by finds to the 6th century BC. To the east the corner of another colonnaded temple has been found, dated by pottery around 500–450 BC.

# The Peloponnese

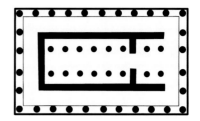

*Aigeira: restored plan of the Doric temple, one of the relatively few colonnaded temples built on the Greek mainland after Alexander the Great (see p. 35).*

The Greek mainland's southernmost land-mass, the so-called 'Island of Pelops', is a peninsula linked to central Greece by the Isthmus of Corinth. Named after a legendary wandering hero from western Turkey, this mountainous region was described by the geographer Strabo (late 1st century BC) as the 'akropolis' of ancient Greece. In classical antiquity its Greek population lived in a number of different regions with distinct ethnic sub-identities and (often) dialects: Achaia in the northwest, Elis and Triphylia in the west, Messenia in the southwest, Lakonia in the southeast, Arkadia in the centre, and in the northeast the Argolid and the Corinthia.

In ancient times the region's most famous communities were the Spartans and the Argives. The Spartans, based on Sparta or Lakedaimon in inland Lakonia, were regarded by other Greeks as culturally eccentric, and never seem to have adopted the colonnaded temple for their sanctuaries (see p. 34). The Argives, centred on the city of Argos, were famous chiefly for their glorious past – Agamemnon, leader of the Greek host against Troy, had been their ancestral king. In the 7th and early 6th centuries BC they and their northern neighbours, the Corinthians, were leaders in developing the Doric style of colonnaded temple-building (see p. 24).

The Peloponnese hosted some of Greece's most architecturally impressive shrines, including those of Hera at Argos, Asklepios at Epidauros, Zeus' sanctuary at Nemea and – completing this northeastern cluster – Poseidon's precinct on the Isthmus. Most famous of all, however, was Olympia in the west, where Zeus' temple housed the god's great gold-and-ivory statue, an ancient world-wonder. Inland the Arkadians, oldest of all the peninsula's inhabitants, were also among its most active temple-builders. High up in the mountains, at Bassai, they created what is now often considered the most picturesque of all ruined Greek temples.

The following sequence of temple sites works round the Peloponnese in an anti-clockwise direction, starting with the region of Achaia in the north and northwest, continuing down the peninsula's west side, thence through Arkadia in the centre to the Argolid and the rest of the northeast.

## Aigeira

This small Achaian citizen-state occupied a highland site commanding fine views across the central Corinthian gulf. There are scrappy remains of a small (?) 3rd-century BC temple at the east end of the theatre-terrace, with dimensions of 11.82 x 20.4 m (39 x 67 ft), 6 by 11 Doric columns and walls reusing older architecture, perhaps from an earlier temple. The central intercolumniation in front is wider than the others.

## Lousoi

In a scenic and now rather remote area of northern Arkadia, Lousoi was once a flourishing little polis or a city, later absorbed by its neighbour, Kleitor. Lousoi is best known for its hillside sanctuary of Artemis, with an architecturally peculiar temple combining Doric with local traditions. Down below, just over 1 km (½ mile) to the southwest, was the ancient urban centre, where a set of limestone foundations came to light in 2001 for a colonnaded temple of 6 by at least 12 columns, with overall dimensions of 15.07 x 33.4 m (50 x 103 ft). The date is uncertain – possibly 6th century BC. The cult is unknown.

## Ano Mazaraki

This Achaian site southwest of modern Patras lies in an upland valley on the southeast side of Mount Kombovouni, near modern Ano Mazaraki. Here foundations survive of an early temple with curved ends, one of them forming a front porch, entered through a row of wooden columns on sandstone blocks. Another colonnade of the same construction surrounded most of the building, except the porch. The temple had estimated dimensions of 27.5 x 7.5 m (90 x 25 ft), and in ancient terms was a hundred-footer (*hekatompedon*). Finds indicate a date in the early 7th century BC and a cult of Artemis. The temple was destroyed in the 4th century BC.

## Olympia

This inland site halfway down the west coast of the Peloponnese lies in a lush wooded valley at the confluence of two rivers. In antiquity the most renowned of all the Greek precincts of Zeus, Olympia was home to a four-yearly panhellenic ath-

letic festival, celebrated near-continuously from 776 BC to at least AD 385. For most of this period the cult was administered by nearby Elis.

## Temple of Hera

In the Doric style, this is one of the earliest colonnaded temples anywhere, firmly dated by pottery around 600–590 BC, Overlying an 8th-century predecessor, it was built by the citizens of nearby Skillous, says Pausanias, who gives the deity as Hera, although nowadays Zeus is thought to have been the original deity here, with reconsecration to Hera after the construction of Libon's new temple (see next entry, Temple of Zeus).

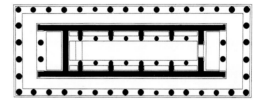

*(Above) 19th-century artist's impression of the Olympia sanctuary based on the excavations of the German Archaeological Institute. The temples of Hera and Zeus are to left and right respectively. Looming in the background is a Roman-imperial fountain-house, nowadays restored rather differently.*

*(Centre right) Restored plan of the temple of Hera, Olympia, its elongated plan reflecting its early date.*

*(Right) General view of the (partly restored) temple of Hera, Olympia, the entrance facade in the foreground.*

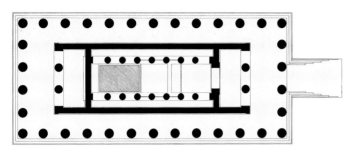

*(Left) Restored plan of the temple of Zeus, Olympia, showing the frontal ramp and the arrangement of the shrine, with the base for the great statue, the shallow rectangular pool with olive oil (see text) and the intercolumnar security grilles.*

The elongated plan measures 18.76 x 50.01 m (62 x 164 ft) on the top step, with 6 by 13 columns. Pausanias draws attention to a wooden column in the rear porch – usually seen as evidence of an originally wooden colonnade, gradually upgraded to stone, although this interpretation has recently been queried, and there are stone Doric capitals which apparently date to the original construction.

The inner building, of mudbrick on a stone base, comprised a long shrine between two porches. Pausanias mentions an attic (p. 88). In his day the inside was basically a museum, filled with miscellaneous dedications (see p. 94). When Olympia was fortified about AD 267, the Heraion was abandoned, losing its roof to an earthquake shortly before AD 400.

## Temple of Zeus

A monument to Greece's inter-state rivalries, Zeus' temple was built by Elis to vaunt her conquest of

*(Below) A serene Apollo surveys the surrounding mayhem of Greeks fighting with centaurs who attack the Greek womenfolk. From the east gable of Zeus' temple at Olympia.*

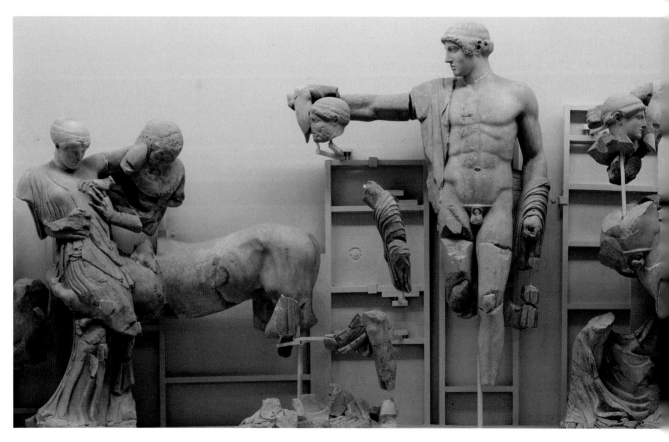

Pisa and other neighbours, and its great statue inside may have aimed to rival the colossus in the Parthenon. By 457 BC the temple was finished. Measuring 27.68 x 64.12 m (91 x 210 ft) on the top step, it was the largest in the Peloponnese, with 6 by 13 Doric columns and the usual two porches framing a shrine with bronze doors and a corridor of two rows of superimposed columns leading up to the statue. Pausanias mentions a spiral staircase to the attic. Built from the local shell limestone, stuccoed and painted, the temple used Parian marble for relief metopes of the Labours of Herakles over the two porches and groups showing the chariot-race of Pelops and the battle of Greeks and centaurs in, respectively, the west and east gables.

Inside the shrine sat one of the ancient Wonders of the World, an enthroned Zeus in gold and ivory (see illustration on pp. 78–79). An estimated 12.27 m (40 ft) high, it was commissioned from the Athenian Pheidias as a change of plan. The traces of the massive base, squeezed into the central aisle, show that a smaller statue was envisaged first. Details of the viewing experience in the 2nd century AD are given by Pausanias, including a pool of black stone filled with the olive oil used to maintain the ivory, but also with reflective qualities; painted barriers 'made like walls', to keep people off; a viewing gallery 'up above'; and, somewhere, a purple woollen curtain, 'let down to the pavement', a gift of

*General view of the site of the temple of Zeus at Olympia, showing column-drums and capitals still lying where they fell in the earthquake during the 6th century AD.*

153

*(Below) Final arrangement of imperial statues inside the Metroon, Olympia, based on the reconstruction by German archaeologist Konrad Hitzl.*

*(Bottom) The site of the Metroon, Olympia, viewed from the east.*

the Seleukid king Antiochos IV (died 163 BC). The remains point to a further security grille in metal, wall-to-wall at the level of the second columns.

Functioning for over eight centuries, this working temple received repeated and extensive repairs, such as replacement figures in the gables and the Augustan reflooring of the front porch in pavonazetto, a coloured marble beloved by Romans (see pp. 70–71 for this and other ancient repairs to the temple). Around AD 267, for its own protection the temple was built into a hastily constructed fortress. About AD 300 the roof received a last major repair. With the abolition of cult in AD 391, the statue was transferred to Constantinople for a connoisseur's art collection, and the temple fell into ruin. The columns were toppled by earthquake in the 6th century AD.

## Temple of the Mother (Metroon)

This small limestone temple measures 10.62 x 20.67 m (35 x 68 ft) on the top step, had 6 by 11 Doric columns, and on style dates around 410–400 BC. Created for Meter, the Mother of the Gods, it was more or less rebuilt to accommodate the worship of Augustus, whose monolithic image in the pose of Jupiter, over 4 m (13 ft) high, could only be installed by dismantling the inner walls. Another five imperial statues were found (see p. 99), the latest from the Flavian dynasty (AD 69–95). The temple was demolished when Olympia was fortified about AD 267.

## Makiston (mod. Mazi)

This small Triphylian city lay about 20 km (12½ miles) south of Olympia in the vicinity of Mazi village. On a nearby hill are the foundations of a major temple in the local stone dated on style

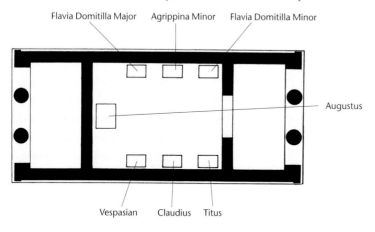

Flavia Domitilla Major — Agrippina Minor — Flavia Domitilla Minor

Augustus

Vespasian — Claudius — Titus

around 500–450 BC. Measuring 15.85 x 35.10 m (52 x 115 ft), it had a Doric colonnade, a shrine and porches. Marble sculpture from the gables, dated early 4th-century on style, belonged to a later upgrade. The deity was Athena, as an inscription shows. After destruction by earthquake, the site became a quarry.

## Lepreon

Within the fortified akropolis of this small city on Triphylia's mountainous border with Arkadia are the foundations of a small Doric temple sited near the edge of a conspicuous terrace commanding

views to the gulf of Kyparissia. Of local limestone, once stuccoed and painted, the temple measures 10.44 x 20.22 m (34 x 66 ft) on the top step, and had 6 by 11 Doric columns and a shrine and front porch. If this is the shrine of Demeter mentioned by Pausanias, it also used brick construction, no doubt for the inner building's walls. On style a date around 400–390 BC is likely.

## Messene

Northwest of modern Kalamata in the southwest Peloponnese, ancient Messene is dramatically sited on the slopes of Mount Ithome, a centre of Messen-

*(Above) The site of the Doric temple of Lepreon, looking west towards the Messenian coast and the sea beyond.*

*(Below) Model of the Asklepieion complex at Messene, with the temple of Messene dominating the open courtyard.*

*(Above) Ruins of the temple of Messene and its axially aligned altar (in the foreground).*

ian resistance under Spartan rule. In 369 BC, shortly after Messenia's liberation, the city was founded as a new centre for the region. The Doric temple, dedicated to the local heroine Messene, after whom the city was named, dominated the colonnaded court of the Asklepieion, south of the ancient agora. Axially aligned with a monumental altar and also the main entrance to the complex, both to the east, it measures 27.97 x 13.67 m (92 x 45 ft) and is provisionally dated to the 3rd century BC, replacing a predecessor on the same platform. There were 6 by 12 columns, a shrine flanked by porches of equal size, and a ramp leading down to the altar. Inside was Messene's statue in gold and Parian marble; paintings of the ancient Messenian kings were placed in the rear porch. Now only preserved up to the lowest course of the walls, the temple is still surrounded by a cluster of bases in situ for lost dedications.

## Bassai

On the southwestern confines of ancient Arkadia, the lofty site of Bassai lies on a ledge of Mount Kotilion visible for many kilometres. Its well preserved temple of Apollo Epikourios ('Helper') won praise from Pausanias (2nd century AD): 'Of all the

temples in the Peloponnese, next to the one at Tegea, this may be placed first for the beauty of the stone and its harmony'. It was begun by the nearby Arkadian citizen-state of Phigaleia to the southwest after 429 BC, and completed about 400 BC (the dating is on grounds of style). As well as the local blue-grey limestone, marble was imported for the sculpture, roof tiles and other details.

In its proportions and in its north-facing orientation the temple followed a predecessor on the same site, resulting in an unusually long structure for the period of 14.54 x 38.32 m (48 x 126 ft) on the top step with 6 by 15 Doric columns. The inner building

*(Right) Plan of the temple at Bassai, showing the window (not the door as once was thought) in the east colonnade, the semi-engaged Ionic columns of the shrine, and the solitary Corinthian column aligned with the temple's lengthways axis.*

*(Far right) Bassai: the view into the interior from the front porch.*

Cutaway perspective of the temple at Bassai (after Fred Cooper). Note (centre) the grilled window in the east wall of the interior.

(Below) Bassai: the temple of Apollo in its mountainous setting in southwest Arkadia, Peloponnese.

comprised the usual porches. But the ornate shrine was revolutionary, bearing out the claim of Pausanias that the architect was Iktinos, who designed the Parthenon. Its long sides were lined with Ionic columns semi-engaged to spur walls and carrying an ill-fitting all-round frieze depicting Greeks fighting amazons and centaurs (see pp. 66–67) which continued over the most startling feature of all, an isolated Corinthian column opposite the entrance, the earliest known example of this style (see p. 44). It has been suggested that this lone pillar had a sacral significance, a distant echo of the sanctity which some modern scholars claim for the isolated column of Mycenaean times (see p. 63).

Behind was a back room of uncertain function with a door-like opening facing east, in fact a window, originally with a fixed grille (see pp. 52 and 90). Its purpose, according to Fred Cooper, was to funnel the rays of dawn into the southwest corner of the back room, where he places the twice-lifesize bronze statue of Apollo from Bassai, which by Pausanias' day had long been in Megalopolis.

Metopes from above the porches have slots for sculptured slabs, perhaps removed by the Romans. Otherwise the temple was intact when Pausanias visited, and remains of a divine statue of Roman

date have been found. In early medieval times the temple was vandalized for its metal clamps, resulting in the loss of the roof and walls. Partly rebuilt in 1902–8, in 1999 the whole structure was covered by a tent for further conservation.

## Alipheira

The ruins of Alipheira are in the remote countryside of western Arkadia. On a terrace south of the akropolis, commanding spectacular views, are the foundations of the Doric temple of Athena, chief deity of this small Arkadian polis. Dated around 500–490 BC on style, the elongated temple measured 10.65 x 29.6 m (35 x 97 ft), with 6 by 15 columns and a simple shrine without porches. The temple faced north, which the site more or less compels, but the altar looked east. A Byzantine chapel (since demolished) once overlay the foundations.

## Gortys

North of modern Karitaina in west-central Arkadia, overlooking the picturesque ravine of the river

*Alipheira: foundations of the temple of Athena, photographed from the northwest. The stupendous view that the temple commanded suggests how visible the temple must have been to the local population.*

Lousios, the small city of Gortys was well-known for its cult of Asklepios. In the so-called 'lower' Asklepieion, laid out on a natural terrace overlooking the ravine, are the foundations of an east-facing colonnaded temple with dimensions of 23.99 x 13.44 m (79 x 44 ft), suiting a plan of 6 by 11 columns with a front porch and shrine. The complete absence of any signs of a superstructure suggests that the project was abandoned, perhaps after Gortys' unsuccessful revolt from Megalopolis (about 362 BC).

## Peraitheis (?)

In south-central Arkadia, the scanty ruins of a large Doric temple have been found on a natural terrace below the summit of Mount Aghios Elias near modern Arachamiti. The site has a commanding view of the valley of ancient Asea, 5 km (3 miles) away. The temple measured 11.95 x 29.27 m (39 x 96 ft) on the top step and is restored with 6 by 14 columns framing an elongated shrine and porches. Some upper parts, of Doliana marble from Tegea, survive. On style a date around 500 BC is suggested. This may have been the sanctuary of Pan in ancient

Peraitheis, subsumed into Megalopolis in 369/368 BC. The remains were built into a church in more recent times.

## Vigla

In the same part of south-central Arkadia, at the top of the pass carrying the ancient route between Megalopolis and Tegea, are slight remains of a Doric temple in Doliana marble. South-facing and overlying a wooden predecessor, it measured 24.7 x 11.55 m (81 x 38 ft), with 6 by 13 columns framing a shrine and porches, and is dated about 575–550 BC. If this is the sanctuary of Athena Soteira and Poseidon on Mount Boreion (Mount Kravari), the temple would have belonged to the little polis of Asea, and was in ruins (like Asea itself) when Pausanias saw it.

## Tegea

Dominating the southern half of the great upland plain of eastern Arkadia, Tegea was one of the most important and wealthy Arkadian citizen-

states throughout antiquity. Its famous temple of Athena Alea, the chief local deity, 'far surpasses all other temples in the Peloponnese, both in size and style' (Pausanias). Replacing a predecessor burnt down in 395 BC, in turn built over two simple cult-buildings from the 8th and early 7th centuries BC, the temple, in the local Doliana marble, had as architect the famous sculptor Skopas, who worked on the Mausoleum of Halikarnassos in Asia Minor. It dates to about 340 BC on style. Its elongated proportions of 47.52 x 19.16 m (156 x 63 ft) on the top step, with 14 by 6 columns, echoed its predecessor, but the nearly 9 m (30 ft) high columns embodied the 4th-century quest for slenderness. Two ramps of almost equal size approach respectively the east facade and a great door in the north side of the shrine which allowed ritual communication with the adjacent sanctuary (see p. 90). Both gables had marble sculpture, and there were carved metopes above the porches, their figures from local myth identified by inscribed captions. The richly decorated shrine had an innovative design, superimposing Ionic over Corinthian columns,

engaged into the walls (see the illustration on p. 88). A 6th-century AD earthquake brought the temple down. A Byzantine church was installed in the ruins.

## Orchomenos

The remains of this important city in northeast Arkadia are scenically sited on a prominent hill commanding a rural hinterland surrounded by mountains. On the lower slopes of the hill, in what was the lower town, are the limestone vestiges of a colonnaded temple, measuring 31.22 x 13.33 m (102 x 44 ft) on the top step with 6 by 13 Doric columns and a front porch and shrine, where traces of a large statue-base were found. On style the date is around 500 BC.

## Hermione (mod. Ermione)

On the south coast of the Argolid promontory, opposite the island of Hydra, ancient Hermione was a small but flourishing citizen-state with a good harbour. Once within the walls of the ancient polis, on the highest point of the modern Bisti peninsula, are the foundations for a temple with estimated dimensions of 31.46 x 15.03 m (103 x 49 ft) on the top step. The plan is restored with 6 by 12 Doric columns, a shrine and porches. On style the date is around 500 BC. A medieval church was built on the foundations. The deity may have been Poseidon.

## Kalaureia

On the eastern flank of the Argolid promontory, this offshore island opposite modern Poros was the home of a famous sanctuary of the sea god Poseidon belonging to a maritime organization of 'dwellers-around' (*amphyktyones*), including Athens and Aigina. The Athenian orator and statesman Demosthenes, leader of the Greek resistance to Macedon, committed suicide here in 322 BC. The site of the temple is on a high mountain plateau in mid-island. The temple's dimensions are estimated at 14.4 x 27.5 m (47 x 90 ft) on the top step, with 6 by 12 Doric columns. On style the date is around 500 BC. Little is now left, with many blocks recycled in the churches of the nearby island of Hydra.

## Troizen

The ruins of this small city are sited in attractive countryside near the southeast tip of the Argolid promontory. This was where the mythical Athenian hero Theseus was raised, and where the women and children of Athens were sent for safety during the

*(Below) Doric capital of the 'flattened' early type from the temple at Orchomenos.*

*(Right) Arkadian Orchomenos – restored plan of the Doric temple.*

*(Left) Foundations of the Doric temple at Troizen, dating probably from the second half of the 4th century BC.*

*(Below) Limestone columns from the 4th-century BC temple of Zeus, Nemea. Originally they were covered with a layer of plaster and painted.*

*(Below left) Plan of the temple of Zeus, Nemea, showing the frontal ramp, and the crypt to the rear with its access steps.*

invasion of the Persian king Xerxes I (480–479 BC). Outside the ancient city walls are the foundations for a colonnaded temple, with restored dimensions of 15.04 x 29.46 m (49 x 97 ft) on the top step and a plan of 6 by 11 columns, with a shrine and porches. The extremely shallow rear porch indicates a date not before 350–300 BC. The deity is uncertain.

## Nemea

In a side-valley northwest of the Argive plain, the Nemean sanctuary of Zeus was one of Greece's four panhellenic religious centres. But the festival had migrated to Argos by the 1st century BC, and when Pausanias visited (around AD 150), the temple was roofless and the god's statue had vanished. Four columns still stand today, one recently reerected. The temple was built during Nemea's revival in the 4th century BC, and had the shortened proportions of the time. Approached by a ramp, it measures 20.09 by 42.55 m (66 x 140 ft) on the top step, with 6 by 12 Doric columns framing porches and a shrine featuring freestanding colonnades of Ionic superposed on Corinthian on three sides. Unusually, grilles were fitted between the rear columns to screen a back room with an open crypt some 2 m (6½ ft) deep, approached by steps. This feature would suit an oracle (see p. 91), otherwise unknown for Nemea. The material was local limestone, stuccoed and painted, with black and white marble trim.

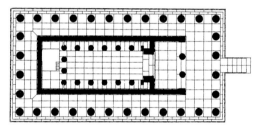

## Isthmia

The venerable sanctuary of Poseidon on the Isthmus, in Corinthian territory, was one of Greece's four panhellenic religious centres. Thought 'not very large' by Pausanias, the god's temple dates on style around the 460s BC, replacing a 7th-century BC predecessor, and was itself extensively rebuilt after a fire in 390 BC. With dimensions of 22.9 x 53.5 m (75 x 176 ft) on the top step, it had a colonnade of 6 by 13 Doric columns, porches and a shrine. Colour was used extensively above the columns, especially red, white and blue. Roman Corinth's colonists veneered the interior in marble. The original statues, on a base partly extant, were upgraded in gold and ivory by Herodes Atticus of Athens (2nd century AD). The temple was demolished, probably in the mid-6th century AD, to build the nearby 'Fortress of Justinian', where many blocks can still be seen. Little now remains in situ, apart from foundation trenches.

## Corinth

Commanding the Isthmus, Corinth was a major centre in antiquity. Destroyed by Rome in 146 BC, it was refounded by Caesar in 44 BC as a Roman colony.

### Temple of Apollo

In a commanding position on a ridge overlooking the centre of Corinth, and on the site of a 7th-century BC predecessor (see p. 20), the temple dates around 540 BC on the basis of the pottery. Measuring 53.8 x 21.58 m (177 x 71 ft) on the top step, it had 6 by 15 Doric columns, limestone monoliths of which a number still stand. The upward curvature on all sides is the oldest example in Greece of this refinement (see pp. 64–65). A masonry cavity in the front porch may have been a sunken treasury (see pp. 92–93). The inner building had two shrines, back to back, with traces of a possible statue base in the smaller one. Above the outer columns votive objects such as shields were once attached. The Roman colonists applied a fresh coat of stucco and removed the interior columns to create (probably) a single inner shrine. Probably damaged by earthquake in the 6th century AD, the temple has served as a quarry.

### Temple E

This marble temple in the Corinthian style, a showpiece of the Roman colony, clearly betrays Greek influence. The chief feature in situ is a massive podium, some 42.7 x 18.2 m (140 x 60 ft), encased by ashlar masonry. On top rose a colonnaded temple of 6 by 12 columns, with gable sculpture inspired by the Parthenon's. Dated to the late 1st century AD or under Hadrian (AD 117–38), the temple almost certainly served the imperial cult. It was destroyed by fire around AD 350.

## Sikyon

Corinth's western neighbour was famous chiefly for its artists. Southeast of the theatre are the foundations of a long thin limestone temple measuring 38.07 x 11.55 m (125 x 38 ft). The colonnades were Ionic, framing a shrine and porches. The date is late 4th or early 3rd century BC, but

*Plan of the temple of Apollo at Corinth in its original (Greek) phase.*

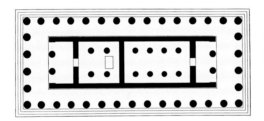

*The temple of Apollo with Akrocorinth, the Corinthian akropolis, in the background.*

*(Below) Remains of temple E, Corinth, showing reassembled elements from the colonnade, including Corinthian capitals, and the masonry casing of the podium.*

the reused foundations were those of a building of similar plan now dated about 575–550 BC. In late antiquity the temple was converted into a church.

## Argos

On manmade terraces in the foothills of Mount Euboia commanding spectacular views westward across the Argive plain towards ancient (and modern) Argos, the Heraion was the chief sanctuary of the Argives, celebrated for its rich offerings. According to a later tradition known to Vitruvius, this was the site of the oldest Doric temple.

The first temple with an outer colonnade stood on the highest terrace and dates to the 7th century BC. The mudbrick interior has vanished, but a stretch of the limestone top step survives, covered with stucco on the visible side and with marks for wood columns. Either originally or as part of a later repair, it seems to have had clay roof tiles. The temple burnt down in 423 BC when the lamp of the priestess Chryseis, who was asleep inside, 'caught the [woollen] strips' hanging from the statue (Thucydides: see p. 80).

Probably towards 400 BC the temple was rebuilt on a new terrace built just below by an Argive architect, Eupolemos. The reasons for this unusual change of site are unclear. The massive limestone foundations measure roughly 39.5 x 20 m (130 x 66 ft) and once supported 6 by 12 Doric columns, a shrine and porches, with a ramp on the east side.

The roof-tiles were marble, as were the sculptured metopes and gables. The goddess' seated colossus, by the Argive Polykleitos, was in ivory and gold (see 'Temples and Divine Statues', pp. 74–75). The temple's final days have yet to be reconstructed, but many of its blocks can be seen in nearby churches.

*(Right) Plan of the 'old' temple of Hera, Argive Heraion.*

*(Below) Remains of the 'new' temple of Hera and its ramp, overlooking the Argive plain.*

## Epidauros

Laid out in a natural hollow, the Epidaurian sanctuary of Asklepios was the Greek mainland's most celebrated healing sanctuary from the 400s BC into late antiquity. The host city, Epidauros, was some 7 km (4½ miles) away on the Saronic coast.

### Temple of Asklepios

Poorly preserved, the god's limestone temple is grouped with the other main structures on somewhat higher ground overlooking the stadium. A ramp linked the temple and its altar to the east. Measuring only 11.76 x 23.06 m (39 x 78 ft) on the top step, it had 6 by 11 Doric columns and a shrine and rear porch only. Before entering the visitor could read an inscribed *gnome* or maxim, 'Pure must one be to enter the incense-fragrant temple, and purity is thinking holy thoughts.' Above the columns there was bright paintwork, and marble sculpture adorned gables and metopes. The great doors of precious woods and ivory are described in the building accounts. A cavity in the shrine for the god's gold and ivory statue was probably a treasury (see pp. 92–93). Dated around 375–370 BC, the temple was included in the sanctuary's fortifications over six centuries later. It may have succumbed to earthquake in the 6th century AD.

*Remains of the temple of Asklepios, Epidauros. The ramp can be made out, along with the clutter of bases for ancient offerings still in situ.*

*(Below) Restored plan of the temple of Asklepios, Epidauros, showing the probable treasury set into the paving of the shrine.*

probable treasury

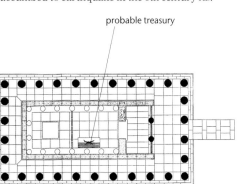

# Central and Northern Greece

Divided geographically by the formidable spine of Mount Pindos, the Greek-speaking peoples of central and northern Greece in ancient times formed a mosaic of polities and local cultures. Immediate neighbours of the Athenians were the Euboian islanders, who had been at the fore of early Greek trading ventures in the 8th century BC, and the Boiotians, a famously agricultural people whose chief city, Thebes, briefly enjoyed a military empire in the mid-4th century BC. North of the Boiotians, still on the east side of Greece, Greeks of the Phokis region shared their mountains with the precipitous sanctuary of Delphi, where a revered temple hosted Apollo's most famous oracle.

Further west, along the north coast of the Corinthian gulf, lived the Aitolian highlanders, whose ill-gotten wealth as brigands on land and sea may have helped to fund several major temples, above all Thermon, their tribal centre. Their tribal neighbours in northwest Greece were the Akarnanians, and beyond them the Epeirots, whose lands shaded into what is now Albania. In the 5th century BC this area seemed backward to the more urbanized Athenians. Prosperous Greek colonies on the Adriatic coast, however, explain the appearance of major Greek temples here at an early date, with a pioneering all-stone colonnaded temple built at Kerkyra (Corfu) in the early 6th century BC.

In east-central Greece the Thessalians occupied fertile plains and developed important cities, including Demetrias, a Macedonian royal capital. The colonnaded temple was adopted by the Thessalians but not, it seems, by their northern neighbours, the Macedonians, whose ancestral lands edged the Thermaic gulf near modern Thessaloniki. It appears in northern Greece only in the Greek colonies dotting the Aegean coastline hereabouts. In several cases here the slight remains leave the existence of a colonnade suspected, but unconfirmed.

The following tour starts on the island of Euboia and works westwards as far as the Adriatic colonies. It then returns to east central Greece, before concluding in Macedonia and the northeast.

## EUBOIA

## Eretria

On the west coast of Euboia, Eretria was a leading Greek power in the 7th and 6th centuries BC, with a powerful fleet and far-flung colonies in Greater Greece. Its sanctuary of Apollo was one of the major shrines of the Greek mainland at this time. Early in the 5th century BC the Eretrians fought against the Persians and, much later, the Romans, both times seeing the sack of their city. Eretria survived into the Christian era, a shadow of its former self. Like the ribs of a skeleton in the sand, remains of the ancient city emerge from the ground all over the modern town of the same name.

### Temple of Apollo

The chief sanctuary, dedicated to Apollo Daphnephoros (Laurel Bearer), was sited just above sea-level in the middle of the walled city. Dated on style

*Eretria: the temple of Apollo showing some of the earlier foundations (see pp. 50–51) still preserved beneath what is left of the temple substructure after many centuries of quarrying.*

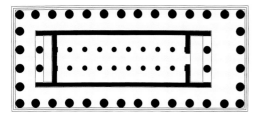

around 530–520 BC, the limestone temple here was partly built on the foundations of its 7th-century BC predecessor, in turn overlying various earlier buildings (see pp. 50–51). Measuring 46.40 x 19.15 m (152 x 63 ft) on the top step, it is restored in plan with 6 by 14 columns, a wider hall and deeper porch emphasizing the east front, and a long narrow shrine with two colonnades. Nearby were found unweathered remnants of marble sculptures from the west gable, piously buried, it seems, after the Persian sack of Eretria (490 BC). Major reconstruction followed, including new gable-sculpture, dated on style about 450–425 BC. For unclear reasons the temple had been abandoned by the late 1st century BC, when its gable-sculpture turned up in Rome

(see p. 40). By the 1st century AD it was a quarry. Foundations only survive in situ.

## Temple of Dionysos

Only foundations survive of this short limestone temple, reconstructed with 6 by 11 Doric columns, a deep shrine and a front porch. On style the date is about 350 BC. It formed an architectural ensemble with the theatre, 25 m (82 ft) to the southwest, and was evidently damaged in the Roman sack of Eretria in 198 BC, since three of its triglyphs were reused in the city walls about this time.

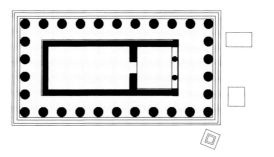

*(Left) Plan of the temple of Apollo, Eretria.*

*(Below) Plan of the temple of Dionysos, Eretria.*

*(Bottom) The site of the temple of Dionysos, Eretria, with part of the theatre visible (upper left of the photograph).*

## BOIOTIA

### Plataiai

Site of the Greek victory over the Persians in 479 BC, the tiny citizen-state of Plataiai in southern Boiotia was an important cult centre, with festivals in memory of the battle celebrated into the 3rd century AD. Inside the walls are foundations of an elongated Doric temple, measuring 49.9 x 16.7 m (164 x 55 ft) and restored in plan with 8 by 18 columns, and porches, shrine and back room. This may be the temple of Hera built by the Thebans after 427 BC. A coin of the emperor Licinius (AD 307) may indicate continuing use under Roman rule. The site has since been quarried.

### Thebes

In the centre of Boiotia, Thebes was one of Greece's most ancient and famous cities, reputedly the birth-place of the hero Herakles. Archaeological finds show that in the 14th century BC the bronze age settlement here was one of the major centres of the Mycenaean world. In historic times the chief city of the Boiotian Greeks, Thebes was briefly the leading power of Greece in the 4th century BC. It was destroyed by Alexander the Great (335 BC), although subsequently refounded (316 BC). Remains of its ancient grandeur, buried beneath a bustling modern town, are few and far between.

#### Temple of Apollo Ismenios

The Ismenion, on a low hill inside the ancient walls, was one of the chief Theban shrines. Named after a local river, the Ismenos, it was dedicated to Apollo, whose cedar-wood statue in the temple here, a work of the 5th century BC, was seen by Pausanias (mid-2nd century AD). Poorly preserved remains have been found of a large limestone temple with marble roofing, possibly never finished. The third and last temple of Apollo Ismenios, it measured 46.25 x 22.83 m (152 x 75 ft) on the top step with 6 by 12 limestone Doric columns and a shrine flanked by two porches. The remains suggest a date around 400–350 BC.

### Ptoion

This oracular sanctuary of Apollo Ptoios (mod. Perdikovrysi), belonging to nearby Akraiphia, a small city in eastern Boiotia, is sited in a mountainous valley on the west slopes of Mount Ptoion. Apollo's limestone temple sits on a manmade platform on the highest of the sanctuary's three terraces, with spectacular views to the west. The foundations measure 24.72 x 11.65 m (81 x 38 ft), and the elongated plan is restored by Greek archaeologist A. K. Orlandos with 6 by 13 columns, a long shrine and a front porch. Dates in both the mid-5th and the late 4th century BC have been suggested.

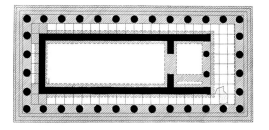

*(Below) Doric capital from the Ismenion with ΕΞΩ ('outside') inscribed on the underside, telling the builders which side of the capital should face outwards. The contact surfaces of the column drums were angled so that the colonnade inclined inwards – one of the 'refinements' discussed on pp. 64–65.*

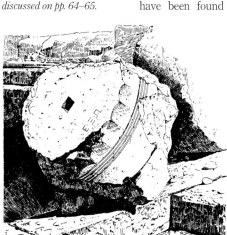

*(Above) Plan and restored facade (right) of Apollo's temple at the Ptoion.*

## Lebadeia (mod. Livadhia)

Pausanias (*c.* AD 160) considered Lebadeia, in the northwest corner of Boiotia's great central plain, 'in style and splendour equal to the most flourishing cities in Greece'. A pile of debris marks the site of its temple of Zeus Basileus atop the hill of Prophitis Elias, southwest of the modern town, 'left half-finished, by reason either of its size or of a succession of wars' (Pausanias). The site has suffered from robbing and Second World War bombs; a better guide to the plan comes from building inscriptions offering contracts for the work (see p. 71), envisaging a limestone temple measuring roughly 46 x 22.6 m (151 x 74 ft) on the top step with a front porch and shrine, a semi-circular base for divine images at the far end. Work began probably in the 3rd century BC.

## Orchomenos

The site of a major settlement in Mycenaean times (14th century BC), Orchomenos in northwest Boiotia was the chief regional rival of the Thebans, who eventually destroyed it in 364 BC. Rebuilt by the Macedonian kings, it survived into late antiquity. On the lower slopes of the akropolis, within the ancient walls, limestone foundations measuring about 11.5 x 22 m (38 x 72 ft) once supported a Doric temple with (probably) 6 by 11 columns. Inscriptions suggest that the deity was Asklepios and mention building works in the temple around 250 BC.

*The temple at Orchomenos, commanding fine views over the lower ground where much of today's fertile land was an inland lake, drained in modern times.*

## Elateia

Elateia was one of the two main cities of ancient Phokis, a mountainous region in central Greece stretching from the Corinthian gulf to the Aegean, its inhabitants organized politically into an armed federation. The modest remains of Elateia's rural temple of Athena Kranaia sit on a hill some 4 km (2½ miles) northeast in a setting 'like that of so many ancient temples in Greece, remarkably fine' (James Frazer), with superb views of Mount Parnassos and the hills of Boiotia. The limestone temple was orientated north–south on a manmade platform, measured 27.5 x 11.5 m (90 x 38 ft) on the top step, and is restored with 6 by 13 Doric columns. Clay roof ornaments help give a date in the early 5th century BC.

## Hyampolis (Kalapodi)

This small Phokian polis, near the modern village of Kalapodi, was destroyed by the Persians (480 BC) and again by Philip of Macedon (346 BC), but still existed, impoverished, in imperial times. The chief sanctuary of the Phokians, dedicated to Artemis Elaphebolos (Shooter of Deer), lay in its mountainous hinterland, some 5 km (3 miles) north of the city on a hillside near modern Kalapodi.

### The 5th-century BC temple

Measuring 44.20 x 17.70 m (145 x 58 ft) on the top step, the temple dates to the late 5th century BC and was the fifth on the spot in a sequence going back to 850–800 BC. Its foundations were built for an immediate predecessor (early 5th century BC) of much the same plan and dimensions, destroyed by earthquake probably in 426 BC. The temple is restored with 6 by 14 columns and had porches, a shrine with foundations for a statue-base, and a back

169

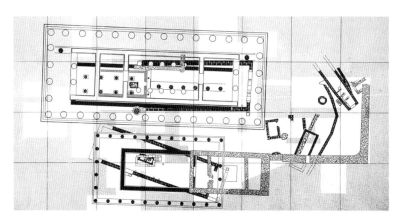

*Plan of the sanctuary at Kalapodi, showing the successive temples of Artemis (above) and Apollo (below).*

room. The temple and its cult were abandoned by AD 350–400, when the inner room was seriously disturbed by digging, perhaps by Christians. The site has since been quarried away, with much of it built into modern Kalapodi.

### The 6th-century BC temple

Just to the south are the remains of a small 6th-century temple of Apollo on a parallel alignment with a twin to the north, the third of the sequence of temples on the same site as the 5th-century temple (see above). The second on its own site, it measured 26.28 x 13.62 m (86 x 45 ft) on the top step, with 6 by 11 Doric columns, some wooden, framing a one-room shrine without porches, and was approached by a ramp. An early Greek inscription in monumental script may have named the donor. Both this temple and its twin were burnt down, doubtless by the Persians in 480 BC. This southern temple was not rebuilt, but amid the ruins a shaft was rigged up from reused blocks to receive offerings.

## Delphi

Delphi, a small citizen-state of the Phokian Greeks, was home to the sanctuary of Apollo, most prestigious of the ancient Greek oracles. The site is spectacular, on one side of a long narrow mountain valley beneath the steep cliffs of Mount Parnassos, with the valley bottom far below (see pp. 52–53). Delphi's heyday fell in the 6th and 5th centuries BC. But it remained one of the holiest Greek shrines until the Christians got the upper hand here from the 360s AD on.

### Temple of Apollo

On a manmade platform approached by a winding sacred way, the temple is the centrepiece of Apollo's precinct (see pp. 46–47). Special sanctity was claimed for the spot, as the tomb of the god Dionysos and as the earth's centre or navel, marked by an ovoid stone. The temple also housed an altar with a perpetual fire, conceived as the communal hearth of Greeks everywhere. It replaced a late 6th-

century BC predecessor on the same site, destroyed by earthquake in 373/2 BC.

As found, the structure had been demolished to the foundations, having served as both quarry and mine (for metal clamps). Its elongated dimensions, echoing its predecessor's, are 21.64 x 58.18 m (71 x 191 ft) on the top step, with 6 by 15 Doric columns framing porches and a shrine, where a sunken area at the back housed the oracle, and a ramped approach. Ancient writers describe a waiting room in or near the sunken area, 'in which they seat those who would consult the oracle'. The Pythia or priest-

ess would 'go down' to utter her prophecies in the sunken area, where she sat on a sacred tripod (see p. 91) in a state of trance. These writers insist on the inspirational role of natural fumes from a chasm in the bedrock in this area, but there is no modern confirmation of this alleged geological phenomenon. Funded in fits and starts, construction was long drawn out (roughly 370–325 BC), and economical. A soft limestone from Corinth, plastered and painted, was used for most upper parts, with additional marble trim, notably the roof tiles and gable-sculpture. The front porch housed the maxims of the

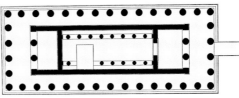

*(Above) Delphi, general view of the temple of Apollo from the west and (left) a plan, showing the sunken area or 'adyton'.*

Seven Wise Men including 'Know thyself', and 'Nothing in excess', inscribed on pillars topped with busts. From the 2nd century BC the wall of the south hall was used for an inscribed 'archive'. The fabric

*The Doric temple in the lower
sanctuary, Delphi, showing
the buckling of the platform
in ancient times from
earthquake damage.*

was maintained by the Romans, including a repair
by Domitian (AD 84). Surviving the advent of Christianity, the temple was finally abandoned during the
Slav incursions (later 6th century AD on).

### Doric temple

A lower sanctuary of Athena, now known as
Marmaria from its ancient marbles, has a row of
temples and treasuries, including the remains of
this short temple on the site of a predecessor, with
its colonnade partly restored. Facing south, it measures 13.25 x 27.45 m (43.5 x 90 ft), with 6 by 12 Doric
columns framing a deep shrine and front porch
only, and is dated on style around 500 BC. The upper
parts and the gable sculpture were the local soft
limestone, plastered and painted; the roofing
system was painted clay; coloured pebbles set in
mortar served as flooring. The long sides are visibly
buckled by ancient earthquakes, and the columns in
the northeast corner at some stage were shored up
with the intercolumnar walls now visible. The proximity of the massive altar to the east suggests that
the cult here was of Athena.

---

## AITOLIA

---

## *Velvina*

---

Crowning Mount Prophitis Ilias in ancient Aitolia,
about 2 km (1¼ miles) southwest of modern Velvina,
are the ruins of a walled sanctuary in a remote,

*(Right) Velvina, general view
of the site of the Doric
temple in upland terrain
controlled by the powerful
Aitolian Confederacy based
on Thermon.*

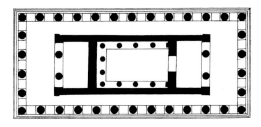

rural setting. Its older identification with Poseidon's sanctuary at ancient Molykrion is now disputed, but it was important enough to display public documents and have a major limestone temple, perhaps the second on its site. Of this only foundations survive, measuring 14.37 x 31.45 m (47 x 103 ft), with 6 by 13 columns and an inner colonnade around three sides of the shrine. From the decoration of the platform steps a date in the late 4th or the 3rd century BC has been suggested.

## Thermon

A sprawling site in the Aitolian countryside, the sanctuary of Apollo at Thermon was the main centre of the Aitolian people and state, its acme falling in the 3rd century BC, when the Aitolians headed a powerful central-Greek federation. The historian Polybius (2nd century BC) described it as 'the natural citadel of all Aitolia'. By the 3rd century BC the sanctuary was also a town, sur-

*(Above left) Velvina, restored plan of the Doric temple showing the internal colonnade framing the shrine.*

*(Above) Thermon, part of the fortified sanctuary of Apollo.*

(Above) One of the painted clay panels from the temple of Apollo, Thermon, showing a row of three seated women. Although the style looks as early as the 7th century BC, ornamental details such as the paired griffins (right) are much later (3rd century BC). An older panel was perhaps restored or recreated after damage in one of the Macedonian sacks.

rounded by fortifications to protect its wealth, since 'the houses in the vicinity of the temple and around about were full of valuables' (Polybius, referring to 218 BC). The south-facing temple of Apollo, the third of three on the same site, is no earlier than the late 3rd century BC, as shown by a dated inscription reused in the foundations. Its archaizing plan was a pious rebuild of a venerable predecessor, perhaps burnt in one of the Macedonian sacks by Philip V (218 and 196 BC). A colonnade of 5 by 15 Doric columns (in stone, possibly replacements for wood) framed an exceptionally long and narrow shrine with a central row of wooden columns and a rear porch only. The walls and the roofing system were of fired clay, as were ten panels with paintings found along two sides of the temple, all but one assigned to about 630–620 BC on style. These originally sat on the preceding temple, whose date of construction is indicated by their style. How, if at all, they were displayed on the 3rd century temple is unknown.

## Kalydon

This Aitolian citizen-state was chiefly famous for the sanctuary of Artemis Laphria just outside its walls, a pan-Aitolian precinct where state documents were displayed. In 30 BC the Kalydonians and this cult were forcibly transposed to the Roman colony of Patrai. Commanding panoramic views, the limestone temple of Artemis sat on the cramped summit of a natural col. The latest and largest of three temples on the same spot, it required the support of a massive platform with handsome

(Above) Kalydon, the temple of Artemis: general view with the Aitolian hill-country behind.

(Right) Kalydon, the temple of Artemis: drawing by the Danish excavators reconstructing the view of the temple from the base of its platform.

masonry. Measuring 14.02 x 31.63 m (46 x 104 ft) on the top step, it had 6 by 13 Doric columns, porches and a shrine with (probably) Ionic colonnades against three walls. One sculptured metope survives, and the roofing was marble. The date on style is about 360 BC. Its superstructure may also have been robbed (or transposed?) in Roman times.

## THE NORTHWEST

## *Stratos*

Stratos was the largest city of the Akarnanian Greeks, but declined into a village after the foundation of Nikopolis to the west by the emperor Augustus (about 30 BC). The walled site, just north of the modern trunk road from Athens, is huge, and may never have been fully built up. The substantial remains of a temple of Zeus belong to the ancient city's chief shrine. They sit on a manmade platform which breached the older city wall at a high point commanding superb views of the great plain to the southwest. The cult, identified by an inscription, may have been pan-Akarnanian. Measuring 32.44 x

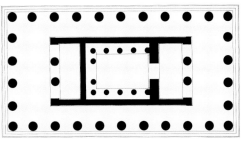

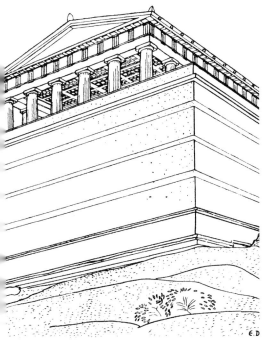

*(Left) Plan of the Doric temple of Zeus, Stratos, showing the compact proportions of the period.*

*(Below) General view of the temple of Zeus, Stratos, from the east. Beyond, the ground falls away sharply; the temple would have been visible for miles to the ancient population working the fertile land below.*

*The solitary standing column
from the Doric temple at the
site of the Greek colony of
Apollonia, Albania.*

16.54 m (106 x 54 ft) on the top step with 6 by 11 Doric columns framing porches and a shrine, the temple was built in local limestone around 320 BC and sat on the foundations of a non-colonnaded 5th-century predecessor. A colonnade framing the divine statue was either Ionic or Corinthian. Unfinished column fluting shows that the temple was incomplete. The interior paving shows ancient earthquake damage.

## Ambrakia

Beneath modern Arta, Ambrakia in Epeiros was founded from Corinth about 625 BC, flourished as the capital of king Pyrrhos (319–272 BC), but declined with the foundation of Nikopolis (about 30 BC). Inside the ancient walls are the foundations of a colonnaded temple measuring 20.75 x 44 m (68 x 144 ft), with a front porch and long narrow shrine with a base, not for a statue, but for a circular fetish, probably a stone cone or baetyl, the local symbol of the city's patron god Apollo, featured on its coins. An inscription from the site confirms the deity as Apollo. The date on style is around 500 BC, and clay roof-tiles, dated 450–425 BC, may belong to repairs. The site was already a quarry in Roman times.

## Kassope

This mountain capital of the Kassopaians, an Epeirote tribe, was founded about 360 BC and abandoned with the foundation of Nikopolis to the south. The lofty site is one of the most spectacular in Greece, in a mountain bowl with breathtaking views south to Actium and the Ionian sea. Thanks to its remoteness the ancient remains, laid out on a grid, are well preserved, and the sense of walking ancient streets is particularly strong here. Outside the walls, 300 m (984 ft) from the east gate, are the limestone foundations of a Doric temple with rough dimensions of 10 x 17 m (33 x 56 ft) – one of the smallest known. A colonnade of 6 by 10 columns can be restored, and an inner plan of deep front porch and shrine, with foundations for a statue-base. The plan would suit the 4th century BC. The vanished superstructure conceivably was transposed to Nikopolis sometime after 30 BC.

## Passaron

Near Radotovi in a rural valley some 10 km (6 miles) northwest of Ioannina is the site of ancient Passaron, a common sanctuary of Zeus Areios for the Epeirote tribe of the Molossians. Foundations survive of a small limestone and marble temple, measuring 19.30 x 11 m (63 x 36 ft), and allow a restored plan of 6 by 11 columns, shrine and front porch. Both Doric and Ionic capitals survive, suggesting a date on style in the late 4th century BC. To judge from a layer of limestone shards over the site, the temple was deliberately destroyed, probably in the Roman sack of Epeiros (167 BC).

## Apollonia (mod. Pojani)

This joint colony of Corinth and Kerkyra in what is now Albania was founded in 588 BC on a hilltop site near the Adriatic sea. Outside the city-wall, on the low hill (Sthyllas) overlooking the river Aous, foundations for a Doric temple were visible in the mid-19th century, with estimated dimensions of 23 x 40 m (75 x 131 ft) and a restored plan of 6 by 11 columns with shrine and front porch. A solitary limestone column survives in situ, its capital dateable around 500 BC.

## Epidamnos

This colonial Greek polis (beneath mod. Dürres, Albania), founded probably by Corinth and Kerkyra, occupied a peninsular site on the Adriatic coast about 30 km (20 miles) west of Tirana. In 2002 remains of a Greek temple were discovered here at the modern locality Spitalla, the outside colonnade possibly of wood. A provisional date of around 550 BC is suggested.

## Kerkyra (Corfu)

The citizen-state of Kerkyra was founded from Corinth in 734 BC. Remains of three colonnaded temples

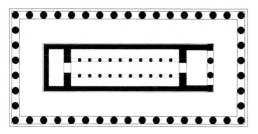

have been uncovered in its urban centre on a peninsula in the southern suburbs of modern Corfu town.

## Temple of Artemis

Foundations of this early Doric temple indicate an elongated building measuring 47.50 x 21.94 m (156 x 72 ft) on the top step, with 8 by 17 columns framing double-width halls, porches and shrine and a frontal ramp. Ten stone relief plaques in the west gable are centred on the protective Gorgon Medusa (see p. 65). Dated around 580 BC on style, this is the earliest known stone temple-sculpture from Greece proper. Originally the roofing system was fired clay, replaced in marble about 535–525 BC. An inscription identifies the cult.

## Kardaki temple

The remains lie in a hollow on the northern flank of the ancient akropolis, overlooking the sea. The temple had (restored) dimensions of 11.91 x (?) 25.59 m (39 x 84 ft), and 6 by (?) 11

Doric columns (some reerected), again enclosing unusually wide halls. With no Doric frieze, the temple would have had a squat appearance. Inside the shrine are remains of a base, wide enough for two statues. On the style the date is around 510 BC. The cult is unknown.

## Doric temple

On the ancient akropolis, slight remains are known of a large limestone temple, measuring roughly 20.6 x 46 m (68 x 151 ft), with 6 by at least 14 Doric columns, and dated *c*. 400 BC from the superstructure, which included a marble roof and possibly gable sculpture. Systematic quarrying took place in medieval and Venetian times. An inscription mentioning Akria (?Hera) may identify the cult.

---

## THESSALY

---

## *Demetrias*

In Thessaly on the Gulf of Volos, this huge planned city was founded around 290 BC by Demetrios I, one of the most colourful of the Macedonian kings who succeeded Alexander the Great. The scrappy remains scarcely hint at the place's ancient strategic and commercial significance, although the sprawling modern port of Volos nearby suggests the region's economic importance. The ancient walls on the low-lying plain south of

*(Left) The temple of Artemis, Corfu: restored plan. The elongated proportions are typical of the early date and the colonnaded shrine creates an imposing approach to the back room, where divine statuary may have been positioned.*

*(Below) General view of the Kardaki temple, Corfu, showing the foundations of the base inside the shrine and elements of the Doric superstructure.*

General view of the stepped platform for a major Doric temple at ancient Pherai.

the ancient royal palace are evidently the 'sacred agora of Artemis Iolkia' of inscriptions. Inside are the foundations of the goddess' limestone temple, measuring 9.6 x 16 m (32 x 53 ft), with 6 by 10 columns of uncertain style, a front porch and shrine, with traces of a statue-base. The date is probably 3rd century BC.

## Pherai

Now the town of Velestino, Pherai was the most important Thessalian city in the 5th and 4th centuries BC. As the fertile plain round about suggests, this would have been a rich farming town in antiquity. On the outskirts of the modern town, hedged by pine trees, are the slight remains of a major temple on a marble platform, its foundations reusing blocks from a 6th-century BC predecessor. Archaeologist Erik Østby estimates the rough dimensions as 15.81 x 32.6 m (52 x 197 ft), restores 6 by 12 Doric columns, and argues for a close resemblance with the 4th-century BC temple of Apollo at Delphi, suggesting a date about 300 BC.

## Metropolis

A place of some importance throughout antiquity, this ancient city in Thessaly's western plain now lies beneath its modern namesake. At Lianokokkala, 2 km (1 ½ miles) to the west, lay an important rural sanctuary of Apollo, identified by inscriptions. Extensive remains have been found here of a primitive temple built in the mid-6th century BC and destroyed in the 2nd century BC, apparently by fire. The inner building had mudbrick walls on a stone base, and the outer colonnade, with 5 by 11 columns, seems to have been made of wood, gradually upgraded to stone. Inside the east-facing building a mudbrick partition divided a back room from the shrine proper, where a central base was found in place. It may once have

supported the fragmentary bronze statue of a helmeted warrior, found by the base.

## MACEDONIA AND THE NORTHEAST

## Thessalonike

Cassander, ruler of Macedon, founded this Greek-style city around 316 BC, probably on the site of the pre-existing Greek city of Therme. Named after his wife, Alexander the Great's sister, the new city quickly became the most important port of the region, as it has remained ever since. Remains of a monumental marble temple in the Ionic style have been found in different parts of the modern city. Capitals, drums and bases give a date by style around 500 BC. Masons' marks show that this was an itinerant temple, moved in Roman-imperial times from an unknown site and reassembled in Thessalonike, probably on a site in what is now Krystallis Street, where the largest concentration of blocks was found. The existence of a colonnade is likely but not certain. The original site was probably a sanctuary belonging to 6th-century BC Therme.

## Aphytis

Aphytis was a Greek city on the westernmost prong of the Chalkidike peninsula. About 2 km (1¼ miles) south of the ancient city near the modern village of Kallithea, on rising ground overlooking the shore, are foundations for a Doric temple of Zeus Ammon, measuring roughly 10.51 x 21.43 m (34 x 70 ft), with 6 by 11 columns, and dated about 350–300 BC on style. The upper parts were limestone and marble, with a fired clay roof. Inscriptions identify the deity. Later stone robbers included Orthodox monks, to judge from a cornice block in the monastery of Panteleimon on Mount Athos.

*(Left) View of the probable
temple-site on the Lekythos
promontory at Torone.*

## Torone

This Greek city on the tip of the Chalkidike's middle prong was an important port-of-call for coastal shipping. In the 2nd or 1st century BC many fragments of a limestone temple of 6th-century BC date were thrown down an ancient cistern on the Lekythos promontory, probably from a temple of Athena which existed here by 423 BC. A Doric colonnade is likely.

## Stageira

On the eastern flank of Chalkidike, near modern Olympias, this coastal Greek colony of the Cycladic island of Andros was chiefly famous in ancient times as the birthplace of Aristotle (384–322 BC). Destroyed by Philip II of Macedon (349 BC), the city was soon rebuilt thanks to Aristotle's influence at court. There are significant remains, including those of a large Doric temple, its discovery in 1996 reported in the Greek press. The details are not yet published. But fragments of gable-sculpture from this temple strongly suggest an outer colonnade.

## Amphipolis

Near the mouth of R. Strymon in western Thrace, this major Athenian colony was founded in 437 BC, passing to the Macedonians in 357 BC. The extensive remains, on a low plateau flanked by the twisting river, command panoramic views, including Mount Pangaion to the east, with ancient goldmines which help explain why Philip II was so keen to seize the city. A modern village near the site was the findspot of an ancient marble metope showing a naked Greek fighting a barbarian. Its original home must have been a major Doric temple in Amphipolis or its territory, probably with colonnades. An alleged similarity with another sculptured metope now in Rome, also ancient Greek work, is now doubted.

## Neapolis

On the site of modern Kavala, Neapolis was a colony of Thasos, founded probably about 650 BC. Chance finds of Ionic capitals and other elements belong to a monumental temple in Thasian marble dating about 500 BC on style, its site probably on the seaward side of the promontory where the ancient city was. A capital with the mason's mark *phi*, 'twenty-two', may signal that the temple was colonnaded. Inscriptions give the deity as the city's patroness, the Maiden ('Parthenos', in origin probably Thrakian), and mention as dedications 'the chairs and the tables' and the 'archive of public debtors' (*chreophylakion*).

## Thasos

East of Kavala, just 8 km (5 miles) from the mainland, this attractive north-Aegean island was colonized from Cycladic Paros around 680 BC. It quickly prospered, its rich resources including timber and marble, as well as wines much in demand for export. The ample remains of its urban nucleus on the north coast are nowadays dotted among the houses of modern Thasos town. Ruins of the only known Greek temple of Herakles, the ancient island's patron, sit on an artificial terrace within the ancient walls, some 300 m (984 ft) west of the agora. It began (*c.* 500 BC?) as a single-roomed marble shrine measuring 9.13 x 12.45 m (30 x 41ft), on the site of a small predecessor. In the 3rd century BC an Ionic colonnade of 6 by 11 columns was added, measuring 20.07 x 23.39 m (66 x 77 ft). A marble door frame, richly carved with bands of Ionic ornament, is probably a 3rd-century replacement of a much older original, and is deliberately carved in the style of the 6th century BC. The site had been razed to its marble foundations by the middle ages. Blocks were reused in a Byzantine chapel built on the spot.

# The Aegean Islands and the Black Sea

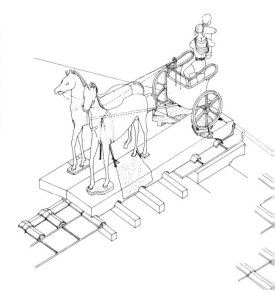

Linking the Greek mainland with Turkey, the crystal waters of the Aegean Sea contain three major groups of inhabited islands much favoured by modern holidaymakers, including the Cyclades in the south-central area and a series of large islands off the Turkish coast. To the south lies Crete, the largest of all the Greek islands. In ancient times a few of these islands were rich and powerful enough to make an impact on the wider political scene, such as 6th-century Naxos and Samos, or Rhodes, in a class of its own as the region's major seapower in the 3rd and 2nd centuries BC. Most played a more modest part in Greek affairs, as waystations for mariners and exporters of natural resources such as Cycladic marbles. A few were places of religious pilgrimage, notably windy Delos in the central Cyclades, birthplace of Apollo, and Kos, with its great shrine of Asklepios.

The northeast Aegean is linked to the Black Sea by a navigable stretch of water separating Europe from Asia, entered at either end by narrow straits which open out into the Sea of Marmara (the ancient Propontis). Greeks early on discovered the great inland sea at the northern end of these straits, calling it the Hospitable (Euxine) Sea, in ironic reference to its cold and stormy waters. These they braved, however, in search of what eventually became a rich trade in regional products such as grain, slaves and salt-fish. Greek colonies followed in the 6th century BC, many claiming the Greek city of Miletos in southwest Turkey as their mother-city. One of them, prosperous Pantikapaion (mod. Kerch) in the Crimea, may well have bequeathed us the northernmost colonnaded temple of Greek antiquity.

The following itinerary works its way roughly from west to east across the Aegean, then north along the Turkish coast, and finally into the Black Sea.

## Keos

In ancient times this Cycladic island (mod. Kea) off the southeast coast of Attike was divided into four tiny citizen-states, of which one was Karthaia, modern Aspri Vigla, its fortified akropolis over-looking the east coast. Karthaia was a prosperous place in the 6th century BC. Below the akropolis summit, on a laboriously contrived artificial plat-form, are the remains of a Doric temple, measuring

23.2 x 11.1 m (76 x 36 ft) on the top step, with 6 by 11 columns, and a shrine and front porch only. The temple faces south, looking out to sea, and was built in the local marble, with imported sandstone and Parian marble for roof tiles. There are many fragments of two-thirds lifesize gable sculpture, including the torso of a central Athena, whose temple this almost certainly was. A Doric capital dates the temple around 500 BC.

## Delos

This small island in the central Cyclades had developed by 600 BC into a major sanctuary of Apollo common to all Ionian Greeks, attracting

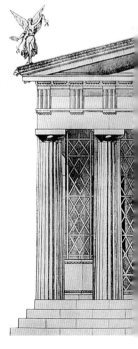

*Delos: restored elevation of the temple of Apollo, showing the columns as if finished (see text).*

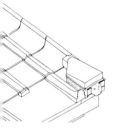

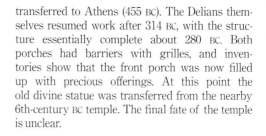

(Left) Keos, Doric temple: this unusually elaborate skyline group on the apex of the main gable (after the restoration by Alexandros Papanikolaou) was a mid-4th-century BC addition. Perhaps it advertised local loyalties to Athens at this time, since it shows Theseus (the Athenian hero) abducting the amazon Antiope.

transferred to Athens (455 BC). The Delians themselves resumed work after 314 BC, with the structure essentially complete about 280 BC. Both porches had barriers with grilles, and inventories show that the front porch was now filled up with precious offerings. At this point the old divine statue was transferred from the nearby 6th-century BC temple. The final fate of the temple is unclear.

## Naxos

This fertile Cycladic island was a prosperous 6th-century BC citizen-state with a strong fleet and close links with Delos to the north. The rocky peninsula of Palatia, linked by a slender isthmus to the seafront of modern Naxos town, is dominated by the massive door of a marble temple, nearly 8 m

Naxos, door of the unfinished Ionic temple. The tenons or projections for lifting the blocks (see p. 60) were never removed.

outside investment, especially from Athens, which controlled it for long periods. The only temple here with colonnades was the grandest in a row of three which faced west on a central hillock in the walled sanctuary, appearing suddenly to ancient seafarers approaching the harbour. Measuring 29.78 x 13.72 m (98 x 45 ft), the temple, in blue and white marble, is restored in plan with 6 by 13 Doric columns (never fluted), porches and a shrine. It may have been commissioned by the Delian League (see p. 33), since work began about 475–450 BC, stopping before the roof sometime after the League treasury was

(26 ft) high and probably honouring Delian Apollo, since it faced northwest towards Delos, visible on a clear day. Measuring 55.27 x 24.32 m (181 x 80 ft), the plan envisaged 6 by 12 or 13 Ionic columns, doubled across the short sides, with porches and a shrine with double colonnade. The walls were more or less finished when building ceased, and pottery suggests abandonment of the cult by the 5th century BC. The temple is usually linked to Lygdamis, Naxian tyrant about 540–524 BC. The ruin was converted into a church in the 5th or 6th century AD.

## Diktynnaion

The Cretan Greeks, perhaps under the influence of their Minoan ancestors, developed their own peculiar form of temple without colonnades. The Diktynnaion may have been an exception. On a conspicuous promontory on Crete's northwest coast, this remote site was the chief sanctuary of the Cretan goddess Diktynna. The foundations of the latest temple (2nd century AD) reused soft limestone fragments of a Doric predecessor, including a capital for a column with an estimated height of 6 m (20 ft), tall enough to have served in a colonnaded temple – the only one in all Crete. If so, the project, begun sometime in the 2nd or 1st century BC, was abandoned.

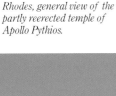

*Rhodes, general view of the partly reerected temple of Apollo Pythios.*

## Rhodes

The island of Rhodes in the southeast Aegean was inhabited in ancient times by Greeks of the Dorian branch, who united into a single citizen-state in 409/8 BC. Its strategic position at a confluence of ancient sea routes gave it a new importance after Alexander's conquest of the near east, which the islanders exploited to become a major maritime power in the 3rd and 2nd centuries BC. Riches flowed in, and the akropolis of the ancient city (on the same site as Rhodes town today) developed into a landscaped park, 'full of terraces and sacred groves' (Aristeides, Greek writer, 2nd century AD).

Two temples have been found here. Prominently placed on the east brow, overlooking the lower city and harbours, is a massive manmade platform once supporting a central temple approached by a monumental staircase on the same alignment. Dated to the 2nd century BC on style, the limestone structure had six Doric columns across the short sides and was partly rebuilt in the last century. Apollo Pythios, the deity, had an oracle here, served by a male prophet.

Higher up to the north, another large complex had a central Doric temple with colonnades, of which foundations and limestone fragments survive. Inscriptions identify the deities as Athena Polias and Zeus Polieus. Both temples were despoiled for the walls of medieval Rhodes.

## Kos

Off the Turkish coast northwest of Rhodes, Kos was also settled by Dorian-speaking Greeks. The island was famous for the practice of medicine. Its suburban sanctuary of Asklepios, a renowned healing centre, is spectacularly sited on three terraces facing northwards so as to command a panorama of coast and sea, including the nearby city (see p. 106).

### Temple of Asklepios

This Doric temple was artfully sited on the uppermost terrace, facing north-northeast in order to look out to sea. It was centred between two colonnades, and aligned with a monumental staircase forming the approach from below. Now only the lower parts survive. It measured 18.79 x 33.28 m (62 x 109 ft) on the top step, with 6 by 11 columns framing a front porch and shrine, with remains of a statue base. The upper parts were white marble, thriftily reserved for the outer face only of the limestone walls. An 'antidote against venomous animals which is inscribed in verse upon a stone in the temple' (Pliny the Elder, 1st century AD) was somewhere on display. A small Byzantine church, now destroyed, was built over the front porch, its floor preserving the original pavement.

### Corinthian temple

On the middle terrace stood a small temple in white marble facing west towards the nearby altar of

*Kos, restored view of the Asklepieion, viewed from the north.*

*Kos, remains of the temple of Asklepios, showing the spectacular marine view.*

Asklepios, its foundations full of reused blocks. Measuring 10.30 x 15.74 m (34 x 52 ft) on the top step, it had 6 by 9 Corinthian columns with unusually wide spacing, porches without columns and a shrine with remains of the statue base. On technique and style the date is around AD 150–200. The deity is unknown.

*Samos: the temple of Hera with its one surviving column in situ.*

## Samos

Separated by a narrow strait from the Turkish coast, this large island was settled in ancient times by Greeks of the Ionian branch. It was among the richest and most powerful states in 6th-century Greece, above all under its tyrant Polykrates (died about 522 BC). The extra-mural Heraion was the chief sanctuary of the Samians.

### Temple of Hera

A much restored Ionic column still stands from this largest of all Greek temples. Measuring 55.16 x 108.63 m (181 x 356 ft) on the top step, it stood on foundations reusing parts of a predecessor, itself the second or third temple on the site. The plan envisaged a forest of 155 columns, including two rows each of 24 on either long side, three rows of 8 across the front, and three of 9 across the back. The columns were limestone or marble, with wooden elements above, and a figured frieze decorated the walls of the porch or shrine. Probably begun by Polykrates, work continued on and off for centuries, and was never finished. The complete absence of roof-tiles shows that there was never a proper roof, although a *pinakotheke* or picture-gallery was housed here under Augustus, when (probably) a Roman-style marble staircase was added along the length of the east front. By the 3rd century AD quarrying had begun. The surviving column probably served as a landmark for transport ships.

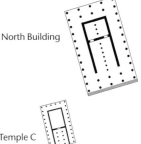

North Building

Temple C

*Samos, Heraion: abridged plan of the sanctuary showing the interrelationships between the colonnaded temples. All five are angled towards the main altar of Hera (not shown), just east of the Roman temple.*

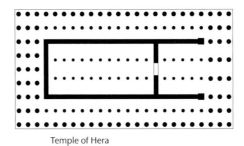

Temple of Hera

Roman temple

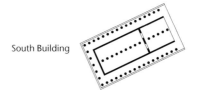

South Building

## Temple C

Known only from incomplete foundations, this temple, built about 550–500 BC, faced southeastward towards the sacred way and the main altar, with 11 by 6 columns on the long and rear sides only, a front porch and shrine. In the 1st century AD the inner building was rebuilt and Roman-style front steps added. By AD 200–50 the temple had been demolished and replaced by a non-colonnaded successor on the same orientation. The deity is unknown.

## Temple ('North Building')

Foundations of this temple face southeast overlooking the sacred way. The inner building dates around 570 BC. Later in the century a colonnade was added, with 12 by 5 Ionic columns, doubled on the short sides. The temple now measured 25.8 x 41.2 m (85 x 135 ft). The deity is unknown.

## Temple ('South Building')

Of this 6th-century BC temple in the southern part of the sanctuary only foundations survive, measuring 22.8 x 45.6 m (75 x 150 ft). It faced northeast and is restored with a colonnade on three sides only, framing a porch and shrine. Columns were limestone, the elements above probably wood. The deity is unknown. The temple was a ruin by imperial times. In late antiquity, some kind of structure was erected on top.

*This Roman-period coin of Samos shows the ancient image of Hera inside what is often identified as the Roman temple. On another view the scene combines in a non-literal way the two best-known sights of the sanctuary – the giant but unfinished temple and (kept elsewhere?) the ancient image.*

## Roman temple

About 20 m (66 ft) east of the temple of Hera, facing the altar of Hera, are remains of a small colonnaded temple of Roman date. Measuring 20.35 x 18.96 m (67 x 62 ft), it had 6 or 7 columns on the long sides and 5 at the rear. Across the front were two pairs of 2, separated by a wide central opening. Details suggest that the temple was designed to echo the appearance of its giant neighbour. No earlier than the 3rd century AD it was extended to allow the installation of a large statue base. The cult is unknown.

# Chios

Another large offshore island, Chios was settled in antiquity by Ionian Greeks. One of the wealthiest island citizen-states, Chios had a powerful fleet in

*Phanai: partial view of the foundations of the temple's east front.*

the 5th and 6th centuries BC. At its southwest end, on a low hill overlooking the sheltered bay of Phanai (mod. Kato Phana), lay the major state precinct of Apollo Phanaios. Foundations have been found here for a large Ionic temple, the second on the spot on an artificial terrace approached by a monumental staircase. Upper parts in white and blue marble show the influence of Ionic work at nearby Ephesos. The preserved column diameters (from 0.76 to 0.92 m / 2½–3 ft) indicate sizeable dimensions, and a possible temple length of around 50 m (164 ft) has been suggested. The temple had been demolished by the 6th century AD, when a three-aisled church, now ruined, was built on its foundations. The presence of lime kilns suggests the fate of much of the superstructure.

## Lesbos

The northernmost of the big Greek islands off the Turkish coast, in antiquity this prosperous island was inhabited by Greeks of the Aiolian branch. Three colonnaded temples have been found here.

### Klopedi

In the northern half of the island near modern Agia Paraskeve, remains of two colonnaded temples have been found side by side on the small plateau of Klopedi. The deity is unknown.

Of the older temple only foundations survive, measuring roughly 26.5 x 14 m (87 x 46 ft) and suggesting an outer colonnade and a three-roomed inner building. A date late in the 7th or the 6th century BC is possible.

Of the much larger temple, measuring 16.25 x 37.5 m (53 x 123 ft), mainly foundations survive

on site, indicating a long narrow shrine with an interior colonnade of wood and a masonry feature at the west end, apparently a statue-base. A colonnade of local stone, restored with 8 by 17 columns, had capitals in the so-called Aeolic style (see pp. 62–63), five of them reused in a nearby Byzantine church. Walls may have been of dressed stone. The fired clay roof decorations suggest a date in the late 6th century BC. Finds suggest that both temples were still in use in the 3rd century BC.

### Messon

In this major rural precinct on the island's central plain (mod. Mesa), the Lesbians worshipped a sacred triad of Zeus, Dionysos and the Aiolian Goddess. Extensive foundations and fragmentary upper parts survive here of a large and precisely built temple on the site of a predecessor. On marshy ground, it measured roughly 22.09 x 39.75 m (73 x 130 ft) on the top step, which slopes outward for rainwater to drain off. A creamy local stone for most of the upper parts, red conglomerate for the middle band of the entablature, and white marble for the lion's-head guttering created a polychrome effect. The plan is restored with 8 by 14 Ionic columns flanking double-width halls, porches and a shrine. The architectural ornament suggests a date around 340–320 BC, perhaps after the liberation of Lesbos from Persian rule by Alexander the Great (334–332 BC). In the 5th–7th centuries AD a church, now in ruins, was built on top of the temple, reusing many of its blocks.

*(Right) Messon: architectural drawing showing details of the Ionic columns and superstructure.*

## Olbia

A Black Sea colony, Olbia was founded around 600–550 BC on the Hypanis (Bug) river, east of modern Odessa in the Ukraine, by Greeks from Miletos. Always a frontier settlement, the colony retained a Greek identity as late as the 2nd century AD, when the Greek philosopher Dio of Prusa observed of its inhabitants that 'almost all at least know the *Iliad* by heart'.

In the walled sanctuary of Apollo Delphinios next to the agora are temple-like foundations of 3rd-century BC date, overlooking the altar, which have been linked with fragmentary Ionic columns from elsewhere on the site. A colonnaded temple can be restored with dimensions of 17 x 34–40 m (56 x 112–130 ft) and 13 by 6 columns, although this identification of the building has been challenged.

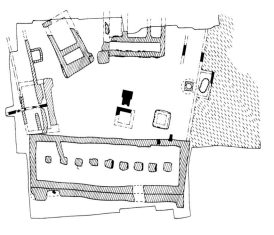

## Pantikapaion (mod. Kerch)

A Greek colony in the eastern Crimea, Pantikapaion was founded by the Milesians in the late 7th or early 6th century BC. It went on to become the chief city and port on the Kimmerian Bosporos, the straits linking the Black Sea to the Sea of Azov. Much of the ancient site lies under the modern town of Kerch. The ancient akropolis was the site of a monumental Ionic temple, probably colonnaded, from which a capital and other fragments survive. Its estimated dimensions are about 20 x 40 m (66 x 131 ft), and its date on style about 475–450 BC. The deity may have been Apollo, god of Greek colonizers.

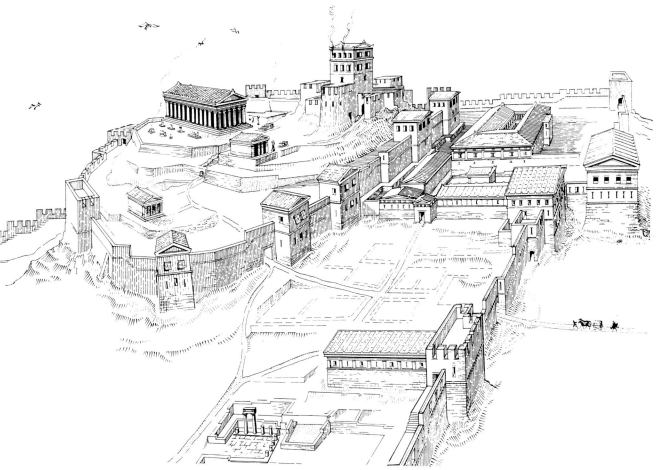

*(Left) Olbia, plan of the sanctuary of Apollo: the putative colonnaded temple is the structure partially shown in the upper centre.*

*(Below) Pantikapaion: artist's impression of the ancient Greek city, showing the Ionic temple and its commanding position.*

# Asia Minor

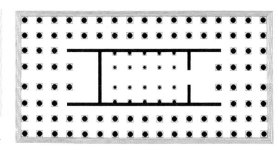

(Right) Kyzikos: reconstructed plan of the Hadrianic temple, showing its forest of Corinthian columns – three rows of 8 on the short sides and two of 17 on the long sides.

Roughly equating with modern Turkey, Asia Minor ('Lesser Asia') was the name which the ancients gave to the westernmost peninsula of continental Asia. Geographically this huge landmass divides roughly between the coastal regions with their rich plains and the upland interior. The ancient population was extremely mixed in language and culture. Early on, Greeks had settled on the west coast, giving their ethnic names to the areas of Aiolis (northwest), and Ionia (central west). A civilization developed here characterized by fruitful interaction between Greeks and their non-Greek neighbours, especially the Lydians, Karians and Lykians, among whom Greek culture had already made deep inroads long before Alexander the Great in 334/3 BC replaced the Persian king as the suzerain of much of Asia Minor.

In the following centuries Alexander's political heirs as rulers of Asia Minor, including the Attalid kings of Pergamon in northwest Turkey, encouraged Macedonian and Greek immigrants to settle in Asia Minor and founded new cities on the Greek model – one to which indigenous communities such as Lydian Sardis or Lykian Xanthos also now aspired. Roman rule from 133 BC continued this encouragement of Greek-style urbanization. As a result, in the first and second centuries AD, when Asia Minor was one of the richest zones of the Roman empire, it was this part of the Greek world, rather than 'old' Greece, which witnessed the final wave of Greek temple-building.

In what follows sites are divided into, firstly, the coastal regions and their immediate hinterland, beginning in northwest Turkey and working down the west, followed by the south, coasts; and, secondly, the interior, travelling roughly from north to south.

## THE NORTHWEST

## Kyzikos

This colony of the Ionian Greek city of Miletos was founded on the Asian coast of the Sea of Marmara (ancient Propontis). In some respects the Asian counterpart of nearby Byzantium (mod. Istanbul) on the European coast, Kyzikos became a major Greek centre thanks to excellent harbours, a strategic position on the seaway between the Aegean and

(Right) Kyzikos: half-column with rich grape-vine decoration, now in the Erdek Open Air Museum nearby.

Black Seas, and a rich hinterland. In Roman times, when Kyzikos belonged to the province of Asia, the city was famed for its public monuments, above all its Corinthian temple in white marble from the island of Prokonnesos in the Propontis, likened by the orator Aelius Aristides (AD 166) to a beacon or signal fire for seafarers (see p. 67). A great mound of debris near the beach now marks the site. Founded by Hadrian in AD 123, the temple was probably dedicated in 138. The dimensions, estimated at 106.56 x 48.84 m (350 x 160 ft), rivalled Didyma or Ephesos, and suggest a special place for the temple in Hadrian's schemes (see p. 40). The plan is tentatively restored with 8 by 17 Corinthian columns, doubled on the long sides and tripled on the short sides. A complex of vaulted rooms in the foundations, to which an internal staircase gave access from the temple above, probably served ritual as well as structural functions; Aristides called them 'underground walks'. The rich decor included half-columns with vine-leaf decoration and a figured frieze of Greeks battling barbarians. The temple was still intact in the 6th century, when it was rated as a Wonder of the World by the Byzantine writer John Malalas. He also records an inscribed bust on the apex of the main facade

depicting Hadrian, who may originally have been worshipped inside. In 1431 the Renaissance antiquary Cyriaco of Ancona (see p. 43) saw statues in the front gable, including a Zeus, probably the temple's chief deity. Quarrying had already begun to take its toll.

## Ilion

Ilion was one of the Greek cities of Aiolis. This region in northwest Asia Minor owed its name to Aiolian Greek immigrants who arrived here from mainland Greece via Lesbos, where the Aiolian Goddess was worshipped at Messon (see p. 186). Ilion occupied a commanding site overlooking the Aegean entrance to the Dardanelles, and was identified with Homer's Troy. On top of the akropolis (modern Hissarlik), the temple of Ilian Athena has more or less disappeared thanks to the combined efforts of stone-robbers and, from 1872, excavators of the earlier levels below. The temple was marble, with 6 by 12 Doric columns, and measured 32.39 x 15.13 m (106 x 50 ft) on the top step, with porches and a shrine lined with Doric half-columns. The east facade carried an inscribed dedication by Augustus (after 27 BC), who rebuilt the temple after a Roman general had destroyed its predecessor (85 BC). Julian, the last openly pagan emperor, was shown round the temple in AD 354 by a sympathetic local bishop who protected it from Christian zealots:

'"Let us head", I said, "for the precinct of Athena Ilias." He took me there very eagerly, opened the temple, and, as if I were a witness in a court case, showed me all the cult statues perfectly intact. He did this with none of the usual carry-on of those miscreants [i.e., Christians], tracing on their brow the sign of impiety, or hissing.' (Julian, *Letter* 79)

## Neandria

Some 13 km (8 miles) from the coast, on the upper slopes of Mount Cigri, this Aiolian Greek city was eventually subsumed into nearby Alexandria Troas (late 4th century BC). On a site inside the walls commanding panoramic views out to sea are remains of a 6th-century temple with foundations measuring 25.71 x 12.87 m (85 x 42 ft). The first column-capital of the so-called Aeolic style (see pp. 62–63), with vertically rising spirals, was discovered here in 1882. The one-room shrine has a paved platform at the far end, perhaps an offerings-base or hearth, and bases for a central row of columns. The existence of two sets of columns, however, may reflect an outer colonnade of 7 by 12 columns as well. The altar, oddly, was placed behind the temple. Above the columns there was a wooden superstructure with fired clay roofing, dated on style around 575–550 BC. An ash-layer shows that the temple was burnt down, thereafter serving as a quarry.

*Kyzikos: Cyriaco's drawing showing elements of the temple, including Corinthian capitals, the giant carved doorway, labelled '40 feet' high, and a Greek inscription, now lost: 'With all Asia helping, noble Aristenetos raised me up from the foundations, [?] a great wonder.' This extremely rare naming of the architect suggests the prestige attached to this project.*

*Neandria: reconstruction of the interior, showing the divine image, offerings, and the 'Aeolic' colonnade.*

## Chrysa

This coastal locale lay in the territory of Alexandria Troas, a Greek city founded in 310 BC on the coast south of Ilion by the amalgamation of a number of older Aiolian Greek cities in the vicinity. Chrysa was home to an important rural sanctuary of Sminthian Apollo on sloping ground below modern Gülpinar. Only lower parts of the marble temple survive in situ. Measuring 41.65 x 23.2 m (137 x 76 ft) on the top step, it is restored with 8 by 14 narrow Ionic columns, double-width halls, a shrine and porches, shallow to the rear, deep at the front. In the front gable were door-like openings as at Ephesos (p. 85). The decoration included an exterior frieze and sculptured drums (columnae caelatae) below the column capitals (pp. 200–1), some with figures, others with garlands and ox skulls. On style the carved ornament dates to the mid-2nd century BC.

## Assos

This Aiolian Greek city occupied an akropolis on the south coast of the Troad, the ancient name for the geographical unit formed by the mountainous northwest corner of Asia Minor, to which Ilion and Chrysa also belonged. The temple of Athena at Assos was one of only four colonnaded Doric temples known so far in Asia Minor. Marked now by reerected columns, the site occupies a natural platform on the summit of the akropolis and commands superb views over the ancient city below and out to sea. Measuring 14.03 x 30.31 m (46 x 99 ft) on the top step, the temple was built in a brittle local stone (andesite) with 6 by 13 columns, a long and narrow shrine, and a front porch with an intercolumnar grille and cuttings for bases and inscr-

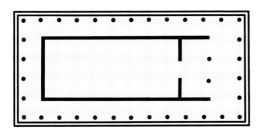

(Above) Temple of (?) Athena, Assos: general view showing reerected columns and the commanding view out to sea.

(Left) Plan of the temple of (?) Athena, Assos. A sculptured frieze that ran around the outside of the columns is now in the Archaeological Museum at Istanbul.

iptions. As well as painted decoration the front metopes were carved and, uniquely for a Doric building, a continuous frieze ran above the outside columns, showing the Herakles myth and other scenes. The deity was probably Athena, the city's patron deity.

## Pergamon

This mighty natural citadel lay some 24 km (15 miles) from the Aegean coast opposite Lesbos, dominating the fertile plain of the River Kaïkos in a region of indigenous settlement which the Greeks called Mysia. By the later 4th century BC the Pergamene community had reinvented itself as a Greek city, one which in the 3rd–2nd centuries BC saw spectacular redevelopment as a royal capital under the kings of the Attalid dynasty. Their kingdom, bequeathed to Rome in 133 BC, went on to

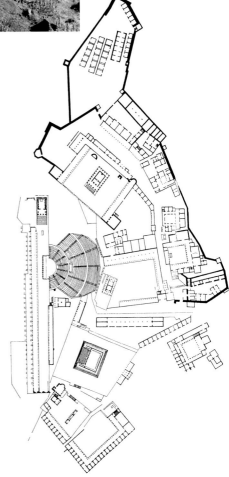

(Right) Pergamon, plan of the akropolis in the 2nd century AD: the temple and colonnades of the sanctuary of Athena are immediately above the theatre.

191

Pergamon: general view of
the temple of Athena Polias,
looking out onto the plain of
the River Kaïkos.

form the nucleus of the province of Asia, with Pergamon one of its three chief cities.

### Temple of Athena Polias

On a manmade terrace near the akropolis summit are the poorly preserved remains of the limestone temple of Athena Polias, the city's patron deity, on a north–south orientation. Measuring 12.27 x 21.77 m (40 x 71 ft) on the top step, the building is restored with 6 by 10 Doric columns, unfluted and unfinished, and perhaps a double shrine. On various grounds a date in the late 4th century BC is likely.

### Temple of Jupiter and Trajan

Crowning the highest level of the akropolis, this temple could not have been more conspicuously placed. Identification with the 'temple of Friendly Jupiter and Trajan' known from a Latin inscription is confirmed by finds of imperial statues. Built out on massive substructures faced by a retaining wall some 23 m (75 ft) high, the temple was set in the middle of an open court framed by colonnades. In design the marble temple shows Roman influence,

(Right) Pergamon: restored
plan of the temple of Jupiter
and Trajan, Pergamon.

(Far right) General view of
the temple of Jupiter and
Trajan, Pergamon.

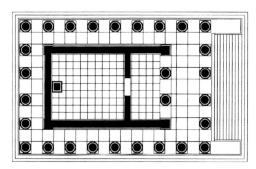

192

set on a marble-clad podium with a frontal staircase flanked by parapets. Measuring about 26.75 x 17.8 m (88 x 58 ft), it had 6 by 9 Corinthian columns, a shrine and a front porch. Probably finished by Hadrian (AD 117–38), at the end of antiquity it became a quarry for lime-burners.

## Aigai

Small and relatively unimportant, this Aiolian Greek city some 30 km (20 miles) south of Pergamon was laid out on the natural terraces of a lofty akropolis, a pale imitation of its famous neighbour. Its Ionic temple of Oracular Apollo in the brown local stone was sited on the upper terrace of the akropolis, where the door frame still stands. With six columns on the short sides, a front porch led into the shrine, and there was an outer frieze of the standard ox skulls, garlands and libation bowls. An inscription over the front columns dates the temple to 46 BC and describes it as a thanks offering in gratitude to the Roman governor, Publius Servilius Isauricus, who had 'saved' the city.

## IONIA, LYDIA AND THE MAEANDER VALLEY

*(Above) Aigai: restored facade of the temple of Oracular Apollo. An inscription mentioning the Roman governor Publius Servilius Isauricus (see text) ran above the columns on the epistyle (see p. 63).*

### Sardis

Connected to the coast by the rich valley of the River Hermos, Sardis lies 150 km (90 miles) inland in the heartland of the ancient Lydians, whose metropolis it was. As capital of the Lydian kings (7th–6th centuries BC), Sardis was one of the great cities of western Asia Minor. It remained a major centre of the successive powers controlling Lydia, including the Persians, the Seleukids (who sponsored the adoption of Greek civic institutions after 213 BC), and finally Rome. Artemis, here a Greek deity with Asiatic roots, was the patron goddess of the Sardians, who honoured her with one of the most ambitious Greek-style temples in Asia Minor.

#### Temple of Artemis

Two columns have been reerected to their full height from this marble temple, the third largest in Asia Minor, lying outside the city proper on the western slope of the akropolis, overlooking a major ancient route. The temple was unfinished, although construction may have dragged on into the mid-2nd century AD. Measuring 45.73 x 99.16 m (150 x 325 ft) on the (hypothetical) top step, its building history is controversial and complex. The inner building was begun first, probably around 300–250 BC, with upward curvature and facing west like the Artemision at Ephesos towards an older altar. Inside the front porch a Greek document was inscribed about 200 BC recording the conveyancing to Artemis of lands belonging to a certain Mnesimachos, a colonial magnate of the vicinity; coins give the same date for the massive base for a divine statue. In a second phase (about 200–150 BC?), an exterior colonnade of

*(Above) Sardis, temple of Artemis showing the west (main) front, its colonnade partly restored.*

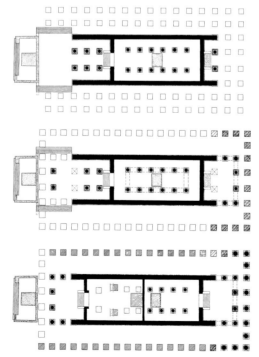

*(Right) Sardis, temple of Artemis: plan of the different phases after Hans Gruben, in chronological order from top to bottom: respectively 3rd century BC, early 2nd century BC, and mid-2nd century AD.*

8 by 20 Ionic columns, with double-width halls, was begun. Either now, according to American excavators, or only much later, in the mid-2nd century AD (in the view of Hans Gruben), a monumental door was opened up to the east, and a cross-wall inserted to create a double shrine. Inside, remains of several colossal statues have been found, including heads of the emperor Antoninus Pius (AD 138–61) and his empress, Faustina, whose joint cult must have been installed here. Marble tiles show that part of the temple was roofed. A major repair, perhaps after earthquake damage, is revealed by an inscribed column base of Roman date declaring 'of all [the columns] I am the first to rise again'. Around AD 600 blocks were broken up for lime kilns in the vicinity. Landslides went on to bury most of what was left.

## Roman temple

At the foot of the akropolis, overlooking the centre of Roman Sardis, the remains indicate a marble Corinthian or Ionic temple with double-width halls and a date in the 1st century AD. A (?) gable block inscribed with the name 'Adramyttion', a Greek city some 200 km (124 miles) away, suggests a provincial cult of the emperors, with the cities of provincial Asia depicted in the gable.

## Smyrna (mod. Izmir)

A harbour-city like its modern successor Izmir, ancient Smyrna was the northernmost of the string of Greek settlements making up Ionia, as the Greeks called the central stretch of Asia Minor's west coast. Like other Ionian cities, it claimed a foundation in the hoary past by Ionian Greek colonists from the mainland. The original settlement, nowadays referred to as Old Smyrna, was destroyed by the Lydians around 580 BC. The city was refounded by the Macedonians (late 4th century BC) on a new site nearby. The location at the head of a deep gulf ensured the city great prosperity throughout antiquity. Both the temples described below bear witness to Smyrna's importance in different phases of antiquity.

### Temple of Athena

This important all-stone temple was an ambitious project begun around 610 BC by the people of Old Smyrna, and was still unfinished at the time of the Lydian sack. The foundations survive, but the superstructure of white stone was entirely dismantled in ancient times and is now known only from fragments. The temple was meant to replace a much smaller and non-colonnaded predecessor, itself the second temple on the site. Its intended plan has been restored with a colonnade of 15 x 11 columns and an inner building comprising a porch with columns fronting a single room. The temple seems to have been planned in stages, with the west and south colonnades begun first. Work on the other two colonnades seems to have been deferred, the intention being first to free up space for them by moving the city wall. The columns, apparently of varying diameter, were made up of drums, faceted rather than fluted; their luxuriant carved capitals were in the 'Aeolic' style (see pp. 62–63). Finds from the sanctuary point to Old Smyrna's close ties with Egypt – the probable source of the technology which made this pioneering structure possible at such an early date.

### Hadrianic Temple

Now robbed and built over, remains of a huge Corinthian temple once stood on the hill called Dierman Tepe inside the walls of the refounded city. This seems to have been the 'temple that can be seen from afar, the one on the height that seems to challenge Mimas' – ancient name for the modern Kara Burun headland to the west (the Greek writer Philostratos, 3rd century AD). Funded by Hadrian,

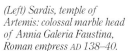

*(Left) Sardis, temple of Artemis: colossal marble head of Annia Galeria Faustina, Roman empress AD 138–40.*

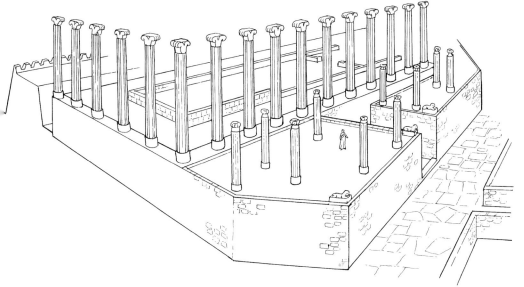

*Smyrna, reconstruction of the unfinished 'Aeolic' temple of Athena, showing isolated dedications in the foreground and two completed colonnades to the rear.*

the marble temple is restored with 10 by 23 columns, the lower column drums about 1.8m (6 ft) in diameter – as big as those of the Olympieion in Athens (see pp. 134–35). The cult would fit that of Zeus 'dwelling on the height' ('Akraios'), who is depicted on Roman Smyrna's coins. As in Athens, Hadrian was probably worshipped here (see p. 40).

## Teos

This Ionian Greek city occupied a headland site 40 km (25 miles) southwest of Smyrna and claimed to be Dionysos' birthplace. His famous temple inside the walls was held up by the Roman writer Vitruvius as an example of the 'beautiful-columned' proportions of its 3rd-century BC architect Hermogenes (see pp. 38, 64), who described it in a book. The remains are those of a thorough-going restoration, the second of at least two in Roman times, by the emperor Hadrian (see p. 40), whose name appeared in large letters on the east facade. Built on sloping ground, the temple sat on a rock-cut podium and then a high platform of six steps, with an additional seven on the east side. Measuring about 19 x 25 m (62 x 82 ft) on the top step, its Hadrianic version is restored with 6 by 11 Ionic columns, a shrine and porches veneered in white marble. An outer frieze showing a company of Dionysiac wor-

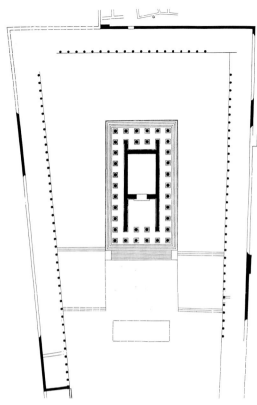

*(Right) Teos, plan of the temple of Dionysos showing the surrounding colonnade and rock-cut terracing at the east (front) end, presumably used by spectators or participants in religious rituals (see pp. 84–85 for ceremonies performed at the opening and closing of the doors of this temple).*

*(Below) General view of the temple of Dionysos and surrounding sanctuary.*

shippers belonged to the original building and was now restored and partly recarved. Many parts of the original building, evidently destroyed by earthquake, were reused in Roman work on the sanctuary and share ornamental details with Hermogenes' temple at Magnesia-on-the-Maeander (see pp. 201–2). A dossier of official documents from 'the pilaster [*parastas*] of the temple of Dionysos', the earliest dating from (probably) about 204/3 BC, helps to date Hermogenes by showing that at this time work on the original temple was well under way.

## Klaros

This rural sanctuary in a narrow wooded valley 50 km (34 miles) south of Izmir and some 2 km (1¼ miles) from the sea, belonged to the nearby Ionian Greek city of Kolophon. Its oracle of Apollo was celebrated, above all in the 2nd century AD, when it was consulted by Greek cities far and wide. The prestige of the cult was reflected in its royal and imperial connections.

### Temple of Apollo

This interesting temple rested on a platform of five finely dressed steps, their vertical joints decorated with bronze appliqués of sheep's ankle-bones (astragals), symbolizing Apolline prophecy. It was 26 m (85 ft) long, with 11 by 6 Doric columns in the white marble used for all the upper parts, with a front porch and shrine for a colossal statue group in marble, 8 m (26 ft) high, depicting Apollo, Artemis and Leto. Stratigraphy shows that the temple was started in the 3rd century BC, with work well advanced when the base for a statue of the future

Antiochos IV was set up in the northeast colonnade (209–193 BC). An inscription over the main facade identifies Hadrian as the temple's final dedicator (AD 135–38), although according to Pausanias (mid-2nd century AD) the temple was still unfinished. Many official inscriptions are carved on the terminals of the porch's side walls, the flutes of the front columns and the vertical faces of the front steps, including some 220 lists (2nd–3rd centuries AD) of delegates sent by Greek cities to consult the oracle.

From the front porch two staircases in a sombre blue marble lead down into a network of cramped tunnels of carefully jointed masonry, wide enough for one person only, leading to a linked pair of vaulted crypts under the floor of the shrine, the

*(Below) Klaros: a sandal-clad foot from the colossal statue-group of Apollo, Artemis and their mother Leto inside the shrine.*

*(Bottom) General view of the two temples during the French excavations, begun in the 1950s.*

## Ephesos

Founded by Ionian Greeks at the mouth (since silted up) of the Kayster river, north of modern Kusadası, this great harbour city flourished in the 7th–6th centuries BC and again from the 4th century BC. The ancient city developed at the foot and on the lower slopes of Mount Koressos and the adjacent Mount Pion, and the remains here, partly restored, are the most impressive of all the Greek cities of Asia Minor. The same sadly cannot be said for the sanctuary of Artemis, adored patron deity of the Ephesians, whose magnificent temple here was an ancient Wonder of the World, but has now all but vanished.

### Temple of Artemis (Artemision)

The sanctuary of Artemis (Artemision) lay outside the city walls on the flood-plain between Mount Pion and what is now the Ayasuluk hill with its medieval fortress. Greek Artemis here, as usually in Asia Minor, had indigenous roots way back in the period before the 8th century BC when Greek historical records began. The sanctuary was famous

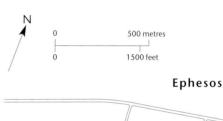

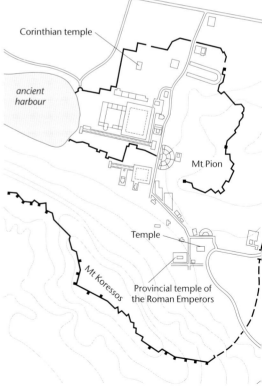

innermost housing a spring, source of the water which nowadays floods the tunnels. This was the seat of the oracle, since ancient writers refer to the prophet descending into the crypt and drinking from the sacred spring for inspiration.

In late antiquity the temple was deliberately demolished for its marble by sapping the columns. Many blocks were taken to the coast nearby, although others still lie where they fell. Gradually the ruins were covered by alluvium.

### Ionic temple of Artemis

Close by, more or less parallel to the north, a small colonnaded temple of Artemis was begun in the 3rd century BC, with further work in the 2nd century AD. It had a shrine and front porch. The upper parts have more or less disappeared, and it remains unclear whether the temple was ever finished.

enough for Alexander the Great to offer to pay for a new temple (and the Ephesians proud enough to turn this offer down: see pp. 36–37). Centuries later, just before the apostle Paul's first visit (AD 52), a Roman governor could describe the Artemision as 'the jewel of the whole province because of the size of the work, the antiquity of the goddess' worship and the abundance of her revenues.'

On site, foundations and a single column, re-erected in 1973, constitute the disappointing remnants of the latest of three colonnaded temples on this hallowed site, replacing a 6th-century BC predecessor burnt down in 356 BC (see p. 28). The

architects included Paionios, who also worked at Didyma (see pp. 204–7). With the same westward orientation, the new temple was even larger, measuring about 51.44 x 111.48 m (169 x 366 ft) on the top step, and stood on a higher platform, of ten steps, as protection against flooding (see the artist's impression, p. 35). The temple's size was one source of wonder. The 36 'sculptured drums' (Pliny the Elder) were another. These belonged to a forest of Ionic columns, some inscribed with the names of male and female donors. Double rows of 21 flanked the long sides, a double row of 9 the rear, and three rows of 8 the front. Nearly all stood on high plinths

*(Right) Ephesos, temple of Artemis: general view with the reconstructed column.*

Temple of Artemis

modern roads

# A mystery solved

For a long time it was debated whether Pliny the Elder's 'sculptured drums' from the temple of Artemis at Ephesos were placed at the top or bottom of columns. Archaeologist Burkhardt Wesenberg has now reexamined this well-preserved example in the British Museum (right) and shown conclusively that it formed the bottom drum of a column. It rested in turn on a square plinth carved in high relief, as in the reconstruction (far right).

on the site of the older ones. Ephesian coins showing three openings in the main gable, liturgical rather than structural (see p. 85). The deep front porch, with two rows of columns framing a processional way, also served as a treasury and meeting place for city councillors. Through the great door, instead of a roofed chamber, steps led down into an open court called the Parthenon, housing a small shrine for a divine statue, presumably the destination of the procession of 'bearers of the dinner'. The rear porch, with its own scribe, was also a treasury or archive. Plundered by Goths in AD 263, the temple's final demise came with the visit (401) of bishop John Chrysostom of Constantinople, hailed as its 'overthrower'. The zeal with which the locals joined in the assault on their erstwhile goddess is suggested by an Ephesian inscription of the time in which one Demeas records his destruction of 'a deceitful image of demonic Artemis'. Dismantlement of the temple now began, with blocks found in the adjacent church of St John (c. 390–420). A church was built inside the court in the 6th century, with signs of later repairs. Eventually the remains were buried by river silt.

*(Below) Silver coin of Ephesos (AD 117) showing the famous image of the goddess and the three door-like openings in the front gable (see p. 35).*

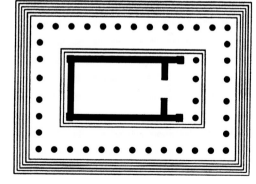

## Provincial temple of the Roman emperors

West of the 'Upper Agora' an artificial terrace, some 100 x 50 m (330 x 160 ft), supports the remnants of the temple described in inscriptions as 'the temple of the emperors in Ephesos, common to [the province of] Asia', where Domitian (AD 82–96) was the first to be worshipped and to whom (or possibly Titus, his brother) belongs the marble head and lower left arm of a statue, four-times lifesize, found in the substructure. The temple, with foundations measuring 33.82 x 23.97 m (111 x 79 ft), had 8 by 13 columns, double-width halls, shrine and front porch. The structure was robbed to the foundations in late antiquity.

## Corinthian temple

Between the akropolis and the ancient harbour are the scant remains of a grand precinct scarcely smaller than the Artemision, with a major Corinthian temple in the centre, now reduced to foundations measuring 85 x 87 m (279 x 285 ft). The upper parts were marble with an estimated total of 74 columns. Probably this was the provincial 'temple of the deified Hadrian' of an Ephesian

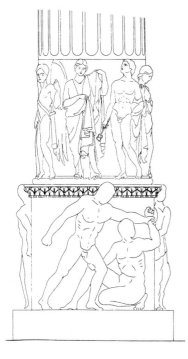

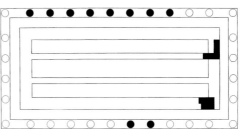

*(Left) Nysa: restored plan incorporating the scanty remnants in situ of the Doric temple in the extra-urban sanctuary of Pluto at ancient Acheraka.*

(improbably) to descend from Spartan colonists. In the 1st century BC their city was famous as an educational centre. Unusually the Nysans worshipped Pluto, Greek god of the underworld, whose famous rural sanctuary (the Ploutonion) was in ancient Acheraka (mod. Salavatlı), 2 km (1¼ miles) southwest of the ancient urban centre. The scant remains of the temple of Pluto and Kore here, which unusually faced north, are restored with 6 by 12 (or more) Doric columns and dimensions of roughly 34.6 x 17 m (114 x 56 ft) on the top step. Official documents were inscribed in 1 BC on blocks from the temple (see pp. 94–95), which evidently is early Roman in date. It was later converted into a church.

## Magnesia-on-the-Maeander

South of Ephesos, the valley of the River Maeander cuts a great swathe of fertile land running northeastwards from the Aegean coast just below Samos. The scant ruins of Magnesia-on-the-Maeander lie inland to the north of the river. This Ionian Greek city had White-browed Artemis (Leukophryene) as its patron deity. Her sanctuary achieved a far-flung renown after an epiphany or 'manifestation' of the goddess in 221/220 BC, recorded in local inscriptions. Designed by the architect Hermogenes (pp. 38, 64), who wrote a book about it, her famous temple was cited by Vitruvius as a classic exemplar of the *pseudodipteros*, that is, with double-width halls. Now little more than a mass of fallen blocks, the west-facing marble temple stood in the ancient city centre on low ground near the river, overlying a predecessor on a high platform of seven steps to avoid flooding. Measuring roughly 31.6 x 57.89 m (104 x 190 ft) on the top step, the elongated plan is restored with a colonnade of 8 by 15 Ionic columns

inscription. About AD 400 it was destroyed, apparently by Christian zealots. Lime kilns were set up on the spot, and the foundations were quarried for their metal clamps.

### Temple

On the middle axis of the so-called Upper Agora a set of foundations belongs to a temple measuring roughly 20.28 x 12.58 m 67 x 41 ft) on the top step, with 6 by 10 columns, a shrine and front porch, dated by sherds to the second half of the 1st century BC. Augustus is a strong candidate for the deity.

## Nysa

Nysa was a Greek city further up the Maeander valley, some 37 km (27 miles) east of modern Aydin at the foot of ancient Mt Messogis, where its plentiful remains are worth visiting. The Nysans claimed

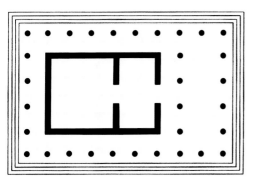

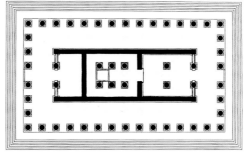

*(Left to right) Plans of the provincial temple of the Roman emperors, the temple in the Upper Agora (both at Ephesos), and the temple of Artemis, Magnesia-on-the-Maeander.*

Magnesia-on-the-Maeander: reassembled section of the entablature of the Ionic temple of Artemis, including sections of the sculptured frieze and guttering.

brated builder of the temple of Minerva [Roman Athena] at Priene', who wrote a book on this temple of the city's patroness, Athena Polias. On a man-made terrace in the city centre with a commanding view over the valley below, later blocked by a flanking portico, the marble temple measures 19.53 x

(Above) Priene, temple of Athena Polias: plan. Note the grooves from the opening and closing of the great double doors into the shrine and the bases for statues found in situ in the front porch.

enclosing an inner building made up of porches at either end flanking the shrine, where remains of the statue-base have been found; the front porch was noticeably deep. An outer frieze showed Greeks battling amazons, and the front gable had three door-like openings (see p. 35). An inscription records the great ceremonies marking the installation of the statue of Artemis in the shrine, called 'Parthenon' or 'Room of the Maiden'. With Hermogenes now dated to the later 3rd century BC (see pp. 196–97), the temple was probably commissioned after the goddess' epiphany, with work continuing into the period 150–125 BC, to which the latest carved ornament belongs. In the 1st century BC the side-intercolumniations in both porches were walled up to a certain height with masonry screens, as if to shield the interiors from outside view.

## Priene

This small Ionian Greek city was refounded in the 4th century BC on the lower slopes of Mount Mykale at the mouth of the Maeander. It was one of several Greek cities in the vicinity to be left high and dry in later antiquity by the progressive silting up of the river mouth. The well preserved site, delightfully set among pine trees, commands spectacular views of the intensively cultivated river valley below and to the south. Vitruvius records 'Pythius, the cele-

(Right) Priene, temple of Athena Polias: general view with some reerected columns. For a translation of the inscription in the foreground, see p. 99.

37.17 m (64 x 122 ft) on the top step, with upward curvature on all four sides. It was laid out on a mathematical grid of squares with 6 by 11 Ionic columns with outward bulging, porches and shrine. Exterior decoration, as well as carvings and red, blue and gold paintwork, included the high-up lids of the ceiling coffers in the halls, showing the battle of gods and giants in relief (see pp. 66–67). In the shrine, approached by steps, was found the statue base for a larger-than-lifesize adaptation of the Parthenon Athena in marble and wood, dated around 158 BC by coins from inside the base, with setting marks for a screen. During the 3rd–2nd centuries BC an 'archive' of official documents about Priene's affairs was inscribed on the walls of the temple (see pp. 94–95), beginning on the north pilaster or wall-terminal of the front porch after the dedication by king Alexander (see pp. 36–37) and spreading onto the wall of the north hall. An inscription on the main facade records the addition of a cult of Augustus (after 27 BC), to which other emperors were added (see p. 99). The east end seems to have been standing to ceiling height by the time of Alexander (334–323 BC), officially the donor, but the temple may not have been finished before the 2nd century BC. At some point the rear porch was converted into a closed room with a door from the west colonnade, perhaps to guard the 400 silver talents which the Kappadokian prince Orophernes deposited in the sanctuary (see p. 93). An ash-layer shows that the temple's timbers were destroyed by a fire, probably not before the late 3rd century AD. An earthquake brought down the stonework soon after, sealing the destruction layer.

# Myous

South of the River Maeander in its present bed, this small Ionian Greek city was founded on a coastal site and declined when the inlet of the sea on which it lay was blocked up by alluvium from the river. On the northern slope of a hill which in antiquity jutted into the sea are two manmade terraces, one above the other, with traces of two colonnaded marble temples. The upper temple, almost completely disappeared, was the more recent, never finished. The lower temple was smaller; some upper parts are preserved. Dating to the 6th century BC, it had six Ionic columns across the front and a frieze showing a wagon race. With the decline of Myous, stone from both was shipped to Miletos for reuse, including an inscribed block with official documents (3rd–2nd centuries BC) from the 'wall-terminal of the temple of Apollo Termintheus'. As for the other deity, Pausanias (2nd century AD) gives a clue: 'The people from Myous withdrew to Miletos with everything they could carry, including the images of the gods; in my time there was nothing left at Myous but a white stone temple of Dionysos'.

# Miletos

Miletos was one the greatest Ionian centres, the centre of the first flowering of Greek philosophy and science. Hard to credit now, it owed its prosperity to the splendid harbours of its promontory site in what once was the delta of the ancient River Maeander. Silting in later antiquity has left the extensive ruins over 14 km (8 miles) from the Aegean. The city's 'younger' temple of Athena, of which scrappy remnants have been found, dates to the later 6th century BC and is restored with dimensions on the top step of 17.2 x 28.2 m (56 x 93 ft), 8 by 14 Ionic columns, doubled on the front, and double-width halls and an extra colonnade across the front. The thorough quarrying of the site dates from the Persian sack of Miletos in 494 BC.

# Didyma

Didyma was the seat of the most famous of Apollo's oracles after Delphi, and its temple takes the palm as Turkey's most awe-inspiring classical ruin. The sanctuary here was usually controlled by the Milesians. It lay some 24 km (15 miles) south of Miletos itself, and the two were connected by a sacred way, eventually paved. The oracle enjoyed a final flowering in the 2nd–3rd centuries AD.

Famed for its huge size, Apollo's temple was the third on the site, replacing a predecessor damaged by the Persians. It shared an architect, Paionios, with the Artemision at Ephesos (see p. 198). Work

(Right) Didyma: general view of the temple of Apollo looking towards the main facade.

was under way by 300/299 BC, aided by gifts from Seleukos I, but the temple was unfinished, never receiving gables. In the mid-1st century BC a brother of Cleopatra gave ivory for 'the great door', and the style of the carved decoration reveals a last major effort in the early 2nd century AD. The material is

(Right) Didyma: a richly carved Ionic column-base from the temple of Apollo.

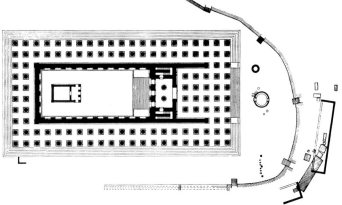

(Right) Didyma, plan of the temple, showing the circular altar outside to the east.

Milesian marble, brought by ship to the nearby harbour of Panormos. Measuring 51.13 x 109.34 m (168 x 359 ft) on the top of seven steps, the temple sat on a platform with gentle upward curvature on all sides. It had a double colonnade of 11 by 21 Ionic columns with richly carved capitals and bases of varied styles and dates. The inner building is unique to Didyma, since its lofty walls framed, not a roofed shrine, but a colossal open court, the *adyton* ('not to be entered') of inscriptions. Other features

also reflect the operation of the oracle, little understood. There was a front porch (*prodomos*), with three rows of four columns. In place of the usual door into the shrine rose a huge portal 14 m (46 ft) high, resting on an insurmountable threshold just under 1.5 m (5 ft) high. Epiphanies may have been staged in this door, which clearly had a religious significance. On either side, dim descending passages (p. 39) provide the sole access from the porch down into the walled court. On any view, the ritual sought to distance the consultant from the source of prophecy in the court. Here, to the rear, are the foundations for a small marble building with colonnaded front of uncertain function: on one view a shrine for a sacred statue, on another the house for the sacred spring from which, as texts show, the prophetess drew inspiration. Across the east end, between the two passages, runs a majestic staircase (*anabasis*) giving access through three doors to a chamber with the great portal on its far side and side doors to a pair of stairwells (*labyrinthoi*). Their destination is uncertain (an attic?), but their decoration and monumentality indicate liturgical activity at a higher level.

In AD 262/63 the threat of Gothic attack prompted the fortification of the inner building by walling up the porch's front row of columns. Inscribed poems from the *adyton* show that fugitives now squatted in the open court. A bishop's church arose there in the 5th or 6th century AD, the first of two. An earthquake in 1493 left only three columns still erect. In 1905 the site was a mound of collapsed blocks 8–10 m (26–33 ft) high, crowned by a windmill.

## KARIA AND THE SOUTHWEST

## *Aphrodisias*

The impressive ruins of this inland city, where excavations continue to produce major surprises, are sited in a river valley which branches off the south side of the Maeander plain beyond ancient Nysa. The Aphrodisians were Karians, an indigenous people who inhabited the upland districts of southwest Asia Minor (known to the Greeks as Karia) and on whom Greek culture had made a major impact early on. Aphrodisias was founded probably in the 2nd century BC and flourished under Roman control, when the city was home to flourishing local schools of Greek sculpture and philosophy.

The chief deity was Aphrodite, whose marble temple stood in a colonnaded court of later date. Fourteen columns still stand. Measuring about 18.45 x 31 m (61 x 102 ft) on the top of five steps, it had 8 by 13 Ionic columns, double-width halls, a shrine unusually fronted by an antechamber (*prodomos* in an inscription) and a front porch. An inscription on the lintel of the main door records the local donor of the first phase, some time in the 30s or 20s BC, as the priest of Aphrodite, Gaius Julius Zoilus, an imperial freedman or ex-slave. The colonnades were a later addition, with individual columns naming married couples who paid for them. The temple was converted into an imposing cathedral-church, perhaps in the 5th century, by

*Aphrodisias: general view of the site of the temple of Aphrodite, where the surviving columns owe their good state of preservation to the conversion of the temple into a church, enjoying a longer life as a place of worship than its pagan predecessor.*

*Aphrodisias: the rich priest Gaius Julius Zoilus, who funded the first phase of the temple of Aphrodite, is shown in this relief (centre) from his local tomb-monument.*

so-called agora was known to Vitruvius, who names one Menesthenes as the architect (see p. 107). Measuring 34.52 x 21.66 m (113 x 71 ft) on the top step, it is restored with 8 by 13 Ionic columns, double-width halls, a front porch, shrine and perhaps a rear porch. A date of about 75–50 BC is suggested by the carving. A colonnaded court surrounding the temple was added probably under Claudius. After complete demolition the temple site was partly overlaid by an early Christian baptistery.

### Doric temple

The lower parts have come to light of a second temple at Alabanda, measuring 27.7 x 15.18 m (91 x 50 ft) on the only step, with 6 by 11 Doric columns, a porch and shrine with a marble threshold, the material otherwise being 'granite' coated with plaster which simulates masonry. A coin-hoard of 280–260 BC from the shrine indicates the date. The deity is unknown.

stripping out the inner building, extending the long colonnades with columns relocated from the short colonnades, and enclosing this three-aisled space with walls. A major renovation took place in the 10th–11th centuries.

## Euromos

This old Karian city (modern Ayaklı) to the southwest of Alabanda was an important regional centre. Its chief claim to fame is its well preserved Corinthian temple, now standing alone among olive trees (see p. 229). Dedicated to the local Zeus Lepsynos and dating to the 2nd century AD, the partly restored temple has 16 Corinthian columns still standing and lies outside the city gates on a slight

## Alabanda

The site of this important Greek city in the Karian interior, on roughly the same latitude as Myous, lay in a side valley branching south from the Maeander plain opposite modern Aydin. In the 1st century BC the inhabitants claimed a Spartan origin (in rivalry with Nysa's, and just as improbable), and were renowned for their luxury. The ruins lie scattered in picturesque fashion among the houses of the modern village. The patron deity of the Alabandans was Apollo Isotimos ('Equal in Honour'), whose sanctuary was an official asylum for fugitives. His west-facing marble temple near the

*(Right) Euromos: the temple of Zeus, showing some of the inscribed panels naming local worthies who paid for individual columns.*

*Alabanda: restored plan of the temple of Apollo Isotimos ('Equal in Honour') at Alabanda in the Karia region, southwest Turkey.*

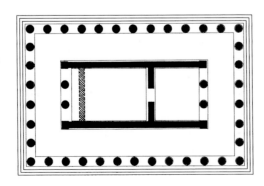

elevation overlooking the surrounding plain. A fragmentary inscription identifies the deity, important enough to have official documents displayed here. Measuring 27.45 x 14.37 m (90 x 47 ft) on the top step, the temple had 6 by 11 columns, doubled across the front, two porches and a shrine with a statue-base in a marble statue-house against the back wall. Panels record that seven columns were donated by a local official, Leon Kointos, another five by the official physician (*archiatros*) and his daughter. Unfluted drums show that the temple was never finished. An ancient fire brought down the wooden roof. Earthquakes have wreaked further damage.

## Labraynda

This major Karian sanctuary of Zeus Labrayndos is reached by a difficult but rewarding journey into pine-clad hills where it sprawls over man-made terraces on a steep hillside in remote and beautiful countryside. In the 4th century BC Labraynda fell under the dominion of the Karian dynast Maussolos and his family. Normally it was dependent on Mylasa 13 km (8 miles) to the south, and the two were linked by a sacred way. Lower parts of the god's temple survive in situ; many elements from the superstructure have been reassembled by the Swedish archaeologists who work here. The upper parts were in Mylasan marble; local stone was used only where it would not be seen. The temple measured 3.87 x 18.71 m

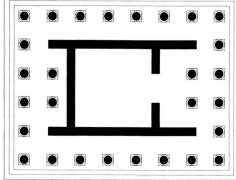

(13 x 61 ft) on the top step of a platform with upper curvature, a feature probably derived from the Greek mainland. Its 6 by 8 Ionic columns were uniformly spaced as if based on a grid of equal squares. The unusual proportions reflect two building phases. In the first there was just a square shrine-building with a porch and no identifiable architectural features. This was later rebuilt, with the addition of colonnades and a shallow rear porch of mainland type. Coins of the imperial age show the statue of a standing Zeus, with chains of woollen fillets, gifts of the faithful, suspended from the arms to the ground. Reused blocks in Byzantine structures come from the temple, perhaps destroyed by the major fire in the sanctuary (4th century AD). Roof tiles are very rare, probably because they were burnt in the lime kilns found on site.

*(Above) Temple of Zeus, Labraynda: general view from the west, showing the woodland highland setting and parts of a reassembled gable.*

*(Left) Plan of the temple of Zeus. Above the columns of the east front ran a Greek inscription naming the dedicator of the rebuilt temple as Idrieus – younger brother of the famous Maussolos and satrap (Persian governor) of Karia 351–344 BC, when the rebuilding took place.*

*(Below) Roman-period coin of Mylasa showing the image of Zeus Labrayndos, hung with woollen fillets (p. 80).*

# Mylasa

'Mylasa is sited in a remarkably fertile plain, with a mountain peak above, where a white stone of great beauty is quarried. Now this quarry is a great benefit, as it offers abundant building stone from nearby… as a result this city is superbly adorned with colonnades and temples.'

Strabo, Greek geographer, late 1st century BC

Now the pleasant modern town of Milâs with its Ottoman mosques and wonderful agricultural markets, ancient Mylasa lay some 13 km (8 miles) southeast of Euromos. It was a far more important place, the seat of the Persian governor (satrap) when Karia formed part of the Persian empire (late 6th to late 4th century BC), and still a thriving centre in Roman times.

## Corinthian temple

Nestling amid the houses on a hill slope in modern Milâs a white marble podium 3.45 m (11 ft) high supports a solitary Corinthian column from a vanished temple, probably colonnaded with 6 columns on the short sides, which once must have dominated the ancient city. A large precinct wall suggests the importance of the sanctuary. The capital is dated to the end of the 2nd century BC on style. An inscription suggests Zeus for the cult.

## Temple of Roma and Augustus

Not far from the museum in modern Milâs this temple stood intact into the 18th century. Measuring 14 x 18.70 m (46 x 62 ft) on the top level of the foundations, it stood on a podium approached by a broad flight of steps and had 6 by 7 columns with composite Ionic-Corinthian capitals, and a square shrine without porches. A centred opening in the front gable was probably for liturgical use (see p. 85). Below a frieze of bulls' skulls a Greek inscription running over the front columns recorded the dedication by the people of Mylasa to Augustus and the goddess Roma sometime between 12 BC and AD 2. Fittingly, the design reveals a strong Italian influence, notably the podium. The temple was completely destroyed shortly before 1765 for the construction of a mosque.

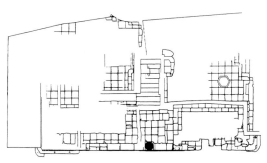

*(Below) Mylasa: general view of the remains of the Corinthian temple, showing the solitary standing column and the temple-podium incorporated into a property in the modern town.*

*(Right) plan of the remains of the Corinthian temple.*

(Right) Mylasa: drawing of the temple of Roma and Augustus by the British traveller R. Pococke, published in 1745.

## Stratonikeia

Some 35 km (22 miles) east of Milâs are the ruins of Stratonikeia (mod. Eskihisar), a Greek-style city of Macedonian colonists founded in the early 3rd century BC and and named after Stratonike, wife of Seleukos I. The city was heir to the older Karian cults of the vicinity, including Lagina.

### Lagina

This lush locale in the rural hinterland of nearby Stratonikeia was home to a celebrated sanctuary of Hekate, Greek goddess of magic and the night,

General view of the temple of Hekate at the extra-urban sanctuary of Lagina in the territory of ancient Stratonikeia. The temple has been partly restored.

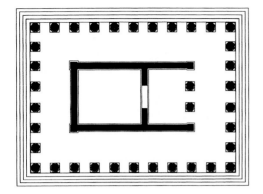

(Left) Lagina: restored plan of the Corinthian temple of Hekate. The squarish proportions and the absence of a rear porch are both signs of a later date.

## Knidos

Below the Gulf of Kos the southwest tip of Asia Minor is formed by two lonely and scenic peninsulas which jut into the Aegean sea on either side of the Greek island of Syme. The northernmost, the modern Reçadiye peninsula, was settled by Dorian Greeks who founded the important city of Knidos here. By the 4th century BC the Knidians had moved to a double-harbour site at the tip of the peninsula. Its delightful windswept ruins by the point command panoramic views of the nearby islands and nowa-

whose cult here was served by eunuchs. In Roman times this was a major festival centre and official refuge. The goddess' richly decorated temple (now partly restored) was reduced to a pile of stones by earthquake. Measuring 18.06 x 24.78 m (59 x 81 ft) on the top of five steps, it had 8 by 11 Corinthian columns, double-width halls, a shrine and deep front porch faced by Ionic columns. An ambitious figured frieze ran round all four sides above the columns showing mythical and historical scenes, including (north) an alliance involving the Karians and Rome. Official documents formed a large mural inscription of five columns in one of the long colonnades, and a pilaster or wall-terminal in the porch carried a local decree describing Hekate's rescue of the city from unspecified 'dangers', probably a reference to Stratonikeia's military resistance to Mithradates (88 BC), which may have divided construction, if begun in the late 2nd century BC, into two phases.

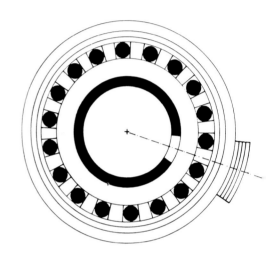

*Lagina: frieze-block from the temple at Lagina showing an armed male and a female shaking hands – perhaps a reference to the renewal of friendship between Rome and Stratonikeia around 85 BC.*

days are best reached by boat. Here the American excavators found remains of colonnaded rotunda which sits on an artificial terrace crowning the city and visible from the sea. A grey marble podium supports a three-stepped platform some 13.45 m (44 ft) in diameter on which once rose 18 Corinthian columns in stuccoed limestone enclosing a circular marble shrine. The base for a marble statue survives in place, and a staircase linked the temple axially to its altar. An earlier identification with the famous Knidian shrine of Aphrodite is mistaken: figurines and an inscription identify the deity as Athena. On style the temple may date to the 2nd century BC.

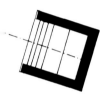

*(Left) Knidos, plan of the temple of Athena formerly identified as that of Aphrodite, showing its relationship to the stepped sacrificial altar outside.*

*(Below) Knidos, rotunda: general view. The large block (centre) is a base for a marble statue.*

## Triopion

Further back along the peninsula at Emecik on the south side, about 12 km (7½ miles) east of Datça, remains have recently been found of the Triopion. This important sanctuary of Apollo, named after the Dorian Greek hero Triopas, served a group of five Dorian Greek cities in the vicinity, among them Knidos. The lower parts survive in place of the god's Doric temple, which measured 11.62 x 21.2 m (38 x 70 ft) on the top step and was probably colonnaded. Parts of an over-lifesize marble figure may belong to the divine statue. The fired clay roof decoration dates the temple to the late 4th or early 3rd century BC. The cult survived into Roman times.

*(Above) Triopion: aerial view of the excavation trenches which have exposed (centre) the ruinous platform of the temple of Apollo.*

## Kastabos

'Standing over the sick in their sleep she gives treatment in person, and many pilgrims, whose condition was desperate, have been restored to health.'

In these terms the Greek historian Diodorus Siculus (mid-1st century BC) described a famous rural sanctuary of a local healing goddess, Hemithea, at Kastabos in the mountainous interior of the Loryma peninsula to the southwest of modern Marmaris. The sanctuary here, controlled by the nearby Rhodians, was so famous for its cures and its riches that by about 150 BC, according to an inscription, the precinct was too small to contain the crowds at festival-time. The remote remains were found about 275 m (900 ft) above sea level on a manmade terrace on the ridge of Mount Evren, commanding panoramic views north and west. Succeeding an earlier shrine

(Left) Kastabos: artist's impression of the temple of Hemithea.

## Xanthos

Xanthos, northwest of modern Kalkan, was the chief city of the ancient Lykians, an indigenous people heavily influenced by Greek culture who occupied a mountainous region with a rugged projecting shoreline east of Karia. The Xanthians controlled the rich southern valley of the River Xanthus. Their chief shrine, the Letoon, on marshy ground near the river mouth, was dedicated to the Greek goddess Leto and her children.

### The Letoon

Worship of Leto and her children Apollo and Artemis was introduced here about 400 BC by Erbinna, ruler of Xanthos and builder of the 'Nereid Monument' now in the British Museum, whose promotion of Greek culture included this Greek 'rebranding' of the much older cult of a local mother goddess. The Letoon went on to become the federal sanctuary of a pan-Lykian federation of cities, admired by the Romans for its good government. The two Greek colonnaded temples mark a total renovation of the sanctuary probably sponsored by the league around 150 BC, accompanied as an inscription records by the regilding of the sacred statues, paid for by voluntary contributions from 68 individuals.

(late 5th century BC?), the limestone and marble temple measured 11.33 x 23.7 m (37 x 78 ft) on the top step, with 6 by 12 Ionic columns, a deep front porch and shrine entered by a lofty threshold. Inside, against the rear wall, was a small statue-house for the axially aligned divine statue, its plinth preserved. On style and finds the date is about 335–300 BC. An inscription records that 'Phileas son of Philonidas, of Hygassos, dedicated the temple to Hemithea', another that two citizens of Halikarnassos, presumably architects, 'wrought' it. Later, a circular altar with sculptured drum was prominently placed before the threshold in the porch to which an even later Corinthian capital belongs, perhaps from a Roman remodelling. In the temple's final decay the superstructure fell in on itself. Most of the marble has disappeared.

(Right) Xanthos, the Letoon: plan of the row of temples. Apollo's is at the top, Leto's at the bottom.

(Below) Kastabos: restored view of the statue-house within the shrine for the image of Hemithea (see p. 88).

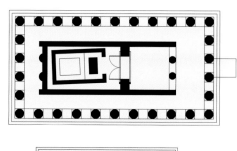

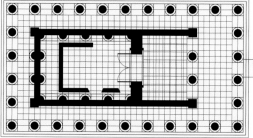

## Temple of Leto

A foundation deposit of some 80 coins from below the door-sill of the shrine dates this temple to about 150 BC. It was the largest in a row of three on a rock-cut terrace, all exactly aligned length-ways and absolutely equidistant, as if part of a single programme. They face south, towards the sacred spring. Of this, the northernmost, two columns have been reerected from the limestone superstructure, found collapsed in a great heap by the excavators. Measuring 16 x 31 m (53 x 102 ft) on the top step, the temple, approached by a ramp, had 6 by 11 Ionic columns, a deep front porch, originally grilled, a wall with two exterior half-columns instead of a rear porch, and a shrine with Corinthian half-columns against the walls. Inside are the polygonal foundations of a small building in the Lykian style, dated by sherds around 400 BC, and still intact when it was piously enveloped within the new Greek-style structure and refloored. An inscription identifies the deity.

Destruction began when metal-hunters felled the columns by cutting them down at the base, like trees. The inner building still stood, now probably a church to judge from Christian graffiti found on its wall-blocks. By the 7th century BC it too had been demolished for its bronze clamps and dowels.

## Temple of Apollo

The easternmost temple, smaller and this time Doric, is also poorly preserved. Measuring 27.97 x 15.07 m (92 x 49 ft) on the top step, it had 6 by 11 columns and a similar interior plan. In the shrine the entire stone substructure is preserved of another older building in the Lykian style, its lost upper parts of wood. Again it was enveloped by the later temple when still intact, and partly refloored with a mosaic, on style no earlier than the 2nd century BC. Its depiction of the bow and the lyre, Apollo's symbols, identifies the deity. The earlier shrines so reverentially preserved inside both Greek temples were probably the work of Erbinna. Like its neighbour, this temple was demolished, at least in part, by metal-hunters.

*(Below) Xanthos, the Letoon: general view of the temples, looking southwest.*

# Side

To the east of Lykia lay the plain of Pamphylia, its inhabitants a partly Greek people of mixed origin. East of modern Antalya, the city of Side prospered as a port for the coast-hugging traffic along Asia Minor's southern shore. During Roman times, when it acquired strategic importance in supplying Roman campaigns beyond the Euphrates frontier, it enjoyed exceptional affluence. Its impressive remains, partly restored, are pleasantly sited by the modern shore.

## Temples of Athena and Apollo

Remains of this pair of partly reerected temples sit on the tip of the peninsula occupied by the ancient city, next to the harbour. The smaller measures 29.5 x 16.37 m (97 x 54 ft) on the top step, with 6 by 11 columns, a shrine and front porch. The larger neighbour, on the same alignment to the north, measures 34.97 x 17.65 m (115 x 58 ft) on the top step, with the same internal plan. Both were Corinthian, their upper parts in marble. From their carved decoration they can be dated about AD 150–200. The deities protected mariners arriving in the city's port; archaeologists have assigned the larger temple to Athena, as the chief local deity. There are no traces of earlier temples. Destruction began in late antiquity, when the area was transformed into the forecourt of a large church, continuing into modern times.

## Temple of Fortune

In the southeast quarter of the agora are poorly preserved remains of a circular marble temple, raised on a podium 9.89 m (32 ft) in diameter and approached by steps, with 12 Corinthian columns enclosing the shrine, and a richly carved frieze. Local coins depict the shrine and identify the deity as Fortune (Tyche). On style the date is 2nd century AD.

*(Below) Side, plan of the temples of Athena and Apollo, and the Christian church (on the right) which later occupied the site.*

*(Bottom) Side: view of the temple of Apollo, partly reconstructed.*

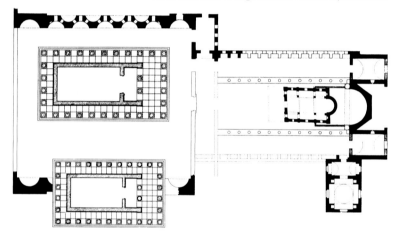

*(Below) Side: plan of the circular temple of Fortune.*

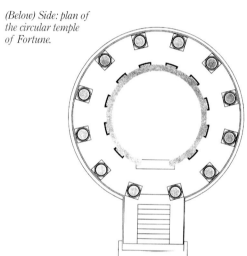

# Seleukeia on the Kalykadnos

Founded by Seleukos I at the fertile mouth of the Kalykadnos River, Seleukeia was the natural capital of the region of Rough Cilicia midway along the south coast of Asia Minor. In the middle of the modern town of Silifke a lone column marks the site of a Corinthian temple, raised on a podium with frontal steps. The top step measured up to 39.15 x 22.53 m (128 x 74 ft), with 8 by 14 columns framing double-width halls, a shrine and front porch, with the possibility of stairwells to the attic left and right of the door. A date in the 2nd century AD is likeliest. Later walling up of the intercolumniations suggests conversion into a church.

*Diokaisareia: general view of the ruins of the temple of Olbian Zeus. Strictly speaking, as at Aphrodisias (p. 206), these are the ruins of the church into which the pagan temple was converted at the end of antiquity – thus accounting for the relatively good state of preservation of the colonnade.*

## Diokaisareia

The impressive ruined temple here is scenically sited in the mountainous hinterland 20 km (12½ miles) north of modern Silifke, midway along the south coast in the region called Rough Cilicia by the ancients. The sanctuary of Olbian Zeus was once subordinate to the city of Olba nearby to the east, but acquired city status in its own right, and its Roman name, in the 1st century BC. The temple now forms part of a ruined city of mainly Roman date, scattered among the houses of the modern village. Much of the temple's colonnade still stands, although the inside has vanished. The temple measures about 21 x 39 m (69 x 128 ft) on the top step, with 6 by 12 Corinthian columns, their details dating the temple around the mid-2nd century BC. A royal donor has often been assumed, such as the Seleukid king Alexander Balas (150–146 BC). Along with the site's remoteness, conversion into an early Christian church, by walling up the intercolumniations and adding an apse to the east, explains the survival of the colonnade.

## Elaioussa-Sebaste

At the end of a low headland overlooking the site of the ancient city, are remains of a limestone temple facing south-east. Some lower columns still stand precariously. Measuring 32.9 x 17.6 m (108 x 58 ft) on the top step, the temple had 6 by 12 Corinthian columns. There were friezes inside and outside, the last depicting a marine revel. The carving suggests a date around AD 50, the subject a marine deity such

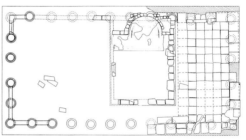

*(Left) Elaioussa-Sebaste: plan of the temple remains, including the later church.*

as Aphrodite. A small church (about AD 500?) was built inside the temple. Stone-robbing continued into modern times.

### THE INTERIOR

## Bithynion-Klaudioupolis

About halfway between modern Istanbul and Ankara in the hinterland behind the southern shore of the Black Sea, Bithynion was a Greek-style city in the Roman province of Pontus-and-Bithynia which claimed – improbably – to be a colony of the Peloponnesian city of Mantineia. Its real claim to some kind of fame was as the birthplace of Hadrian's favourite Antinous, who drowned in the Nile (AD 130) and was then deified by the grieving emperor. In 1964 foundations of a huge temple turned up on the ancient akropolis, along with Corinthian columns. Probably this was a temple of Antinous, perhaps the one shown on local coins. The scale suggests the active interest of Hadrian himself (see p. 41).

## Ankyra (mod. Ankara)

This Greek city was founded in 22 or 21 BC by the
Romans to promote urban life among the Celtic
tribes settled in the ancient region of Galatia. On a
hill in the centre of the ancient city are well preserved remains of a west-facing temple in white
marble. Measuring about 44.2 x 25.3 m (145 x 83 ft)
on the top step, it once had 8 by 15 Corinthian
columns flanking double-width halls, all now vanished, and an inner building, still well preserved to
ceiling height, including the massive door frame,
comprising two porches and a shrine. On the termi-
nal of the north wall of the front porch are listed
'the priests of the commonalty of the Galatians who
have served the deified Augustus and the goddess
Roma', implying a cult of the Roman emperors (the
indigenous Mother of the Gods is a faint possibility
too). On the porch's inner walls two inscribed panels
give the Latin version of Augustus' famous 'accom-
plishments' (*Res Gestae*), with a Greek translation
inscribed in nineteen columns on the wall of the
south hall. A date for the temple late in the reign of
Augustus (30 BC–AD 15) is now favoured. In the 5th
century AD the building was converted into a
church by the addition of an apse and knocking out

some windows. In the late 15th century it became an
Islamic school of theology.

## Aizanoi

Aizanoi was an ancient agricultural centre strad-
dling the Penkalas river in the north of Phrygia,
becoming the most important city of its region
under Roman rule, when it belonged to the province
of Asia. The impressive remains belie the fact that
the city is first heard of in the 1st century BC. They
mainly belong to the 2nd century AD, when the city
fathers encouraged a lavish spending spree, to
which the temple of Zeus belongs.

This is the best-preserved Ionic temple from
antiquity, with 16 columns still standing. It was
centred on the main axis of a colonnaded court (see
pp. 106–7) on a manmade terrace overlooking the

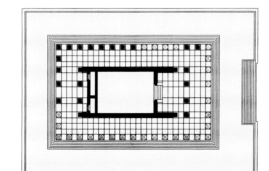

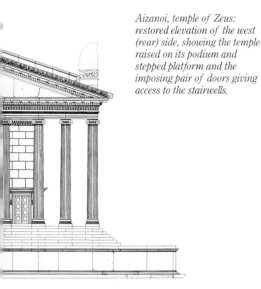

*Aizanoi, temple of Zeus: restored elevation of the west (rear) side, showing the temple raised on its podium and stepped platform and the imposing pair of doors giving access to the stairwells.*

agora and the Penkalas. The exact date is not absolutely certain: probably the mid-2nd century AD. Measuring 36.48 x 21.36 m (120 x 70 ft) on the top step of five, in turn resting on a podium, the temple had 8 by 15 Ionic columns framing double-width halls. The superstructure is a blue-grey marble from a quarry some 17 km (10 miles) away. The inner building comprised a deep front porch, shrine and shallow rear porch. Against the rear wall of the shrine are signs of an unusually wide base for divine statuary. The temple had richly carved ornamentation, including the curious feature of a tiny double-handled vase at the top of each column-flute. Stone blocks with holes show that the main facade above the columns once carried a dedication in bronze letters.

A unique feature is the pair of rooms behind the shrine for stairwells, reached by two monumental doors from the rear porch (see p. 89). The smaller

*(Below) Aizanoi: general view of the temple of Zeus. In the foreground (right) is part of one of the elaborate skyline ornaments (see reconstruction, above left).*

room gave access to the attic, the larger to a crypt, its function disputed. In both cases the staircases were wooden. The vaulted crypt, masonry-lined and lit by openings to ground-level, was 24.9 m (82 ft) long, extending beyond the porches above, with a masonry cavity big enough for a person to stand in set into the floor. Since the local Zeus was an oracle, this was probably its site, evoking an underground cave as at Klaros (p. 198). The equally grandiose treatment of the door to the second stairwell suggests that access to the attic also had religious significance.

Inside the front porch, on the north wall, a long inscription preserves official documents about a dispute over temple-lands, settled under Hadrian. In the north colonnade a closed group of three Greek inscriptions sings the praises of a local potentate, Marcus Ulpius Appuleius Eurycles.

In early Christian times, when the temple was already dilapidated, what was left was converted into a church, with an apse in the front porch. This seems to have burnt down.

## Pessinous

Further inland from Aizanoi but still in ancient Phrygia is the site (mod. Ballihisar) of this former temple-state, a famous centre for the worship of the goddess Kybele. Included in the Roman province of Galatia, it was transformed into a Greek-style city

*(Right) Pessinous: general view of the remains of the Corinthian temple.*

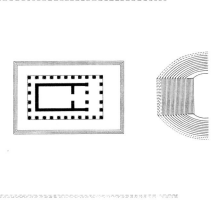

In the mountainous region of Pisidia in southern Asia Minor, this Greek city was founded by a Seleukid king with colonists from Magnesia-on-the-Maeander. The rural sanctuary of its chief deity, the Anatolian Men, lay 3.5 km (2 miles) southeast of the city on a man-made terrace astride a hill-top, overlooking the city plain. Inside a colonnaded court, facing northeast, are foundations of an Ionic temple in contrasting white and dark-grey limestone, measuring 25.25 x 12.53 m (83 x 41 ft) on the top step, with 6 by 11 Ionic columns, a shrine and porches. The design shows the influence of temples on the west coast. A date is suggested between 175 and 125 BC.

*(Left) Pessinous: plan of the Corinthian temple showing its relationship to the theatre below.*

by Roman fiat between 29 and 13 BC. On a hillside above the theatre are remains of a west-facing Corinthian temple in a local white marble quarried about 10 km (6 miles) to the north. Foundations measure 24.1 x 13.7 m (79 x 45 ft), and there were 6 by 11 Corinthian columns framing a shrine and front porch, with an exterior frieze carved on style in the early 1st century AD. Its axial alignment with the theatre below was an arrangement evidently inspired by Roman Italy, and inscriptions suggest that the deities were the Roman emperors.

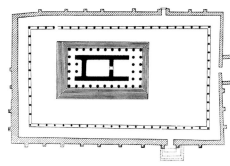

*(Left) Antioch-near-Pisidia, temple of Men: restored plan of the temple in its precinct.*

*(Below) Antioch-near-Pisidia, temple of Men: general view of the temple site.*

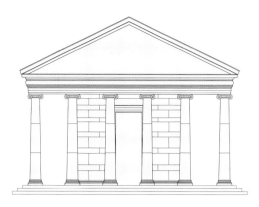

*(Right) Sagalassos, temple of Klarian Apollo and the Emperors: reconstruction of the facade.*

including work on the 'colonnade' (*peripteron*), and the 'veneering (*skoutlosis*) of the walls'. The temple was probably begun under Augustus, with renovations in AD 100–50. In the 5th or 6th century, the temple was converted into a church.

### (?Provincial) temple of Antoninus Pius

This richly decorated temple was built on a prominent terrace extended by buttressing to create an open court framed by colonnades, with the temple in the middle. Measuring 26.8 x 13.8 m (88 x 45 ft) on the top step, it had 6 by 11 Corinthian columns, a shrine and front porch. It was begun under Hadrian to judge from the style of carving. An inscription over the columns of the entrance

## Sagalassos

Southwest of Antioch, Sagalassos was an upland Pisidian centre which adopted Greek culture in the last three centuries BC. Under Roman rule it was one of Pisidia's chief cities.

### Temple of Klarian Apollo and the Emperors

Now a mass of toppled blocks, this marble temple was built on a hillside terrace overlooking the lower agora and measured 24.75 x 13.5 m (81 x 44 ft) on the top step, with 6 by 11 unfluted Ionic columns, a shrine and front porch. An inscription over the columns on the main facade records major repairs to the temple by a local magnate and his family,

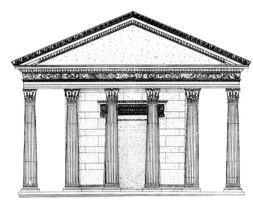

*(Right) Sagalassos, temple of Antoninus Pius: reconstructed facade by Marc Waelkens.*

*(Below) Sagalassos, general view of the temple of Antoninus Pius.*

facade identifies the cult. Partial dismantlement in late antiquity led to the neat rows of blocks to the north of the temple. Final destruction was by earthquake.

## Selge

About 55 km (34 miles) northeast of modern Antalya, the important city of Selge perched about 1000 m (3280 ft) above sea level in the mountains of Pisidia. On the Kesbedion or ancient akropolis are the foundations of a marble and limestone temple of Zeus measuring 33.6 x 17.6 m (110 x 58 ft) on the top step, with 11 by 6 Ionic columns, a shrine and porches. Details betray the influence of Priene's temple of Athena Polias, suggesting a date about 300–250 BC. Sometime after the 4th century AD, an early Christian church was built on the demolished temple's platform.

## Termessos

Scenically sited on the slopes of Mt Solymos in the wooded Pisidian hills northwest of modern Antalya, Termessos, like Sagalassos and Selge, was a major regional centre which fell under the spell of Greek culture in the last three centuries BC.

Remains of an Ionic temple occupy a prominent position between two gullies on the mountainside. Measuring about 22.02 x 11.56 m (72 x 38 ft) on the top step, it had 6 by 11 Ionic columns, front porch and shrine. A block from the sculptured frieze, showing Artemis, probably identifies the cult. The date on style is 3rd century BC.

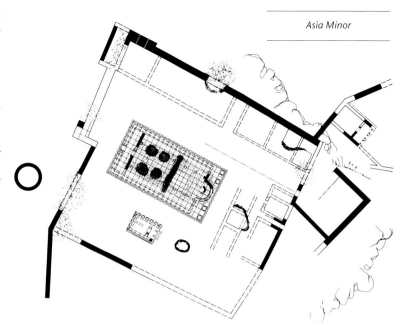

*(Above) Selge, temple of Zeus: plan of the sanctuary showing the temple platform and the apse of the church built on the site of the demolished temple.*

*(Left) Termessos: remains of the temple of (?) Artemis and its monumental gateway.*

# Syria and
# North Africa

## SYRIA

Ancient Syria comprised roughly what are now the states of Syria and Lebanon. After Alexander's conquests its northern part fell to the Macedonian kings of the Seleukid dynasty. In the late 4th and earlier 3rd centuries BC this region was heavily colonized by Macedonians and Greeks. They lived in new cities on the Greek model, the chief of them forming a group of four (*tetrapolis*), including Antioch (mod. Antakya in southeastern Turkey), a royal capital, and the port of Seleukeia in Pieria.

For the ancient Greeks north Africa meant above all Egypt and, to the west, the land of the indigenous Libyans (roughly mod. Libya). Egypt was a mysterious land of high antiquity which the Greeks admired as a source of ancient wisdom. After its conquest by Alexander the Great (332/1 BC) Egypt was acquired by the Macedonian general Ptolemy (died 282 BC), first king of a dynasty which ended with Cleopatra (died 30 BC). Long before Greeks settled in Egypt in large numbers as guests of the Ptolemies, they had colonized the coastal strip to the west (now Libya), attracted by its great fertility. The chief of these colonies was Cyrene, founded in the late 7th century BC and a bastion of Greek culture in this part of north Africa into early Christian times.

## Seleukeia in Pieria

This Greek city-foundation in Syria on the mouth of the Orontes river, some 25 km (16 miles) southwest of modern Antakya, was founded by Seleukos I about 300 BC and developed into a major royal centre. Conspicuously sited in the upper part of the walled city was a large Doric temple measuring 15.84 x 34.14 m (52 x 112 ft) on the top step, with 6 by 12 columns and a deep porch giving access to two successive rooms, the innermost overlying a crypt of excellent masonry, reached by an interior staircase and also (possibly a later addition) a passage from the south hall. The date could be as early as about 300 BC. This may be the Nikatoreion, the temple which king Antiochos I 'built over' the tomb of his father Seleukos I about 281 BC, and still in use about AD 150. Much material was reused in nearby towers of more recent date, and the temple may have been converted into a fortification. Only foundations survive in place.

## Alexandria

This Greek city founded by Alexander the Great near the mouth of the Nile (332/1 BC) quickly became the capital of Ptolemaic Egypt and one of the greatest cities of the ancient world. Curiously it has yet to produce evidence for a colonnaded Greek temple in its central area, where the scant traces of its most famous temple, in the sanctuary of the god Sarapis, suggest a modest structure without an enclosing colonnade (p. 38). Strabo (late 1st century BC) mentions a 'small temple' of Arsinoe Aphrodite on cape Zephyrion to the east of the ancient city commemorating Arsinoe II (died 270 BC), sister-queen of Ptolemy II. Its now vanished site was described in the 1860s, when foundations measuring 10.92 x 7.3 m (36 x 24 ft) were visible, along with fragmentary Doric columns with white stucco. Facing west towards the city, the temple had piers instead of angle columns, and between these had 4 by 2 columns. The interior seems to have been open.

## Hermopolis Magna

On the west bank of the Nile in middle Egypt (mod. El-Ashmunein), this was a Graeco-Roman district capital. Foundations of a Corinthian temple were found beneath an early Christian basilica here, along with a Greek inscription which records the dedication of 'the divine statues, the temple, the other things inside the precinct, and the colonnade' by Ptolemaic military settlers to Ptolemy III (246–221 BC) and Berenike, his queen. Ionic and Corinthian capitals, preserving brilliant paintwork,

*Hermopolis Magna, Corinthian temple: watercolour of a Corinthian capital, found with its original paintwork in good condition.*

may have belonged to the superstructure, thought to have featured an outer colonnade (for another colonnaded temple possibly dedicated to a Macedonian king, see p. 224). The temple seems to have remained in use right up until the time of its demolition to make way for the basilica.

## Cyrene

The Dorian colony of Cyrene (mod. Shahat in Libya) was founded from Cycladic Thera (mod. Santorini) around 630 BC, and quickly became the richest Greek settlement in the region. Devastated in the Jewish revolt of AD 115, it survived into the 7th century AD.

### Temple of Zeus

Some 700 m (2300 ft) above sea level, overlooking the coastal plain to the north, the colony's largest temple has been partly reerected since 1957. Built in the local yellow limestone, it measured about 32 x 70 m (105 x 230 ft) on the top step – comparable in size to the Parthenon. To an older shrine faced by porches a colonnade of 8 by 17 Doric columns was added later, probably (on style) between 500 and 480 BC. A marble torso of a man may come from sculpture in the front gable. By the time of Augustus or Tiberius the temple was dilapidated. A monumental Latin inscription from the east facade, dedicated to 'Jupiter Augustus' by a Roman governor, seems to refer to the complete rebuilding of the east front, including the conversion of the east platform into a Roman-style podium, approached by an oddly off-centre staircase (see pp. 40–41). In the Jewish revolt of AD 115 the rebels attacked the temple, sapping all 46 columns of the colonnade, which was never reerected. Repairs to the inner building were only completed in AD 172–75, as recorded in another

(Above) Cyrene, temple of Zeus: general view showing east side and part of the north. The colonnades were partly reerected in modern times after demolition by rebels in the Jewish revolt of AD 115.

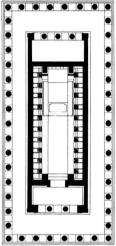

(Left) Cyrene, temple of Zeus: plan of the temple before the destruction of AD 115.

Cyrene, temple of Zeus: the denuded interior as it is now, looking towards the partly reerected east end.

225

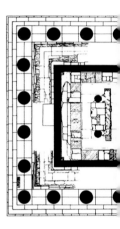

(Above) Cyrene, temple of Zeus: marble head of Zeus, after restoration; suggested restoration (above right) of the new 2nd-century AD statue of Zeus.

local Christians, who broke up the statues in the shrine, including a superb marble head of Zeus that was found shattered into over a hundred pieces.

## Temple of Apollo

On a partly manmade terrace just below the akropolis, this limestone temple of Cyrene's patron deity was a complete rebuilding, down to new foundations, of a colonnaded predecessor (6th century BC), deliberately demolished in the late 4th century BC to make way for a larger and more impressive version. Still visible are the perfectly good inside columns from the old temple which, instead of being reerected, were now relegated to

(Right) Cyrene, temple of Apollo: actual-state plan, showing the fill beneath the floor of the 4th-century BC rebuild, the steps and sunken feature in the east hall, and the Roman staircase.

monumental inscription, in Greek, above the entrance to the shrine. This last was now totally rebuilt with a Roman-style interior using coloured marble, including a green marble from Euboia for the two rows of Corinthian columns, replacing Doric doubled-up predecessors. A new focal statue was commissioned, inspired by the Zeus of Olympia: fragments indicate an eight-times lifesize figure in white marble. There were further repairs before the temple's final destruction by earthquake (probably in AD 365) and by arsonists, evidently the

(Right) Cyrene, the partly restored temple of Apollo, viewed from the east end.

226

serve as fill for the raised floor of the new interior.

With 6 by 11 Doric columns, the temple had marble sculpture in the front gable, much of it preserved, showing figures from local myth. The new inner building consisted of a front porch, the shrine proper, and, behind this a back room on a lower level, with an underfloor masonry treasury. The eastern hall was wider than the other three to accommodate, between porch and outer columns, a sunken rectangle reached by steps from the platform. Ritually important, since its central position displaced the porch entrance to the sides, it was later (3rd century BC) given a mosaic floor with a double border defining an empty central space on

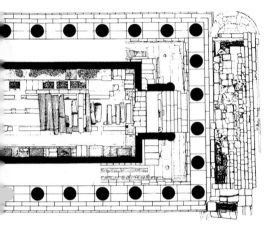

which, originally, an object of some kind would have rested, such as the altar for Apollo's eternal flame, known to the Greek poet Kallimachos (3rd century BC).

Destroyed by Jewish rebels in the revolt of AD 115, the temple was rebuilt with a new Doric colonnade (partly reerected) and a remodelled interior. An inscription provides a date about AD 181 for when 'the temple was finished and dedicated'. Earthquake damage, probably, prompted a further restoration (3rd century), when a Roman-style frontal staircase was added and the interior rebuilt yet again, this time with a raised inner room and a crypt beneath, like the temples of Roman Syria. In the 4th century, with the temple, it seems, in ruins, a small pagan shrine was built over the rear hall and the back of the inner building.

*Cyrene, temple of Apollo: the mysterious sunken feature in the east hall, reached by a flight of steps (shown here partly overlaid by later walls) between the outer colonnade and the front porch. The sheltered location would have made this a suitable place to instal the god's eternal flame.*

## Apollonia

Coastal Apollonia, 20 km (12 miles) from Cyrene and its port, was a Greek city in its own right by the 1st century BC. One km (½ mile) west of the city on the small hill of Ras el Mseied, a rural temple for an unknown deity is known from rock cuttings for foundations and a few fragments of superstructure, including a stucco-coated Doric capital. The plan is reconstructed with 6 by 11 columns, a shrine and front porch. A date around 300 BC is proposed. The temple was evidently repaired under Roman rule, remaining in use in the 2nd century AD.

227

# Epilogue: Exploration and Conservation Today

After they created the colonnaded temple in the late 7th and 6th centuries BC, the Greeks remained loyal to this supreme architectural expression of their religious beliefs for the best part of a millennium. Although building techniques and design underwent further evolution, the latest colonnaded temples of Roman Asia Minor are the instantly recognizable descendants of their 6th-century ancestors. This striking conservatism reflects the abiding appeal of the colonnaded temple as a religious, political and cultural symbol of extraordinary power.

As a building type the Greek colonnaded temple lost its purpose and meaning with the triumph of Christianity in the 4th and 5th centuries AD. Although some converted temples lingered on as churches, many more fell into ruin and disappeared as the result of natural and human action. An inhabitant of mediaeval Athens would have been astonished by the prediction that the obscure ancient ruins still visible in his shrunken hometown would one day be at the centre of a dramatic revival of interest in the colonnaded Greek temple.

But this is exactly what happened in the mid-18th century, thanks to the activities of Stuart and Revett discussed in Chapter 1. On his return from Athens, Nicholas Revett (1720–1804) himself designed a folly with the carefully observed facade of a Doric temple at Hagley in Worcestershire. This was the first 'Doric revival' building in Europe, and was based on the increasingly detailed information about the prototypes in Greece and Italy now becoming available to western architects and their patrons.

The appeal of ancient Greek architecture to the neo-classical mindset of educated Europeans at this time lay in its pre-Roman credentials and therefore its 'purity'. Doric in particular seemed to express this primitive sense of antiquity in its block-like, minimalist appearance. Although not all the Greek structures which antiquaries now studied so carefully were colonnaded temples, these undoubtedly made a particular impact on contemporary taste.

This can be seen by some of the more bizarre expressions of the so-called Greek Revival in the later 18th and the earlier 19th century, such as the church of St Pancras in north London (1819–1922), based on the Erechtheion, or the Walhalla near Regensburg in Bavaria (1830–42), a German national memorial built by Leo von Klenze on the model of the Athenian Parthenon. This monument, which today seems almost more distant in its taste and preoccupations than the ancient Greeks themselves, combined the external look of a Greek temple with an iron roof held up on the inside, inspired by the Karyatids from the Erechtheion – except that here they have morphed into those Teutonic female warriors, the Valkyries.

Such fervour for the Greek historical style clearly could not last. Even in its heyday the style was controversial. Critics decried it as unsuited to modern living, and it is indeed a bit odd, when you think about it, to see the facsimile columns of Paestum or the Parthenon doing late 18th- and 19th-century duty in the facades of banks, libraries, private houses – even, in downtown Manhattan, a customs house.

In the USA the architectural appeal of the Greek temple was to linger well into the 20th century. This is shown nowhere better than in Nashville, Tennessee. Here a full scale replica of – once more – the Parthenon formed the centrepiece of a state fair, the Tennessee centennial exhibition, in 1897. In 1931 the admiring citizenry then rebuilt it in concrete, with the help of the American archaeologist W. B. Dinsmoor. To cap it all, in 1990 a full-scale replica of the original statue of Athena was added – although the budget stretched only to gypsum cement and fibreglass, not the original gold and ivory.

Among modern recreators of ancient Greek temples, this recognition that the originals were in fact religious structures – houses of gods – is rare. The modern history of the ancient Greek temple is an overwhelmingly architectural tale, one which traditionally culminates with the Parthenon. Yet the ancient Greeks, in the words of Moses Finley, remained wedded to 'the monotonous sameness of the column-framed temple, century after century from one end of the Greek world to the other'.

These aspects of the Greek temple – the conservatism of the form, the wide geographical spread, and the chronological longevity – are among the ones which this book has sought to emphasize and explore. In doing so, to some extent it has gone

*Nashville, Tennessee: main front of the replica Parthenon built for an exhibition in 1897 and housing (since 1990) a full-scale replica of the famous statue of Athena by Pheidias (see p. 140).*

against the grain of modern work. The later temple-building of the ancient Greeks, especially after the 2nd century BC, tends to be viewed as part of a slow-fused architectural decline – and therefore less worthy of study. A major temple which served as a great centre of religious belief for generations of Greeks, such as Lagina in southwest Turkey (pp. 211–12), can be happily omitted even from the most up-to-date surveys of Greek temples and sanctuaries.

Part of the problem is that whereas other types of Greek building, such as the theatre or the stadium, housed cultural activities which today are still very much a part of the 'legacy of classical Greece', the Greek temple served a purpose for which the Christian traditions of the 18th and 19th centuries felt little sympathy. To quote Moses Finley again, there was 'no "legacy" of Greek religion as it was practised'. If ancient Greece bequeathed anything to Christianity, it was certainly not image-worship. Even when the cult of statues forms part of modern Christianity, as it does in Roman Catholic countries, it is seen by many as a corruption of Jesus's founding vision, and as a function of the 'simple' piety of the masses.

The relationship between the colonnaded Greek temple and ancient Greek image-worship has been another theme of this book. It deserves more research, especially now that scholars are starting to rethink the place of divine statues in the religious beliefs and practices of the ancient Greeks. More attention needs paying to the layout of temple interiors, their accessibility, and the forms of religious interaction between the statues and their worshippers.

Because the emphasis in modern study of the temple has been so resoundingly architectural, reflection on the meaning of its form has been belated. Here too more research is needed – especially on the question of how much ancient Greek temple architecture, like the sacred architecture of so many other societies, incorporated early Greek ideas about the nature of the cosmos. Archaeologists from the University of Chicago may shed light on this area with their current project, using a Global Positioning Survey unit to assess possible alignments of Greek temples on celestial bodies.

In spite of three centuries of study, the secrets of these inspiring but mysterious buildings have yet to be fully revealed.

*Euromos, temple of Zeus (pp. 208–9): one of the 'late' (2nd century AD) temples proving the extraordinarily long life of this sacred form.*

# Visiting the Temples

## Key sites

Most Greek temple sites are ruinous and at first sight hard to relate to the resplendent restorations in modern books. That said, there is something to be got out of a visit to any Greek temple site, if only in terms of the structure's eventual fate and its topographical setting, often impressive enough to make up for the paucity of remains.

Some of the best-preserved Greek colonnaded temples are in Italy and Sicily, and it is here above all that the achievement of the 6th-century BC temple-builders can be appreciated. The three temples of Poseidonia (Paestum) can easily be reached in a day's outing from the Bay of Naples. In Sicily, the most rewarding sites are Segesta, Selinous and Akragas (Agrigento) in the west, and Syracuse in the east, where the Apollonion and the Athenaion, now the Duomo, remain remarkable sights.

In Greece proper, Olympia, Epidauros and Delphi give a vivid impression of what a major Greek sanctuary was like, even if their temples are rather beaten up. The last can be done in a day (just about) from Athens, but deserves better. Greece's capital with its environs offers the most impressive assemblage of 5th-century temples: the Akropolis, the Hephaisteion, and Sounion, a day trip to the south. Athens also has the Olympieion, the only one of the emperor Hadrian's temples in the Greek provinces that still makes an impact. From the port of Piraeus it is an easy day trip to Aigina, where a bus links the town with the temple of Aphaia. Here, by contrast, you get the feel of a relatively small sanctuary, all in a delightful pine-scented setting.

Back in the Peloponnese, well-preserved Bassai, not far from Olympia, is still worth a visit, although the interior is closed and the whole is currently (2006) under a conservation tent. The two other temples with some columns still standing are Apollo's at Corinth and Zeus' at Nemea.

In the Aegean islands, Apollo's sanctuary on Delos is easily visited from Mykonos. Again, the temple remains are scrappy, but the overall impression made by the site is a powerful one – if the boat trip (notoriously rough) has left you in a state to appreciate it. Other colonnaded temple sites on the islands which reward a visit are the Palatia temple in Naxos town, the Samian Heraion, and the Asklepieion on Kos.

Visiting Greek temple sites in Turkey is something of an adventure – the distances are far greater, and the sites themselves, apart from a few famous ones, less geared up for tourism. Didyma, amid the resorts of the southwest coast, is far and away the best preserved and most impressive of these temples, followed by remote Aizanoi, chronologically the last major Greek temple. In western Turkey, Priene and Euromos merit a visit. By contrast Ephesus and Pergamon, although major archaeological sites, are less rewarding in terms of Greek temples. Along the south coast, Diokaisareia is the most important temple site.

## Museums

It is a truism that to see the Parthenon properly you have to visit the British Museum in London, where the frieze and other items are on display, brought back by Lord Elgin. Generally speaking you have to go to a museum nowadays to see Greek temple-sculpture. Other world-class museums with important material from Greek temple sites include the Louvre, the Munich Glyptothek (the Aphaia marbles from Aigina), the National Archaeological Museum in Athens and the Istanbul Archaeological Museum. The regional museum of Reggio di Calabria has finds from the temples of southern Italy, including an important collection of fire-clay roof decorations, and Palermo from those of Sicily. Local museums with important temple material include Paestum, Olympia, Delphi and the Akropolis Museum (Athens). In all cases it is wise to check in advance where possible for opening hours and gallery closures.

## Books

Apart from the usual recommendations of sensible shoes and sun hat, a decent guide-book helps prepare for a site visit (or may answer your questions after you've visited). As well as the relevant *Blue Guides*, try M. Guido's *Sicily: An Archaeological Guide*, London (1977), or C. Mee and A. Spawforth's *Greece: An Oxford Archaeological Guide*, Oxford (2001). For Turkey, G. Bean's archaeological guides *Aegean Turkey* (1966), *Turkey Beyond the Maeander* (1971), *Lycian Turkey* (1978 ), and *Turkey's Southern Shore*, 2nd edition revised (1979), all originally published by Benn, London, remain unbeatable value.

# Further Reading

What follows is – needless to say – far from exhaustive and emphasizes more recent studies.

## Abbreviations

AA — *Archäologischer Anzeiger*
ABSA — *Annual of the British School at Athens*
AJA — *American Journal of Archaeology*
Fox 1988 — Fox, M. V. (ed.). 1988. *Temple in Society*. Winnona Lake
Hägg 1996 — Hägg, R. (ed.) 1996. *The Role of Religion in the Early Greek Polis*. Stockholm
Hoepfner and Schwandner 1990 — Hoepfner, W. and E.-L. Schwandner (eds). 1990. *Hermogenes und die hochhellenistische Architektur*. P. von Zabern: Mainz
Hoepfner 1997 — Hoepfner, W. (ed.). 1997. *Kult und Kultbauten auf der Akropolis*. Berlin
JHS — *Journal of Hellenic Studies*
Marinatos and Hägg 1993 — N. Marinatos and R. Hägg (eds.). 1993. *Greek Sanctuaries – New Approaches*. Routledge: London
MDAI(A) — *Mitteilungen des deutschen archäologischen Instituts: Athenische Abteilung*
MDAI(I) — *Mitteilungen des deutschen archäologischen Instituts: Istanbulische Abteilung*
Muss 2001 — Muss, U. (ed.). 2001. *Der Kosmos der Artemis von Ephesos*. Vienna
RA — *Revue archéologique*
RE — Pauly, A., G. Wissowa, and W. Kroll, *Real-Encyclopädie der klassischen Altertumswissenschaft* (1893– )

## General books on Greek religion

Bruit Zaidman, L. and P. Schmitt Pantel 1992 (French original 1989). *Religion in the Greek City*. Cambridge
Burkert, W. 1985 (German original 1977). *Greek Religion: Archaic and Classical*. Blackwell: Oxford
Buxton, Richard. 2004. *The Complete World of Greek Mythology*. Thames & Hudson: London and New York
Easterling, P. and J. V. Muir (eds). 1985. *Greek Religion and Society*. Cambridge
Farnell, L. R. 1896–1909. *The Cults of the Greek States*, 5 vols. Oxford
Finley, M. I. (ed.). 1981. *The Legacy of Greece: A New Appraisal*. Clarendon Press: Oxford

Kearns, E. and S. Price (eds). 2003. *Oxford Dictionary of Greek Religion and Mythology*. Oxford UP
Lane Fox, R. 1986. *Pagans and Christians*. Penguin: Harmondsworth
Price, S. 1999. *Religions of the Ancient Greeks*. Cambridge

## General reference

Hornblower, S. and A. Spawforth (eds). 2003. *The Oxford Classical Dictionary*. 3rd edition, revised. Oxford UP

## Ancient Greek architecture

Dinsmoor, W. B. 1975. *The Architecture of Ancient Greece*. 3rd edition revised. Batsford: London
Lawrence, A. W. 1996. *Greek Architecture*, 5th edition revised by R. A. Tomlinson. Yale UP: London and New Haven

## I  Homes of the Gods
### Development, Glory and Decline

Alcock, S., J. F. Cherry, and J. Elsner (eds). 2001. *Pausanias: Travel and Memory in Roman Greece*. Oxford UP
Bammer, A. 1990. A *peripteros* of the Geometric period in the Artemision of Ephesus. *Anatolian Studies* 40: 137–60
Bayliss, R. 1999. Usurping the urban image: the experience of ritual topography in late antique cities of the near east. In P. Baker, C. Forcey and others (eds). *Theoretical Roman Archaeology Conference* 98. Oxford. 59–71
Bietak, M. (ed.). 2001. *Archaische griechische Tempel und Altägypten*. Vienna
Burkert, W. 1986. 'Krieg, Sieg und die Olympischen Götter der Griechen.' In Stolz, G. (ed.). *Religion zu Krieg und Frieden*. 67–87
———. 1988. The meaning and function of the temple in Classical Greece. In Fox 1988: 27–44
———. 1996. 'Greek temple-builders: who, where and why?' In Hägg 1996: 21–29
Frantz, A. 1965. 'From paganism to Christianity in Athens.' *Dumbarton Oaks Papers* 19: 187–205
Hannestad, L. and D. Potts. 1990. 'Temple architecture in the Seleucid kingdom.' In Bilde, P. and others (eds). *Religion and Religious Practice in the Seleucid Kingdom*. Aarhus. 91–123
Knipe, D. M. 1988. 'The temple in image and reality.' In Fox (ed.): 105–138
La Rocca, E. 1985. *Amazzonomachia. Le sculture frontonali del tempio di Apollo Sosiano*. De Luca: Rome
Mazarakis-Ainian, A. 1997. *From Rulers' Dwellings to Early Iron Age Greece (c. 1000–700 BC)* (Studies in Mediterranean Archaeology 121). Jonsered
Polignac, F. de. 1995 (French original 1984).

*Cults, Territory, and the Origins of the Greek City-State*. University of Chicago Press
Popham, M., H. Sackett and E. Touloupa. 1982. 'The hero of Lefkandi.' *Antiquity* 56: 169–74
St Clair, W. 1998. *Lord Elgin and the Marbles*. 3rd edition revised. Oxford
Snodgrass, A. 1980. *Archaic Greece. The Age of Experiment*. Dent: London
———. 1986. 'Interaction by design: the Greek city state.' In C. Renfrew and J. Cherry (eds). *Peer Polity Interaction and Socio-political Change*. Cambridge. 47–58
Stoneman, R. 1987. *Land of Lost Gods: The Search for Classical Greece*. Hutchinson: London
Svenson-Evers, H. 1997. 'HIEROS OIKOS. Zum Ursprung des griechischen Tempels.' In Hoepfner 1997: 132–51
Tsigakou, F.-M. 1981. *The Rediscovery of Greece*. Thames & Hudson: London

## II  Building for the Gods
### Siting, Construction, Decoration and Finance

Alcock, S. and R. Osborne (eds). 1994. *Placing the Gods: Sanctuaries and Sacred Space in Ancient Greece*. Clarendon Press: Oxford
Ashmole, B. 1972. *Architect and Sculptor in Classical Greece*. Phaidon: London
Betancourt, P. 1977. *The Aeolic Style in Architecture*. Princeton UP: Princeton
Barletta, B. 2001. *The Origins of the Greek Architectural Orders*. Cambridge
Burford, A. 1961. 'The economics of Greek temple building.' *Proceedings of the Cambridge Philological Society* 191: 21–36
———. 1969. *The Greek Temple Builders at Epidaurus*. Liverpool
Burkert, W. 1992. *The Orientalizing Revolution: Near Eastern Influence on Greek Culture in the Early Archaic Age*. Cambridge, Mass. (especially 53–55, 'Foundation rituals')
Coldstream, J. N. 1985. 'Greek temples: where and why?' In Easterling, P. and J. V. Muir (eds). *Greek Religion and Society*. 67–97
Cooper, F. 1968. 'The temple of Apollo at Bassae: new observations on its plan and orientation.' *AJA* 72: 103–11
Coulton, J. J. 1974. 'Lifting in early Greek architecture.' *JHS* 94: 1–19
———. 1988. *Ancient Greek Architects at Work*. Oxbow: Oxford
Davies, J. K. 2001. 'Rebuilding a temple. The economic effects of piety.' In Mattingly, D. and J. Salmon (eds). *Economics Beyond Agriculture in the Classical World*.
Doxiades, C. A. 1940. 'Tempelorientierung.' *RE* supplement 7: cols. 1283–93
Fehr, B. 1996. 'The Greek temple in the early Archaic period: meaning, use and social context.' *Hephaistos* 14: 165–81

Haselberger, L. (ed.) 1999. *Appearance and Essence: Refinements of Classical Architecture: Curvature*. Philadelphia

Hoecker, C. 1996. 'Architektur als Metapher: Überlegungen zum Bedeutung des dorischen Ringhalltempels.' *Hephaistos* 14: 45–71

Hoepfner and Schwandner 1990.

Jenkins, I. 1994. *The Parthenon Frieze*. British Museum Press: London

Jenkins, I. and A. Middleton. 1988. 'Paint on the Parthenon sculptures.' *ABSA* 83: 183–207

Korres, M. 1995. *From Pentelicon to the Parthenon*. Athens

Migeotte, L. 1992. *Les souscriptions publiques dans les cités grecques*. Geneva

Onians, J. 1999. *Classical Art and the Cultures of Greece and Rome*. Yale UP: New Haven

Osborne, R. 2000. 'Archaic and classical Greek temple sculpture and the viewer.' In Rutter, N. K. and B. A. Sparkes (eds) *Word and Image in Ancient Greece*. Edinburgh. 228–46

Østby, E. 2001. 'Der Ursprung der griechischen Tempelarchitektur und ihre Beziehungen mit Ägypten.' In Bietak, M. (ed.). *Archäische griechische Tempel und Altägypten*: 17–33

Salmon, J. 2001. 'Temples the measure of men. Public building in the Greek economy.' In Mattingly, D. and J. Salmon (eds.). *Economics Beyond Agriculture in the Classical World*. 195–208

Schilardi, D. and D. Katsonopoulou (eds). 2000. *Paria Lithos*. Athens

Scully, V. 1979. *The Earth, the Temple and the Gods. Greek Sacred Architecture*, revised edition. New Haven and London

Sinn, U. 1985. 'Der sog. Tempel D im Heraion von Samos II. Ein archäologischer Befund aus der nachpolykratischen Zeit.' *MDAI(A)* 100: 129–58

Stanier, R. S. 1953. 'The cost of the Parthenon.' *JHS* 73: 68–76

Tomlinson, R. 1963. 'The Doric order: Hellenistic critics and criticism.' *JHS* 83: 133–45

West, M. L. (ed.) 1966. *Hesiod* Theogony. Clarendon Press: Oxford

———. 1997. *The East Face of Helicon. West Asiatic Elements in Greek Poetry and Myth*. Clarendon Press: Oxford

Wilkinson, R. H. 2000. *The Complete Temples of Ancient Egypt*. Thames & Hudson: London and New York

Wilson Jones, M. 2000. *Principles of Roman Architecture*. New Haven and London

———. 2002. 'Tripods, triglyphs and the origin of the Doric frieze.' *AJS* 106: 353–90

Wright, G. R. H. 2000. *Ancient Building Technology*. I. *Historical Background*. Brill: Boston

## III   The Living Temple
The Parts of the Temple and their Uses

Amy, R. 1950. 'Temples à escaliers.' *Syria* 27: 82–136

Burkert, W. 1997. 'From epiphany to cult statue.' In A. B. Lloyd (ed.). *What is a God? Studies in the Nature of Greek Divinity*. Duckworth: London. 15–34

Catling, H. W. 2002. 'Zeus Messapeus at Tsakona, Lakonia, reconsidered.' *Lakonikai Spoudai* 16: 67–107

Corbett, P. E. 1970. 'Greek temples and Greek worshippers: the literary and archaeological evidence.' *Bulletin of the Institute of Classical Studies* 17: 149–58

Davies, J. K. 2003. 'Greek archives: from record to monument.' In M. Brosius (ed.). *Ancient Archives and Archival Traditions*. Oxford. 323–43

Donahue, A. A. 1988. Xoana *and the Origins of Greek Sculpture*. Scholars Press: Atlanta

Engelmann, H. 2001. 'Inschriften und Heiligtum.' In Muss: 33–44

Gebhard, E. 1993. 'The evolution of a pan-Hellenic sanctuary: from archaeology towards history at Isthmia.' In Marinatos and Hägg: 154–77

Gordon, R. L. 1979. 'The real and the imaginary: production and religion in the Graeco-Roman world.' *Art History* 2: 5–34

Harris, D. 1995. *The Treasures of the Parthenon and the Erechtheion*. Clarendon Press: Oxford

Hollinshead, M. 1999. '"Adyton", "opisthodomos", and the inner room of the Greek temple.' *AJA* 68: 189–218

Hommel, P. 1957. 'Giebel und Himmel.' *MDAI(I)* 7: 1–55

Humphrey, C. and J. Laidlaw. 1994. *The Archetypal Functions of Ritual: A Theory of Ritual Illustrated by the Jain Rite of Worship*. Oxford UP

Kaminski, G. 1991. 'Thesauros: Untersuchungen zum antiken Opferstock.' *Jahrbuch des Deutschen archäologischen Instituts* 106: 63–181

Lacroix, L. 1949. *Les reproductions de statues sur les monnaies grecques: la statuaire archaïque et classique*. Liège

Lapatin, K. D. S. 2001. *Chryselephantine Statuary in the Ancient World*. Oxford

Miles, M. 1985. Stone staircases in Sicilian temples. *AJA* 89: 134

Neumann, G. 1965. *Gesten und Gebärden in der griechischen Kunst*. De Gruyter: Berlin

Parasinou, E. 2000. *The Light of the Gods. The Role of Light in Archaic and Classical Greek Cult*. Routledge: London

Parker, R. 1983. *Miasma. Pollution and Purification in Early Greek Religion*. Oxford UP

Rigsby, K. 1996. Asylia. *Territorial Inviolability in the Hellenistic World*. University of California Press: Berkeley

Robert, L. 1939. *Études anatoliennes*. Paris

Romano, I. B. 1988. 'Early Greek cult images and cult practices.' In Hägg, R., N. Marinatos and G. Nordquist. (eds) *Early Greek Cult Practice*. Stockholm and Athens. 127–34

Roux, G. (ed.). 1984. *Temples et sanctuaires: séminaire de recherche 1981–1983*. Lyon and Paris

Schafer, B. E. (ed.). 1997. *Temples of Ancient Egypt*. Tauris: London and New York

Scheer, T. 2000. *Die Gottheit und ihr Bild*. Munich

Scranton, R. 1946. 'Interior design of Greek temples.' *AJA* 50: 39–51

Servais, J. 1967. STEMMAT' ΕΧΩΝ ΕΝ ΧΕΡΣΙΝ. *L'Antiquité classique* 36: 415–53

Sherwin-White, S. M. 1985. 'Ancient archives: the edict of Alexander to Priene, a reappraisal.' *JHS* 105: 69–89

Steiner, D. 2001. *Images in Mind: Statues in Archaic and Classical Greek Literature and Thought*. PUP

Themelis, P. G. 1991. 'Artemis Ortheia at Messene. The epigraphical and archaeological evidence.' In R. Hägg (ed.). *Ancient Greek Cult Practice from the Epigraphic Evidence*. 101–22

Tilley, C. 1999. *Metaphor and Material Culture*. Blackwell: Oxford

Umholtz, G. 2002. 'Architraval arrogance? Dedicatory inscriptions in Greek architecture of the Classical period.' *Hesperia* 71: 261–93

Versnel, H. S. (ed.). *Faith, Hope and Worship: Aspects of Religious Mentality in the Ancient World*. Brill: Leiden

Wikander, Ö. 1983. 'ΟΠΑΙΑ ΚΕΡΑΜΙΣ. Skylight-tiles in the ancient world.' *Opuscula Romana* 14: 81–99

Winter, F. E. 1978. 'Tradition and innovation in Doric design: Archaic and Classical Doric east of the Adriatic.' *AJA* 82: 151–61

## IV   Encounters with the Gods
The Temple in its Sacred Setting

Aleshire, S. 1994. 'The demos and the priests: the selection of sacred officials at Athens from Cleisthenes to Augustus.' In R. Osborne and S. Hornblower (eds). *Ritual, Finance, Politics*. Oxford. 325–37

Dignas, B. 2002. *Economy of the Sacred in Hellenistic and Roman Asia Minor*. Oxford

Hansen, M. H. and T. Fischer-Hansen. 1994. 'Monumental political architecture in Archaic and Classical Greek *poleis*: evidence and historical significance.' In D. Whitehead (ed.). *From Political Architecture to Stephanus Byzantius* (*Historia Einzelschriften* 87). 22–90

Jantzen, U. (ed.) 1976. *Neue Forschungen in griechischen Heiligtümern*. Tübingen

Lehmann, P. W. 1954. 'The setting of Hellenistic temples.' *Journal of the Society* of *Architectural Historians* 13: 15–20

Mantis, A. 1983. *Problemata tes eikonographias ton iereion kai ton ieron sten archaia ellenike techne*. Thessaloniki

Parker, R. and D. Obbink. 2001. 'Aus der Arbeit der "Inscriptiones Graecae" VIII. Three further inscriptions concerning Coan cults.' *Chiron* 31: 253–75

Price. S. 1984. *Rituals and Power: The Roman Imperial Cult in Asia Minor*. Cambridge UP

Stevens G. P. 1940. *The Setting of the Periclean Parthenon* (*Hesperia* supplement 3)

Stillwell, R. 1954. 'The siting of Classical Greek temples.' *Journal of the Society of Architectural Historians* 13: 3–8

Summerson, J. 1980. *The Classical Language of Architecture*. Revised edition. Thames & Hudson: London

Tomlinson, R. 1976. *Greek Sanctuaries*. Elek: London

# V Temples of the Gods
Seven Journeys through Hellenic Lands

For older bibliography see Dinsmoor 1975 and Stillwell, R. (ed.) 1976. *Princeton Encyclopedia of Classical Sites*, Princeton. What follows is less than systematic and – to repeat – concentrates on more recent major publications and key articles.

## 1 Italy and Sicily

Barello, F. 1995. *Architettura greca a Caulonia*. Florence.

Bernabò Brea, L. 1986. *Il tempio di Afrodite di Akrai*. Centre Jean Bérard: Naples

De Franciscis, A. 1979. *Il santuario di Marasà in Locri Epizefiri*. I. *Il tempio arcaico*. G. Macchiaroli: Naples

Krauss, F. 1976 (1943). *Paestum – die griechischen Tempel*. 3rd revised edition. G. Mann: Berlin

Manganaro, G. 1995. 'L'*elaphos* di oro dedicato dai Selinuntini nell'Apollonion' (IG XIV, nr. 268). *Zeitschrift für Papyrologie und Epigraphik* 106: 162–64

Mertens, D. 1984. *Der Tempel von Segesta und die dorische Tempelbaukunst des griechischen Westens in klassischer Zeit*. 2 vols, P. von Zabern: Mainz

———. 1985. 'Metapont. Ein neuer Plan des Stadtzentrum.' *AA* 645–75

———. 1993. *Der alter Heratempel in Paestum und die archaische Baukunst in Unteritalien*. P. von Zabern: Mainz

———. 1996. 'Greek architecture in the west.' In Carratelli, G. P. (ed.) *The Western Greeks*. Thames & Hudson: London. 415–436

Pedley, J. G. 1990. *Paestum. Greeks and Romans in Southern Italy*. Thames & Hudson: London and New York

Rizzo, L. 1998. *Il tempio dorico di Taranto*. Taranto

Zoppi, Carlo. 1996. 'Esecuzione delle scanalature e interpretazione di un edificio: il tempio F di Selinunte.' *Selinunte* 3: 119–34

## 2 The Peloponnese

Arafat, K. W. 1995. 'Pausanias and the temple of Hera at Olympia.' *ABSA* 90: 461–73

Bammer, A. 2001. 'Neue Heiligtümer in Aigeira.' In Mitsopoulou-Leon, V. (ed.). *Forschungen in der Peloponnes. Akten des Symposions anlässlich der Feier '100 Jahre Österreichisches Archäologisches Institut Athen', Athen 5.3–7.3.1998* (ÖAI Sonderschriften Band 38): 95–105

Cooper, F. 1992–1996. *The Temple of Apollo Bassitas*, 4 vols. American School of Classical Studies: Princeton, NJ

Gebhard, E. 1993. 'The evolution of a pan-Hellenic sanctuary: from archaeology towards history at Isthmia.' In Marinatos and Hägg: 154–77

Hitzl, K. 1991. *Die kaiserzeitliche Statuenausstattung des Metroon* (Olympische Forschungen 19). W. de Gruyter: Berlin and New York

Jost, M. 1985. *Sanctuaires et cultes d'Arcadie* (*Études péloponnésiennes* 9). J. Vrin: Paris

Knell, H. 1978. 'Troizen, Tempel des Hippolytos (?)'. *AA* 397–406

———. 1983. 'Lepreon. Der Tempel der Demeter.' *MDAI(A)* 98: 113–47

Miller, S. (ed.). 1984. *Nemea. A Guide to the Site and Museum*. University of California Press: Berkeley and Oxford

Norman, N. J. 1984. 'The Temple of Athena Alea at Tegea.' *AJA* 88: 169–94

Petropoulos, M. 1996–97. 'New elements from the excavation of the Geometric temple at Ano Mazaraki (Rakita).' *Peloponnesiaka*. Suppl. 22: *Acts of the Fifth International Congress of Peloponnesian Studies* II

Trianti, I. 1986. 'O gluptos diakosmos tou naou sto Mazi tes Eleias.' In H. Kyrieleis (ed.). *Klassische griechische Plastik*. P. von Zabern: Mainz.155–68

Mallwitz, A. 1972. *Olympia und seine Bauten*. Munich

## 3 Athens, Attike and the Saronic Gulf

Bankel, H. 1993. *Der spätarchäische Tempel der Aphaia auf Aigina*. W. de Gruyter: Berlin and New York

Beard, M. 2002. *The Parthenon*. Profile Books: London

Camp, J. 2001. *The Archaeology of Athens*. Yale UP: New Haven

Economakis, R. (ed.). 1994. *Acropolis Restorations*. Academy Editions: London

Hoepfner (ed.). 1997

Korres, M. and others (eds). 1996. *The Parthenon. Architecture and Conservation*. Foundation for Hellenic Culture: Athens

Miles, M. M. 1989. 'A Reconstruction of the Temple of Nemesis at Rhamnous.'

*Hesperia* 58: 133–249

Öhly, D. 1977. *Ägina. Tempel und Heiligtum*. C. H. Beck: Munich

Petrakou. V. Ch. 1999. *Ho Dêmos tou Ramnountos*. 2 vols. Athens Archaeological Society: Athens

Rhodes, R. F. 1995. *Architecture and Meaning on the Athenian Acropolis*. Cambridge UP

Roux, G. 1984. 'Pourquoi le Parthénon?' *Comptes rendus de l'Académie des Inscriptions*. 301–17

Tölle-Kastenbein, R. 1994. *Das Olympieion in Athen*. Böhlau: Cologne, Weimar and Vienna

Travlos, J. 1971. *Pictorial Dictionary of Ancient Athens*. Thames & Hudson: London

———. 1988. *Bildlexikon zur Topographie des Antiken Attika*. E. Wasmuth: Tübingen

## 4 Central and Northern Greece

Bommelaer, Jean-Francois. 1991. *Guide de Delphes. Le site*. Paris

Ellinger, Pierre. 1993. *La légende nationale phocidienne. Artémis, les situations extrêmes et les récits de guerre d'anéantissement* (*Bulletin de Correspondance Hellénique* Suppl. 27). Paris

Felten, F. 1999. Heiligtümer der Makedonen. In [no eds] *Ancient Macedonia. Sixth International Symposium* (*Ancient Macedonia* 6). Thessaloniki. I: 405–17

Grandjean, Yves, and François Salviat. 2000. *Guide de Thasos*. 2nd ed. École française d'Athènes

Hoepfner, W. and E.-L. Schwandner. 1986. *Haus und Stadt im klassischen Griechenland*. Munich

Østby, Erik. 1994. 'A reconsideration of the Classical temple at Pherai.' In *La Thessalie* II. Athens. 139–42

Roux, G. 1976. *Delphes, son oracle et ses dieux*. Belles Lettres: Paris

Stucky, R. A. 1988. 'Die Tonmetope mit den drei sitzenden Frauen von Thermos: ein Dokument hellenistischer Denkmalpflege.' *Antike Kunst*: 71–78

Turner, L. A. 1994. 'IG vii.3073 and the display of inscribed texts.' In J. M. Fossey (ed.). *Boeotica Antiqua* IV. 2–30

Tzouvara-Souli, C. 2001. 'The cults of Apollo in Northwestern Greece.' In Isager, J. (ed.). *Foundation and Destruction. Nikopolis and Northwestern Greece*. Danish Institute at Athens. 233–52

## 5 The Aegean Islands and the Black Sea

Beaumont, L. and A Archontidou-Argyri. 1999. New work at Kato Phana, Chios: the Kato Phana Archaeological Project. *ABSA* 94: 265–87

Bruneau, Ph. 1970. *Recherches sur les cultes de Délos à l'époque Hellénistique et à l'époque impériale*. Paris

Gruben, G. 1972. 'Naxos und Paros.' *AA* 22: 319–79

Heid, W. 1995. 'Wo stand die Hera von Samos?' *MDAI(A)* 45: 13–23

Kyrieleis, H. 1981. *Führer durch das Heraion von Samos*. Athens

Labarre, Guy. 1996. *Les Cités de Lesbos*. Paris

Papachristodopoulou, Joannis. 1992. 'Culti e santuari di Rodi. Nuovi dati e scoperte.' *La Magna Graecia e i grandi santuari della madrepatria. Atti del trentesimo convegno di studi sulla Magna Grecia*. Taranto. 249–73

Papanikolaou, Alexandros. 1998. 'E stege tou naou tes Athenas sten Karthaia.' In Mendoni, L. and A. I. Mazarakis Ainian (eds). *Kea-Kythnos: History and Archaeology* (Meletemata 27). Athens. 583–608

Plommer, H. 1981. 'The temple of Messa on Lesbos.' In L. Casson and M. Price (eds). *Coins, Culture, and History in the Ancient World. Numismatic and Other Studies in Honor of Bluma L. Trell*. Detroit. 177–86

Tolstikov, V. P. 1984. 'Factors leading to the formation of the Bosporan state' (Russian with English summary). *Vestnik Drevnei Istorii* 3 (1970): 24–48

Vinogradov, Jurij and Sergej Kryzickij. 1995. *Olbia. Eine altgriechische Stadt im nordwestlichen Schwarzmeerraum*. Brill: Leiden

## 6 Asia Minor

Berges, D. and N. Tuna. 2000. 'Das Apollonheiligtum von Emecik. Bericht über die Ausgrabungen 1998 und 1999.' *MDAI(I)* 50: 171–214

Bammer, A. and U. Muss. 1996. *Das Artemision von Ephesos*. P. von Zabern: Mainz

Bankel, H. 1997. 'Knidos. Der hellenistische Rundtempel und sein Altar.' *AA* 50–71

Baratollo, A. 1995. 'The Temple of Hadrian-Zeus at Cyzicus.' *MDAI(I)* 45: 57–108

Carter, J. C. 1983. *The Sculpture of the Sanctuary of Athena Polias at Priene*. London

Des Courtils, J. 2001. 'Xanthos et le Létôon au IIe siècle a.C.' In A. Bresson et R. Descat (eds). *Les cités d'Asie Mineure occidentale au IIe siècles a.c.* Bordeaux. 213–24

Fontenrose, J. 1988. *Didyma*. Berkeley

Genière, J. de (ed.). 1992. *Cahiers de Claros* I. Paris

Gruben, G. 1961. 'Beobachtungen zum Artemis-Tempel von Sardis.' *MDAI(A)* 76: 155–96

Hanfmann, George M. A. and K. J. Frazer. 1975. 'The temple of Artemis: new soundings.' In Hanfmann and S. W. Jacobs (eds). *A Survey of Sardis and the Major Monuments Outside the City Walls*. Harvard

Hänlein-Schäfer, H. 1985. VENERATIO AUGUSTI. *Eine Studie zu den Tempeln des ersten römischen Kaisers*. Rome

Hansen, E. 1991. 'Le temple de Létô au Létôon de Xanthos.' *RA*. 323–40

Hesberg, H. von. 1982. Review of Naumann 1979. *Gnomon* 54: 64–70

Le Roy, Chr. and E. Hansen. 1976. 'Au Létôon de Xanthos: les deux temples de Léto.' *RA* 317–35

Le Roy, Chr. 1991. 'Le développement monumental du Létôon de Xanthos.' *RA* 341–51

Mallwitz, A. 1975. 'Gestalt und Geschichte des jüngeren Athenatempels von Milet.' *MDAI(I)* 25: 67–90

Machatschek, A. and M. Schwarz. 1981. *Bauforschungen in Selge*. Vienna

Mitchell, S. 2002. 'The temple of Men Askaenos at Antioch.' In T. Drew-Bear and others (eds). *Actes du Ier Congrès International sur Antioche de Pisidie*. Lyon and Paris. 313–21

Naumann, R. 1979. *Der Zeustempel zu Aizanoi*. Berlin

Parke, H. W. 1986. 'The temple of Apollo at Didyma: the building and its function.' *JHS* 106: 121–31

Pohl, D. 2002. *Kaiserzeitliche Tempel in Kleinasien unter besonderer Berücksichtigung der hellenistischen Vorläufer* (Asia Minor Studien 43). R. Habelt: Bonn

Radt, W. 1992. *Pergamon. Geschichte und Bauten, Funde und Erforschung einer antiken Metropole*. Cologne

Ratté, C., T. N. Howe and C. Foss. 1986. 'An early imperial pseudodipteral temple at Sardis.' *AJA* 90: 45–68

Roueché, C. and K. T. Erim. 1990. *Aphrodisias Papers*. Ann Arbor

Rumscheid, F. 1994. *Untersuchungen sur kleinasiastischen Bauornamentik des Hellenismus*. Mainz. 2 vols

———. 1995. Die Ornamentik des Apollon-Smintheus-Tempels in der Troas. *MDAI(I)* 45: 25–55

Schneider, E. E. (ed.).1999. *Elaiussa Sebaste* I. Rome

Tuchelt. 1992. *Branchidai-Didyma*. P. von Zabern: Mainz

Uz, D. 1990. 'The Temple of Dionysos at Teos.' In Hoepfner and Schwandner (eds): 51–67

Varinlioglu, E. 2002. 'The temple at Ankara.' In T. Drew-Bear and others (eds). *Actes du Ier Congrès International sur Antioche de Pisidie*. Lyon and Paris. 393–99

Waelkens, M. 1986. 'The imperial sanctuary at Pessinus: archaeological, epigraphical and numismatic evidence for its date and identification.' *Epigraphica Anatolica* 7: 37–72

———. 1993. 'Sagalassos. History and archaeology'. In Waelkens (ed.). *Sagalassos* I. Leuven. 37–50

Wesenberg, B. 2001. 'B.M. 1206 und die Rekonstruktion der *columnae caelatae*.' In Muss (ed.): 297–314

## 7 Syria and North Africa

Bonacasa, N. and S. Ensoli (eds). 2000. *Cirene*. Electa: Milan

Grimm, Günter. 1996. 'City planning?' In *Alexandria and Alexandrianism: papers delivered at a symposium organized by the J. Paul Getty Museum and the Getty Center for the History of Art and the Humanities, Getty Museum 22–25 April 1993*: Malibu. 55–74 (63–65 on the Alexandria Serapeion)

Stucchi, Sandro. 1975. *L'architettura cirenaica*. Rome

# Illustration Credits

Abbreviations: a – above, b – below,
c – centre, l – left, r – right

akg-images 10b, 91, 145, 151a, 152–53b
akg-images/Peter Connolly 141b
D.A.I. Aizanoi-excavation 2004 219
Archivi Alinari 18–19, 111b, 118bl, 121b, 127a
Allard Pierson Museum, Amsterdam 84a
Courtesy American School of Classical
    Studies at Athens 33b (G.P. Stevens), 81a,
    86br, 138–39 (Alison Frantz), 157a
American School of Classical Studies at
    Athens, Agora Excavations 146ar
The British School at Athens 146l, 147r
D.A.I., Athens 64, 99b, 139, 144ar, 177
École Française d'Athènes Archives-
    Photothèque 172, 179c&b
Private Collection, Athens 45
L.Beaumont and A. Archontidou-Argyri,
    Kato Phano Archaeological Project 186a
Dietric Berges 213a
Bildarchiv Preussischer Kulturbesitz,
    Staatliche Museen zu Berlin 100l, 105b
After M.T. Boatwright, Hadrian and Cities of
    the Roman Empire, Princeton 1987 121cr
After J.C. Carter, The Sculpture of the
    Sanctuary of Athena Polias at Priene,
    London 1983 67a
C.R. Cockerell, The Temples of Jupiter
    Panhellenicus at Aegina, and of Apollo
    Epicurius at Bassae, London 1860 44
J.M. Cook & W.H.Plommer, The Sanctuary at
    Hemithea at Kastabos, London 1966 214a
Frederick A. Cooper 52
Corbis 228
F. Courby, Exploration archéologique de
    Délos…Les Temples d'Apollon, Paris 1931
    181bl
Delphi Museum 103
Michael Duigan 65b, 199

After Ejnar Dyggave 175bl
Epidauros Museum 57l
Werner Forman Archive/J. Paul Getty
    Museum, Malibu 38r
Werner Forman Archive 162–63
Sian Francis 35b, 79l
J. de Genière, Cahors de Claros I, Paris 1992
    198a&c
Getty Images 82–83
Photo Heidi Grassley © Thames & Hudson
    Ltd 31, 63b, 134–35, 140–41, 141a, 143al,
    143b, 152–53a
Robert Harding Picture Library 99a, 148, 203
After D. Harris1995 88a, 92
Fotoarchiv Hirmer 16, 17a, 94, 188, 205
Archaeological Museum, Istanbul 212bl
D.A.I., Istanbul 85a, 190b
Michael Jenner 2–3, 55, 113b, 126, 128br,
    143ar, 192–93b
Robert Koldeway 186b
M.Korres, From Pentelicon to the Parthenon,
    Athens 1995 33a
After M. Korres 50, 140b
After Krischen 1962 189b
L. Lacroix, Les reproductions des statues sur
    les monnaies grecques Liege 1949 75b, 80al
The British Museum, London 15, 37, 42, 51l,
    66–67, 69a, 87a, 99c, 102a, 142, 185c, 195a,
    200a&b, 209br
R.I.B.A, London 43b
David Lyons 132–33
© Schmuel Magal 182, 190a, 191a, 209a, 211b,
    212–13b, 215, 216, 217, 222, 223, 229
Leonard von Matt 17b
Christopher Mee 155, 158, 161, 178, 179
Stephen Mitchell 220b, 221
Olympia Museum 54, 70, 71
Bodleian Library, University of Oxford 189a
R. Naumann, Der Zeustempel zu Aizanoi,
    Berlin 1979 89a, 106–7, 218ar&br, 220a
Aphrodisias Excavations, New York
    University 208a
Metropolitan Museum of Art, New York 79r,
    57

After A. Papanikolaou 1998 180a
École Nationale Supérieure des Beaux-Arts,
    Paris 46–47
Musée du Louvre, Paris 70b
R. Pococke, A Description of the East,
    London 1743–45 211a
Iris Pojani 176
Zev Radovan 41, 63a
Soprintendenza alle Antichita, Reggio di
    Calabria 119al
Courtesy Robin Rhodes 20
Museo Nazional delle Terme, Rome 40
N.J. Saunders 185a
Scala 84b
P.Schatzmann & R. Herzog, Asklepion, Kos I,
    Berlin 1932 106, 183a
© 2002 René Seindel 111a
Ibrahim Shazli 224
Edwin Smith 123b
Society of Dilettanti, The Unedited
    Antiquities of Attica, London 1817 102–3
Tony Spawforth 10–11, 22–23, 24, 32, 39, 60l
    & r, 68, 69br&l, 74–75, 80–81, 92–93, 104al,
    104b, 104–5, 115b, 116, 117al&ar, 119ar,
    120, 130ar, 154, 155, 156a, 158, 161a, 163b,
    164, 165, 169, 174a, 175br, 178, 179a, 183,
    192a, 194, 196, 197a&b, 206, 207, 209bl, 210
After A. F. Stewart, Greek Sculpture, 1990 87b
Swiss School of Archaeology in Greece
    50–51, 166, 167
P.G. Themelis 80ar
Richard Tomlinson 65a, 88b, 90b, 160bl,
    173a&b, 227a
Biblioteca Apostolica Vaticana 43a
Philip Watson 181br
Philip Winton 76–77
Roger Wilson 1, 4–5, 6–7, 14, 21a ,26, 27, 30,
    48, 49, 53, 58–59, 59b, 61, 72–73, 89b, 96–97,
    100–1, 108–9, 112a&b, 113al&ar, 114c&b,
    115al, 117bl&br, 122a, 123a, 124, 127c&b,
    128bl, 129br, 130al, 131a&b, 132a&b, 133b,
    135a, 136a&b, 144al, 149, 151b, 156b, 157b,
    159, 161b, 170–71, 202, 204b, 225a&b,
    226a&b

# Acknowledgments

I am grateful to Colin Ridler at Thames & Hudson who first suggested this enjoyable project. It is a pleasure to thank all those friends and colleagues in whose stimulating company I have visited Greek temples over the years, including Bob Barber, Robin Barber, Fiona Cameron, Erica Davies, Kerin Hope, Simon Hornblower, Robert Jackson, Marie-Christine Keith, Rosalind Thomas, Babette Young, and fellow-cruisers on the Turkish gulets of Westminster Classic Tours. A special thanks is owed to Chris Mee, old friend and co-author, with whom I toured Greece in the late 1990s. I have been helped in a variety of ways by Hector Catling, Kevin Greene, Simon Hornblower, John Moles, Karen Ni Mheallaigh, Andrew Parkin, Christopher Pfaff, Iris Pojani, Robin Rhodes, Sally Waite, Susan Walker, C. K. Williams II, Mark Wilson Jones and Penny Wilson-Zarganis. My interest in Greek temples germinated in the slide-illustrated lectures of Richard Tomlinson, who taught me as an undergraduate at Birmingham University. I owe a particular debt to him and to Robert Parker, who both at short notice generously read drafts. Their wise comments have greatly improved the book; its remaining shortcomings are of course mine. The library research was done in London, mainly in the Greek and Roman Societies Library in Senate House, where, as ever, the staff deserve the warmest thanks for their helpfulness. Much of this book was tried out on undergraduates at the University of Newcastle upon Tyne on my 'Archaeology and Art of Greek Religion' module. In Newcastle, too, Dawn Robinson in the School of Historical Studies office cheerfully carried out various computing chores. I am grateful to the friends and colleagues who kindly answered appeals for illustrative matter. At Thames & Hudson I am further indebted to Sally Nicholls (picture researcher), Geoff Penna (designer) and Philip Watson (editor), who miraculously transmuted the raw text into an illustrated book. Finally I thank Lee, whose moral support has given new meaning to the ancient Greek concept of 'temple-sharing'.

# Index

Page numbers in *italics* refer to illustrations. Most ancient Greek proper names are more or less literally transliterated, but with the usual inconsistencies.